DATE DUE

DEMCO, INC. 38-2931

The American Direct Primary

This book rejects conventional accounts of how, and why, American political parties differ from those in other democracies. It focuses on the introduction of that most distinctive of American party devices, the direct primary, and argues that primaries resulted from a process of party institutionalization initiated by party elites. Thus, it overturns the widely accepted view that, between 1902 and 1915, direct primaries were imposed on the parties by antiparty reformers intent on weakening them. An examination of particular northern states shows that often the direct primary was not controversial, and only occasionally did it involve confrontation between party "regulars" and their opponents. Rather, the impetus for direct nominations initially came from attempts within the parties to subject previously informal procedures to formal rules. However, it proved impossible to reform the older caucus-convention system effectively, and party elites then turned to the direct primary – a device that already had become more common in rural counties in the late nineteenth century.

Professor Alan Ware taught at the University of Warwick from 1972 to 1990, and he has been a Fellow of Worcester College, Oxford, since 1990. He has been a visiting scholar at American universities, most especially at the Institute of Governmental Studies, University of California, Berkeley. He is author or coauthor of six previous books, most recently *Political Parties and Party Systems* (1996), and editor or coeditor of a number of others.

The American Direct Primary

Party Institutionalization and Transformation in the North

ALAN WARE

University of Oxford

CAMBRIDGE
UNIVERSITY PRESS

PUBLISHED BY THE PRESS SYNDICATE OF THE UNIVERSITY OF CAMBRIDGE
The Pitt Building, Trumpington Street, Cambridge, United Kingdom

CAMBRIDGE UNIVERSITY PRESS
The Edinburgh Building, Cambridge CB2 2RU, UK
40 West 20th Street, New York, NY 10011-4211, USA
477 Williamstown Road, Port Melbourne, VIC 3207, Australia
Ruiz de Alarcón 13, 28014 Madrid, Spain
Dock House, The Waterfront, Cape Town 8001, South Africa

http://www.cambridge.org

First published 2002

Printed in the United Kingdom at the University Press, Cambridge

Typeface Sabon 10/12 pt.   *System* QuarkXPress [BTS]

A catalog record for this book is available from the British Library.

Library of Congress Cataloging in Publication Data available

ISBN   0 521 81492 8   hardback

For Joni, Iain, and Austin
and the many members of the Lovenduski family

Contents

vii

Tables

Abbreviations

DD	Democratic Dominant (state)
DL	Democratic Leaning (state)
DS	Democratic Safe (state)
GOP	Grand Old Party
NDD	Non-Democratic Dominant (state)
NDL	Non-Democratic Leaning (state)
NDS	Non-Democratic Safe (state)
OBSTP	Office Block Ballot with Straight Ticket Provision
POB	Pure Office Block (Ballot)
PCB	Party Column without Box (Ballot)
PPC	Pure Party Column (Ballot)
YMDC	Young Men's Democratic Club (of Massachusetts)

Preface and Acknowledgments

As with several of the books and articles I have written, the origins of *The American Direct Primary* lie in my gradually becoming aware that arguments I had long assumed to be valid might not be. In the mid-1990s I had been rereading articles by Martin Shefter, published originally in 1983, but that had been reissued in his *Political Parties and the State*. One of the points that struck me was that, at the beginning of the twentieth century, party organizations in the eastern United States were no weaker than they had been a few decades earlier; indeed, because there had been pressures toward centralization, in some ways they were stronger than in the 1870s and 1880s. If Shefter's account of the state of the parties were correct, and to me it seemed a highly plausible account, how was the introduction of the direct primary in the eastern half of the United States to be explained? After all, here was a reform that appeared to run counter to the interests of parties but that had been adopted at a time when those parties were arguably still at the peak of their power. Trying to solve that puzzle set me on the path that has led to the publication of this book.

I was fortunate in enjoying the help of a great many people during the period it was being researched and written. Some of my first attempts at formulating the ideas I was developing were in papers presented to the Senior Seminar in American Politics at the University of Oxford. I am grateful to the members of that seminar for their comments, especially its convenor Byron Shafer, Nigel Bowles, David Goldey, and Desmond King. Desmond King also supplied me with various helpful written comments on a number of occasions.

The first extended period of research I undertook on the topic was in the late summer and autumn of 1996 when I was a Visiting Scholar at the Institute of Governmental Studies (IGS) at the University of California, Berkeley. Once again, IGS proved a wonderful place to be based while undertaking a research project. I received the help of a number of people at the Institute, especially its director, Nelson Polsby, and the librarian,

Marc Levin. Marc Levin was instrumental in one of the "breakthroughs" that I made on the project at that time. I had discovered a few references in early-twentieth-century publications to a Conference on the Practical Reform of Primary Elections that had been held in New York City in 1898. I had found no references to the conference since that era, and it was with Marc's help that I tracked down a microfiche copy of its proceedings somewhere in the California state library system. When the microfiche arrived, confirmation that the importance of the document had been misjudged was evident in its appearance – it had been stored on the smallest form of microfiche possible. It was only by using the strongest lens available in the Berkeley libraries that it was possible to reproduce a readable version of this forgotten document.

In the autumn of 1997 I received a Special Lectureship from the University of Oxford, and this enabled me to start writing up some of the material I had gathered over the previous year. Two short research trips to the United States were funded by the Mellon Fund. In 1996 I went to the Massachusetts Historical Society in Boston, where I examined archival material, including material they hold on Richard Henry Dana and on Joseph Lomasney. In 1999 I went to the Wisconsin Historical Society to make use of their extensive holding of newspapers on microfilm. During 2000–1, I was granted sabbatical leave by Worcester College and the University of Oxford, and I was able to complete the manuscript during that year.

I have benefited greatly from the help of an extended family. My stepson, Austin Jones, kindly lent me the Banksville Joinery van so that I could make the trip from Stamford to an archive in Waterbury, Connecticut. Regrettably, this was one of the "leads" that proved not that helpful – the correspondence in the archive of a former Connecticut governor, George L. Lilley, turned out to be nothing but formal responses acknowledging receipt of letters to him. Subsequently, Dianne Nast, of Roda and Nast PC of Lancaster, Pennsylvania, kindly arranged for two legal assistants at the firm, James J. Maksel and Meredith E. Rappaport, to travel to the Pennsylvania state archive in Harrisburg, where they read and photocopied interesting material for me from the papers of Samuel W. Pennypacker. I am extremely grateful to all of them.

Several people have stopped me from making serious errors in the book. I am indebted to David Mayhew, who kindly read the entire first draft of the manuscript, made a great many helpful criticisms of that draft, and directed me toward secondary sources of which I was unaware. I am similarly grateful for the comments on that draft from the referees provided by Cambridge University Press. I also wish to thank Kenneth Finegold, John J. Grabowski, and David C. Hammack, who helped me to identify the Thomas Johnson of Cleveland whose paper was read at the 1898 conference. Without their help I might have leapt to the erroneous conclusion that this was the future mayor of Cleveland, Tom Johnson. Obviously, I assume responsibility for any remaining errors in the book.

An earlier version of the material presented in Chapter 2 was published as "Anti-Partism and Party Control of Political Reform in the United States: The Case of the Australian Ballot," *British Journal of Political Science*, Volume 30, 2000, pp. 1–29. I am grateful to Cambridge University Press for permission to use that material in this book.

Alan Ware
Worcester College, Oxford

July 2001

Introduction

This book aims to shed light on two crucial questions about political parties: Why are America's parties different from those in Europe? And why did the party-centered American politics of the nineteenth century become a candidate-centered system during the twentieth century? The two questions are linked, in that to answer the first adequately requires the availability of an answer to the second. As with many issues in political science, the problem is not the absence of possible answers but that there are too many competing, and sometimes incompatible, explanations. Superficially plausible though some of these explanations are, one of the points that will become evident during the course of the book is that much that has been asserted over the years about America's parties has been taken out of context, is misleading, or is simply untrue.

In attempting to answer the two questions, this study examines how and why direct primary elections were introduced in the United States. The direct primary has been one of the most unusual features of American parties. In each state today the selection of candidates for public office takes the form of an election that is organized by a government agency, rather than the parties themselves, and is subject to state law. Candidates for most elected offices, with the notable exception of the presidency itself, are now chosen in such elections. The direct primary is not just a distinctive institution, however; by some political scientists its introduction is thought to mark an important turning point in the development of America's parties. Thus, in his book, *Curing the Mischiefs of Faction*, Austin Ranney says, "The general adoption of the direct primary by the states from the early 1900s onward is, in my opinion, the most radical of all the party reforms adopted in the whole course of American history."[1]

---

[1] Austin Ranney, *Curing the Mischiefs of Faction: Party Reform in America*, Berkeley, University of California Press, 1975, p. 121.

By examining the origins of the direct primary, and how, and why, it was introduced by most states between about 1899 and 1915, it will be possible to examine both the factors prompting change in American parties, and the constraints on the form that party change can take there. It might be imagined, given the significance of the direct primary, that much original research, on its adoption by the states, would have been undertaken. In fact, it is a subject that attracts virtually no attention. Not since 1928, when the last edition of Charles Merriam's *Primary Elections* was published (an edition he coauthored with Louise Overacker), has a major study appeared.[2] Indeed, as will be seen shortly, one of the weaknesses of much that has been written about direct primaries since then is that political scientists have relied too heavily on Merriam's account of what happened, or on the rather different version of that account produced by his most outstanding graduate student, V. O. Key. Key's work was flawed because it is clear that, except for the South, he had not actually examined the process by which primary elections were introduced.

Before considering further the consequences of the lack of attention to the direct primary, however, it is necessary to return to the questions outlined in the opening paragraph. How have the contrasts between American and European parties been understood? In general, three main factors have been held to account for the variation between the continents – with different scholars placing different emphases on each of them. They are (1) patterns of social division and/or political ideology; (2) political culture; (3) the centralization, or decentralization, of the governmental system within which the parties operate. These factors are discussed briefly in turn.

1. Patterns of Social Division and/or Political Ideology

The crude version of the account that prioritizes social division holds that, while European parties have differed with regard to ideology, American parties have not, and, instead, they are the Tweedledee and Tweedledum of the liberal democratic world. Whatever else might divide the American parties, it has not been ideology. Thus, even those authors who explicitly denied any resemblance to Lewis Carroll's famous twins could still argue, as Ladd did, that "[T]here have been substantial policy differences between the parties, but these have existed as 'controlling tendencies' within each body of party leaders, not as neat doctrinal fissures."[3] Unlike the European democracies, it is asserted, the American parties are not a manifestation of distinct ideological bases. But why not?

---

[2] Charles E. Merriam and Louise Overacker, *Primary Elections*, Chicago, University of Chicago Press, 1928, p. 65.

[3] Everett Carll Ladd, *American Political Parties: Social Change and Political Response*, New York, W.W. Norton, 1970, p. 30.

Social class is often invoked as the relevant variable, though this can be done in one of two ways. One version of the argument is that there was a plurality of cleavages in American society which cross-cut each other, and thereby produced an electorate in which no lines of division were so strong that they could generate an ideology. By contrast, in Europe there were dominant lines of division, often – though not always – class, and this made it possible for distinct party ideologies to develop. America's social pluralism lay at the root of its program-less and ideology-free parties. The second version held that, as a result of industrialization, class was increasingly the only possible line of major social cleavage in any advanced industrial society; societies in which class did not really divide voters could not be expected to have programmatic and ideological parties because there were no firmly shared interests around which the supporters of the different parties could congeal. But whichever version was used, the conclusion was the same; America's parties were, unfortunately, "ideology-less," according to European commentators, or, fortunately, "ideology-free," according to Americans. Whether this crucial difference between parties on the two continents was seen in terms of America having a vice or a virtue tended to vary, therefore, with the national origins of the commentator. The absence of ideology in American parties meant that they were under no pressure to create formal mass-membership organizations that would act as the guardians of party goals and values; older caucus-cadre forms of organization were adequate for their purposes.

These sorts of accounts of differences in the two sets of party systems were especially popular during the 1950s and 1960s, the decades during which there was a widespread assumption among political scientists that politics was essentially about class. While there was, at least, a superficial plausibility to the claim that ideology was the key variable, more recent research on America's parties has undermined it. For example, John Gerring has shown that from the 1820s to the 1990s there were major ideological divisions between the two main parties – divisions that endured for decades. What divided the parties were, to recall Ladd's words, "doctrinal fissures" or, in Gerring's words, the parties were "ideologically motivated."[4] His study of presidential contests shows that the Whig and Republican parties had been parties of nationalism, but that after the mid 1920s the Republican party was a party with a neoliberal ideology. The Democrats' ideology was Jeffersonianism until the early 1890s, populism from then until the late 1940s, and what he calls "universalism" after that. Other studies have focused on particular aspects of political conflict in America, and shown how intense that conflict has been and how it was mediated

---

[4] John Gerring, *Party Ideologies in America*, Cambridge, Cambridge University Press, 1998, p. 257.

through the parties – even in the nineteenth century.[5] For example, Gretchen Ritter has demonstrated how "financial policy was a central political issue around which so much else revolved" between the Civil War and the 1890s.[6] In addition, there is the evidence of comparative studies, which seem to indicate that more recently the distance between the Republicans and Democrats on some major policy issues was actually greater than the gap between the two leading parties in some of the European democracies, most notably Germany.[7]

If American party politics had always had an ideological base, why had so few observers not recognized this earlier? Why were American parties seen as so obviously deficient in this regard by comparison with their European counterparts? There were three main causes of that outcome. First, the obsession among social scientists with class during the mid-twentieth century – and with its primacy as a social cleavage – blinded many scholars to the fact that other sources of division, or divisions that were only partly class-based, could nevertheless spawn ideological politics. Second, it was more difficult in the case of America to understand the links between the group basis of party politics and ideology. It was easy to understand how someone in 1920s' Europe who saw themselves as working class, and who voted for the party that promoted itself as being for the working class, was connected to the party's socialism. It was more difficult to see how in 1880 an Irish American identity that prompted voting for the Democracy, was linked to that party's Jeffersonian ideology. The relationships between the patterns of group loyalties to a party and that party's ideology were complex in the United States. Because of that, American party "ideology" could be dismissed as the mere froth of party politics. Third, the local bases of voter loyalties, combined with the two-party system that presidentialism facilitated, meant that nationally the parties could appear as incoherent electoral coalitions. In the post–New Deal era, both the Southern wing of the Democratic party and the liberal, northeastern wing of the Republican party had few equivalents in Europe. These were moderately large wings of a party, and often they appeared out of kilter with the parties' majority wings. It was all too easy to conclude from this diversity that there was no ideological coherence to the parties.

Nevertheless, much contemporary scholarship has now shown conclusively that American parties were always far more than coalitions relying

---

[5] On the ideological division between the parties that underpinned the founding of the party system in the 1830s see John Ashworth, *"Agrarians" and "Aristocrats": Party Political Ideology in the United States, 1837–1846*, London, Royal Historical Society, 1983.

[6] Gretchen Ritter, *Goldbugs and Greenbacks: The Antimonopoly Tradition and the Politics of Finance in America*, Cambridge, Cambridge University Press, 1997, p. 3.

[7] Alan Ware, *Political Parties and Party Systems*, Oxford, Oxford University Press, 1996, p. 55. Ware used data compiled by Michael Laver and W. Ben Hunt, *Policy and Party Competition*, New York and London, Routledge, 1992.

on short term opportunism in the electoral market. Issues and policies divided them – and did so consistently over time. Given that the parties' elected representatives seem to have become more coherent ideologically since the 1980s, it is perhaps not surprising that such findings have provoked little backlash from those holding an older view of American parties as Tweedledee and Tweedledum. It is easier now to accept that American parties are not quite as free of ideology as was once assumed. Because of the obvious weight of the evidence produced by researchers against the earlier view, this book will not be concerned further with the argument that either the structure of social cleavages or ideology account for the distinctive nature of parties in the United States.

2. Political Culture

Those who argue that the second factor is significant claim that public attitudes toward parties are different in the United States. Political beliefs in America are either not supportive of, or actually hostile to, parties as political intermediaries. The consequence of this lack of trust in parties has been much greater regulation of parties by law than in the European countries. Essentially, this is a view of America's parties that sees them as "victims": they became what they are because of what reformers at various times did to them. American political culture differs markedly from political cultures in Europe, and this is why the parties were forced to develop along such different lines.

In its full-blown form this argument is comparatively recent in origin. However, it emerged out of the much older, Progressive, view of American history which interpreted the political reforms of the early twentieth century as something that was done to the parties by those who were opposed to their *modus operandi*; the conflictual nature of party change at that time is evident, for example, in Merriam and Overacker's claim that "[S]tartling disclosures respecting the betrayal of public trust by party leaders aroused the people to a crusade for responsible party government."[8] Curiously, though, this interpretation of American party development was to be reinvigorated within political science at the very time that historians were reappraising Progressivism.

Among American historians, the 1970s and 1980s were decades of considerable debate about Progressivism. The questions of who the Progressives were, what they had done, and, indeed, whether there really was a unified movement that could be placed under a single label of "Progressivism" were all scrutinized.[9] However, just as this debate was

---

[8] Merriam and Overacker, *Primary Elections*, p. 61.
[9] Among the historians whose research prompted this reevaluation of Progressivism was David P. Thelen, one of whose important early articles was "Social Tensions and the Origins of Progressivism," *Journal of American History*, 56(1969), pp. 323–41; see also Thelen,

developing among historians, political scientists were taking a different path. Instead of a direct challenge to the Progressive orthodoxy, that party reform had been brought about by a popular revolt against the parties' practices, a modification to that argument gained widespread popularity in political science. The originator of (what might be called) this neo-Progressivist account was Austin Ranney. In 1975, Ranney published *Curing the Mischiefs of Faction*, in which he sought to link both the reforms of the presidential nominating system after 1968 and the reforms of the Progressive era, most especially the introduction of the direct primary, to ambivalent attitudes to parties that he claimed had long been at the heart of American political beliefs.

Ranney's claim that there is such ambivalence hinges on there being antiparty attitudes, as well as attitudes supportive of parties, evident in the American political culture. According to Ranney, a strain of antipartism, of which Madison's remarks in the Tenth Federalist Paper were an important early example, prompted support for the reform of political parties that has surfaced from time to time in American history.[10] Certainly, Ranney was not original in pointing to the antipartisanship evident among the Founding Fathers – Hofstadter among others had done that – but he was an innovator in seeking to link it to mid-twentieth century developments in American party politics.[11]

Ranney's conclusion about why the parties had been transformed in the early twentieth century was similar to that of the Progressive interpretation, in that he saw it as the result of what reformers did to the parties; as he noted of that period: "The Progressives' arguments – and formidable political clout – won the day."[12] Nevertheless, Ranney also had an answer to the obvious objection to this view – namely, how did such strong parties, as American parties undoubtedly were in the nineteenth century, become so weak that they were defeated by reformers? The answer was that American attitudes toward parties had always been characterized by an ambivalence; at times the antipartisan elements would come to the fore, and when this happened antiparty reformers could overcome their

The New Citizenship: Origins of Progressivism in Wisconsin, 1885–1900, Columbia, Mo., University of Missouri Press, 1972, Daniel T. Rodgers, "In Search of Progressivism," *Review in American History*, 10(1982), pp. 113–32, and Richard L. McCormick, *The Party Period and Public Policy: American Politics from the Age of Jackson to the Progressive Era*, New York and Oxford, Oxford University Press, 1986, Chapter 7. However, an important earlier study of one state, Massachusetts, in which Progressivism had little influence is Richard M. Abrams, *Conservatism in a Progressive Era, Massachusetts Politics, 1900–1912*, Cambridge, Mass., Harvard University Press, 1964.

[10] Austin Ranney, *Curing the Mischiefs of Faction: Party Reform in America*, p. 23.

[11] Richard Hofstadter, *The Idea of a Party System: The Rise of Legitimate Opposition in the United States, 1780–1840*, Berkeley, University of California Press, 1969.

[12] Ranney, *Curing the Mischiefs of Faction*, p. 81.

opponents. According to Ranney, the reform of the presidential nominating system after 1968 was merely the latest manifestation of an upsurge of antiparty sentiment. Ranney's argument has won wide acceptance among scholars specializing in American parties; in fact, it has been so successful that it has become a commonplace, and Ranney appears to have been forgotten as the originator of it. For example, three sets of leading scholars, Martin Wattenberg, Gerald M. Pomper, and Richard S. Katz and Robin Kolodny all outline variants of this argument without attribution to Ranney.[13] Wattenberg argues that:

Americans have traditionally maintained a rather ambivalent attitude towards parties. The Founding Fathers view[ed] parties as necessary evils. . . . Even after the acceptance of regularized opposition parties in the mid-nineteenth century, major steps were taken to weaken their role. In the spirit of cleaning up government, a number of reforms were instituted, many of which had the effect of forever weakening the parties. . . . It is ironic that parties have been looked upon with such wariness and suspicion in the nation that founded the world's first political party system. Being the first to experiment with democratic political parties has apparently left an indelible imprint on the American ethos.[14]

Pomper places the argument in a more comparative perspective, but the Ranney framework is still evident:

Opposition to political parties is long-standing. . . . Despite such opposition, parties did develop, particularly vigorously in the United States, but attacks also expanded. . . . The progressive and nonpartisan perspectives on party reform convey this hostile tradition. The antiparty attitude continues among contemporary Americans. . . . [One] source of opposition flows from a liberal tradition, which sees strong parties as threats to vital social interests. . . . Madison developed his quintessential American political theory to control and enfeeble factions and parties, the dangerous expressions of political power. In the spirit of Madison, even the most successful American politicians, the presidents, have been embarrassed by parties and prone to wish them gone.[15]

Katz and Kolodny take a rather similar line:

American political culture is profoundly ambivalent about political parties. . . . Ambivalence about parties is reflected in American attitudes toward representation. . . . Especially with the rise of urban (and occasionally rural) political machines in the late nineteenth century, a second ambivalence about political parties came to

---

[13] I wish to make it clear that I am neither implying nor intending any criticism of Wattenberg, Pomper, or Katz and Kolodny in this regard; my point is simply that, like many widely accepted arguments, Ranney's has fallen victim to its very success, in that its originator's role has been forgotten.

[14] Martin P. Wattenberg, *The Rise of Candidate-Centred Politics*, Cambridge, Mass., Harvard University Press, 1991, pp. 32–4.

[15] Gerald M. Pomper, *Passions and Interest: Political Party Concepts of American Democracy*, Lawrence, University Press of Kansas, 1992, pp. 132–4.

the fore, that is a perception that party organizations illegitimately interposed themselves between the people and their representatives . . . ambivalence about party and
particularly the imposition of state authority on parties . . . is reflected in their
organizations.[16]

Following Ranney, all these authors relate the peculiar path of American
party development to antipartism as a supposedly key component of an
ambivalent American attitude to parties.

If Ranney's account were correct, then an important aspect of the
transformation that American parties underwent between the late nineteenth century and the late 1960s would have been explained: the rise of
candidate-centered politics would be the by-product of laws and party
structures that had been designed to frustrate party power. Moreover, this
would help explain the divergence of American party practices from those
in Europe. Unfortunately, there are three major problems with Ranney's
analysis indicating that the entire edifice is one that might be built on sand.

First, if the peculiar development of American parties is to be attributed
to the role played by antiparty sentiments, then it has to be shown that
antipartism has not been a significant factor elsewhere. If antipartism had
been as important in other liberal democracies, then it could not account
for the distinctive and unusual path followed by the American parties. In
fact, no scholar has produced a shred of evidence drawn from comparative
studies to show that the United States was unusual in having widespread
ambivalent attitudes toward parties. A case can be made that, at various
periods in a number of other countries, antiparty attitudes were important,
and quite possibly as strong as in the United States. There was a long tradition of antipartism in much of Europe, for example.[17] Most obviously,
there is the case of France, where Gaullism in the Fourth Republic was a
major source of opposition to the party-based parliamentary regime. (De
Gaulle's attempt to weaken the role of parties in its successor Republic
lasted no longer than his own presidency, and his "nonparty" grouping
quickly became a party in all but name.) Even in Britain, support for a
party-dominated politics has been far from complete, though it has taken
the form of "centrism," and any analysis of antipartism in Britain must
begin by "unpacking" the different elements of "centrism."[18]

[16] Richard S. Katz and Robin Kolodny, "Party Organization as an Empty Vessel: Parties in
American Politics," in Richard S. Katz and Peter Mair (eds.), *How Parties Organize: Change
and Adaptation in Party Organizations in Western Democracies*, London, Sage, 1994,
pp. 26–7.

[17] See, for example, the essays in the Special Issue of the *European Journal of Political Science*,
29(1996) on the "Politics of Anti-Party Sentiment," especially Piero Ignazi, "The
Intellectual Basis of Right-Wing Anti-Partyism," pp. 279–96.

[18] See Brian Harrison, "The Centrist Theme in Modern British Politics," in Harrison,
Peaceable Kingdom: Stability and Change in Modern Britain, Clarendon Press, Oxford,
1982, pp. 309–77.

The assertion that there is something unusual about the presence in the United States of widespread ambivalent attitudes toward parties in the past is no more than an assertion; efforts to demonstrate its truth have not progressed beyond the identification of antiparty attitudes in the United States during the 1790s, in the early 1900s, and in the three decades since the 1960s.[19] That is not enough to support the Ranney view; periods of strong antipartisanship have existed elsewhere. This is not to deny that some major studies, such as Hofstadter's *The Idea of a Party System*, have explored how attitudes toward party were linked to earlier attitudes in Britain.[20] But such studies have not explored how attitudes to party changed in the various countries *during the period of democratization*. For example, they do not compare developments in the United States from 1780 to 1830 with those of the comparable period in Britain's democratization, 1830–80. Consequently, there is at least one major limitation to such studies, irrespective of their undoubted merits – they lack a genuine comparative framework, and this means that they cannot establish whether democratization in the United States was accompanied by greater antipartisanship than that evident elsewhere, or not.

Of course, a counterargument to Ranney, that the European experience of antipartism was different in that much of it did not reflect republican political values, as it may have done in America, might be advanced in his defence. However, for the Ranney argument to be sustainable, it would then be necessary to show that different types of antipartism in Europe actually led to a different approach by their opponents to the practical control of parties than that evident in the United States. So far this, too, has not been demonstrated – either in genuinely comparative studies or in studies focusing primarily, on the European side, on single countries.

Second, political values can change over time, and one of the long-recognized problems with the political culture approach is that it tends to regard values as rather like precious heirlooms that are preserved intact for future generations. However, new social experiences, economic conditions, and political practices can transform previously core beliefs. To take an obvious example: Linda Colley has shown that British identity in the eighteenth century was constructed around a strong set of anti-Catholic beliefs and prejudices.[21] Yet, of all the attitudes that might have characterized the British two centuries later, this was not one of them. Given that the practice of party politics in a democratizing regime always had the potential for

---

[19] McCormick, among others, has pointed out that the view that parties were "evil" was widespread in England in the late eighteenth century, as well as in America; Richard L. McCormick, *The Party Period and Public Policy: American Politics from the Age of Jackson to the Progressive Era*, New York, Oxford University Press, 1986, p. 145.

[20] Richard Hofstadter, *The Idea of a Party System*.

[21] Linda Colley, *Britons: Forging the Nation, 1707–1837*, New Haven, Conn., Yale University Press, 1992.

transforming the antipartisanship evident at the country's founding, the onus is on those who would argue that these values persisted continuously in the United States to show how they did so after the 1830s. There is little conclusive evidence to show that they did, although, as in other democratic regimes, particular instances of antipartism were evident from time to time afterwards.

Third, there is the problem of whether manifestations of antipartism, after parties had become established in the 1830s, actually reflected deep-rooted cultural values in American society, or were merely strategies used at particular times by certain individuals or groups who felt under threat from the exercise of party power. Scholars who claim that antiparty values continued to be a significant element in an American political culture tend to assume that such values must underpin most manifestations of antipartism. Thus, Glenn C. Altschuler and Stuart M. Blumin note of the Civil War period, "That antiparty rhetoric continued to be expressed during these years, even as a faint counterpoint to the partisanship that was invading so many areas of community life, is evidence of its cultural resonance and relevance."[22] However, at any given time antipartism might be an acceptable, and an important, strategy in a society in which there was little evidence of a more permanent hostility to parties; all that would be required would be the absence of such strong proparty sentiments that a display of antipartism would necessarily provoke fierce opposition. Despite the importance of parties in nineteenth-century American life, public support for them was never so strong that antipartism would have faced such difficulties. Moreover, even proponents of the antiparty hypothesis recognize that antipartism could be a strategy in some circumstances. For example, in the paragraph immediately preceding the passage quoted above, Altschuler and Blumin cite an example of its strategic deployment, and conclude that "[B]eneath this epidermal antipartisan rhetoric, however, was thick-skinned party passion."[23] Unfortunately, they simply assume that antipartism could be attempted, and would succeed, only if it were grounded in a deeply-rooted American political value. However, given the constraints imposed by two-partism, antipartism would always be a viable and attractive strategy for those who believed themselves excluded from influence, even if antipartism as a political value was not strongly held by many Americans.

Of course, the argument should not be overstated. Recent critics of the "party period" idea are correct in drawing attention to the presence of non-party groups contesting some local elections and of evident antiparty sen-

---

[22] Glenn C. Altschuler and Stuart Blumin, *Rude Republic: Americans and their Politics in the Nineteenth Century*, Princeton, N.J., Princeton University Press, 2000, p. 169.

[23] Altschuler and Blumin, *Rude Republic*, p. 169.

timents in some third-party campaigns.[24] However, none of them addresses the key issue of whether the instances of antipartism they cite were really a strategy – a response to a form of political organization from which they were excluded – rather than being derived from deeply embedded values of opposition to partisanship.

One of the most remarkable aspects of the Jacksonian revolution was that it was so complete.[25] Even though, as Stampp notes, "the spoils system was not without its critics" in the late 1850s, "those criticisms were always most plentiful among the members of a defeated party"; in other words, opposition to a party regime based on patronage was low, and what people really objected to was not getting patronage themselves.[26] Furthermore, when antipartism was evident, as it was early in the 1850s on the breaking-up of the Whig party, it did not persist. Once a viable new party appeared, that party could then channel those antiparty sentiments into support for it. Although Kleppner is correct in arguing that this process took some time, the central point is that antipartism was inevitable in a two-party system when one party was no longer viable;[27] the antipartism of the early 1850s was the result of a lack of alternative parties for channeling voter support, whereas in a multiparty system revolt would more likely have prompted party fission. The appearance of a new party (the Republicans) that could channel support dissipated the antipartism there had been in the United States.

When a rather more sustained antipartisanship did start to appear in the United States in the later 1870s, it developed among small groups who had a particular "ax to grind." They were middle-class professionals, primarily in the New York and Boston areas, who believed themselves excluded from political influence after the Civil War. It was from this class that the Mugwump revolt of 1884 gained its support – an electoral revolt that, all the attention paid to it notwithstanding, consisted of no more than a few thousand individuals.[28] A plausible interpretation of their behavior is that

---

[24] In addition to Altschuler and Blumin, *Rude Republic*, see also Ronald P. Formisano, "The 'Party Period' Revisited," *Journal of American History*, 86(1999), pp. 93–120, and Mark Voss Hubbard, "The 'Third Party Tradition' Reconsidered: Third Parties and American Public Life, 1830–1900," *Journal of American History*, 86(1999), pp. 121–50.

[25] The books that develop most clearly this argument about the importance of parties in American political life from the 1830s to the 1890s are McCormick, *The Party Period and Public Policy*, and Joel H. Silbey, *The American Political Nation, 1838–1893*, Stanford, Calif., Stanford University Press, 1991.

[26] Kenneth M. Stampp, *America in 1857*, New York, Oxford University Press, 1990, p. 73.

[27] Paul Kleppner, *The Third Electoral System, 1853–1892*, Chapel Hill, University of North Carolina Press, 1979, Chapter 3.

[28] On the Mugwumps see especially Gerald W. McFarland, *Mugwumps, Morals and Politics, 1884–1920*, Amherst, University of Massachusetts Press, 1975, Geoffrey Blodgett, "The Mugwump Reputation, 1870 to the Present," *Journal of American History*, 66(1980),

their antipartisanship was simply a strategy deployed by political "outs" who, compared to many of the earlier "outs" identified by Stampp in the antebellum years, believed that they could not become "ins" via the parties, and so they sought political influence by attacking the parties. Their antipartisanship was a strategic response to powerlessness, rather than reflecting a resurrection of older antiparty political values or ideals. As McGerr notes:

Class concerns underlay the liberals' reconsideration of partisanship and gave it bite. As their interest in suffrage restriction made plain, liberals were not sympathetic to popular political participation. Unable to keep the poor and uneducated out of politics, they tried to reshape the political world in which these voters lived.[29]

Clearly, a strategic response might still be one that drew on an antiparty strand within a political culture, but demonstrating that it does requires evidence other than the adoption of the strategy itself. That evidence has not been produced so far.

There are grounds, therefore, for believing that arguments based on supposedly different political cultures may fail to account for the very different paths taken by American and European parties in the twentieth century. In this book, the antipartism argument is tested by examining the reform that would appear to lie at the heart of an early-twentieth-century reform agenda – the direct primary. If it can be shown that the direct primary was imposed on unwilling parties by reformers who were antagonistic to – or, at best, indifferent to – the interests of parties, the case for the "political culture" argument would be much strengthened. If the evidence of primary reform does not indicate that antipartisan forces played much part in that process, the plausibility of the argument is reduced.

3. Governmental Decentralization

The third main factor that may account for both intercontinental variations in party systems, and also the particular path taken by American parties in the twentieth century, is the decentralization of the political system. Proponents of this view argue that the highly decentralized political system in the United States brought about parties that were similarly decentralized. By contrast, the European states were much less fragmented, and more centralized parties could develop there. There are several differences in governmental structure that it is claimed are relevant in the maintenance of decentralized parties in the United States: federalism; presidentialism, incorporating a system of separated powers, that produced an unusually

pp. 867–87, and Blodgett, *The Gentle Reformers: Massachusetts Democrats in the Cleveland Era*, Cambridge, Mass., Harvard University Press, 1966.

[29] Michael E. McGerr, *The Decline of Popular Politics: The American North, 1865–1928*, New York, Oxford University Press, 1986, p. 67.

autonomous national legislature; and, in the nineteenth century, a limited role for the national government, so that political activity was directed toward the local and state levels of government. The claim is that parties had an incentive to direct their main attention to control of government at these power levels, and that this hindered any attempts at centralizing power in the parties on a national level.

By comparison with the first two factors, which are socioeconomic variables, this third factor is political; its proponents claim that the structure of political institutions is central to any explanation of the conduct of politics. Those who emphasize the significance of this factor argue that the structure of government provides incentives for parties to organize in certain kinds of ways, and constrains how they may change. Parties can be transformed. The French parties, for example, have moved from being loosely structured – groupings of locally powerful politicians – to being more disciplined and centralized. However, they did so in the context of a political system in which governmental reform made it advantageous. In particular, the advent of a directly elected presidency in 1962, following the reforms of 1958 that greatly reduced the powers of the legislature, prompted party reform.

Parties are not constrained to remain what they were like at their founding, even though Panebianco might be correct in arguing that how a party was formed restricts the ways in which it can change later.[30] However, decentralized parties can only transform themselves into more centralized structures over time if the political system becomes less fragmented. The constraints on party transformation in such a system are very different from those in a more centralized polity.

The argument outlined in this book places considerable emphasis on the role played by institutional decentralization in accounting for the developments that led to the direct primary. It does not argue, however, that it played an exclusive role. Certain political values were relevant in explaining why the direct primary was adopted, and the book also argues that antiparty reformers did play some part in the process. However, the evidence presented later will show that only in the later stages of the process that led up to the adoption of the direct primary was antipartisanship of any significance. Rather, much of what happened was the result of constraints facing politicians operating within a highly fragmented political system. It was political institutions, more than culture, that was crucial. Moreover, the values that were really important in constraining these politicians were not ones of antipartisanship but of a long-standing commitment to the practice of democracy within particular political institutions, namely, the parties.

[30] Angelo Panebianco, *Political Parties: Organization and Power*, Cambridge, Cambridge University Press, 1988.

Given the orientation of the book, it might well be that it will come to be labeled as "new institutionalist" in its approach, for it partly reflects March and Olsen's point that:

[P]olitical actors are driven by institutional duties and roles as well as, or instead of, by calculated self-interest; ... routines, rules, and forms evolve through history-dependent processes that do not reliably and quickly reach unique equilibria; the institutions of politics are not simple echoes of social forces.[31]

However, the objective of the book is not to show how the new institutionalist approach can further our understanding of politics but, rather, to account for how the parties came to adopt something that appeared to be against their interest – the direct primary.

One of the ways in which the study is "new institutionalist" is that it operates at the level that Thelen and Steinmo call "midrange theory." It aims to do precisely what they argue institutional analysis does, namely that it

allows us to examine the relationship between political actors as objects and as agents of history. The institutions that are at the center of historical institutional analyses ... can shape and constrain political strategies in important ways, but they are themselves also the outcome (conscious or unintended) of deliberate political strategies, of political conflict, and of choice.[32]

Consequently, the analysis may well not satisfy one potential set of critics. These are scholars who argue that the decentralized structures within which late-nineteenth-century politicians were operating had been created in the first place because of the antipartism present in late-eighteenth-century American society.

If they are correct, then, in some sense, political values would still account for the peculiar development of American parties since the late nineteenth century. This is not the place to evaluate that kind of grand theorizing, although it should be noted that this author remains rather skeptical about it. However, even if it were the case that the political institutions introduced between 1787 and the 1830s were primarily the product of a particular set of social and political values, those institutions still had a "life of their own." That is, how actors perceived their interests and made choices within those institutions still accounts for particular outcomes coming about rather than others. The choices they made affected how American politics would work in the future. In particular, the argument

[31] James G. March and Johan P. Olsen, *Rediscovering Institutions: The Organizational Basis of Politics*, New York, Free Press, 1989, p. 159.
[32] Kathleen Thelen and Sven Steinmo, "Historical Institutionalism in Comparative Politics," in Sven Steinmo, Kathleen Thelen, and Frank Longworth (eds.), *Structuring Politics: Historical Institutionalism in Comparative Analysis*, Cambridge, Cambridge University Press, 1992, p. 10.

presented here is that it was party politicians, initially mainly at the county level and then in state legislatures and in governors' mansions, who were the main actors who brought about the direct primary. Especially in much of the eastern United States, they could have prevented the introduction of the direct primary – had they wanted to do so. But, for the most part, they did not.

This is the kernel of the puzzle about American party development. Why did parties, which seemingly were still so powerful in many ways in the early 1900s, allow the adoption of a reform that would have long-term adverse consequences for them?

4. Explaining the Rise of the Direct Primary

There is no doubt that the rise of the direct primary was quite extraordinary. In 1899, the first legislation in the American north mandating the use of a direct primary was passed by the state legislature in Minnesota. (It required the use of such elections in Hennepin County, which contains the city of Minneapolis.) By the end of 1915, all but three states had enacted legislation for direct nominations, and in most of these states virtually all elective offices were now covered by legislation. However, even more extraordinary, perhaps, is the explanation that political scientists and historians have usually provided for this transformation in American parties; it is extraordinary because it is utterly implausible.

As we have seen, the conventional account holds that direct primary legislation was sponsored by Progressive reformers who were intent on curbing the power of parties. Their reaction against the corruption of nineteenth-century politics took the form of legislation that would make it more difficult for party elites to control the candidate selection process. Supported by mass electorates who shared the reformers' opposition to party organizations, reform politicians took on the parties. Inevitably there was conflict over a policy that would weaken the latter, but in state after state the reformers prevailed. This "heroic" version of what happened is open to a serious objection, though. No one doubts that parties were as powerful in the early twentieth century as they had been for most of the nineteenth century, and their representatives controlled state legislatures. Moreover, in spite of early-twentieth-century reforms, party organizations in many states were still strong at the time of World War I. But, if their supposed opponents had not disintegrated between 1900 and 1915, how was it possible for the reformers to overcome them in those years? That the public supported such reform is a wholly inadequate riposte, because everything that political science has learned about the relationship between mass electorates and elected politicians suggests that a supportive public is neither a necessary nor a sufficient condition for the passage of legislation. Democratic political systems do not work like that, and they certainly do not do so in the United States, where the fragmentation of governmental power made policy initiation difficult. The conventional account is about as implausible as claiming that the driving force behind the direct primary was a large invisible rabbit called Harvey.

Yet the conventional account has been accepted by generations of political scientists, including the present author, so that an obvious point to address is why such an implausible explanation was accepted for so long without question. There appear to be four main reasons for this. The first concerns the role of Charles Merriam in relation to the study of primaries. As noted earlier, no one else published a major study of party nominations after the last edition of his *Primary Elections* appeared in 1928. The strength of that book is its attention to the details of when particular states passed legislation on candidate selection. Its major weakness is that Merriam never investigated the circumstances in which legislation was passed; he was neither interested in why particular legislative proposals should have been introduced nor why some proposals could command majority support in a legislature. He thought this did not need explaining – the parties had been corrupt and in need of reform, so that eventually there was a popular revolt against them. End of story. Nor is it surprising that Merriam should have such views. Before he became the founding father of American political science, he was a reformist politician. In fact, the first edition of *Primary Elections* was published three years before his failed bid of 1911 for the mayoralty of Chicago, in which, to use Finegold's description, Merriam was a "traditional reform" candidate.[33]

Even in the 1928 edition of the book, his "purple prose" in places is more reminiscent of the political hustings than of scholarly debate. Thus, he says of candidate selection:

Having become one of the most important steps in the process of government [it] was open to every abuse that unscrupulous men, dazzled by prospects of almost incredible wealth and dictatorial power could devise and execute. Not all of these evils appeared in one place and one time.[34]

Given that the most important political scientist of his generation had written a major book on party nominations, no one else attempted to do so; when, much later, such constraints were less significant, the issue of how and why the direct primary was introduced was no longer of such central importance in political science. The Progressivist imprint of Merriam persists in the conventional wisdom of political science, even though few political scientists today have actually read anything that he wrote.

---

[33] Kenneth Finegold, *Experts and Politicians: Reform Challenges to Machine Politics in New York, Cleveland and Chicago*, Princeton, N.J., Princeton University Press, 1995, p. 121.

[34] Merriam and Overacker, *Primary Elections*, pp. 6–7.

The second reason is that far too much attention has always been paid to two states in which the debate over the direct primary was marked by intense conflict of a kind that could be characterized in terms of "reformers versus parties." These states were Wisconsin and New York. In fact, the experience of neither state was typical. Wisconsin's importance was that it was the first state to pass legislation requiring the use of the direct primary for all elective offices, and that did have a catalytic effect among reformers in some states, especially in the West. However, the drawn-out conflict evident in Wisconsin was not present in many states, simply because the source of that dispute had been the incompatible political ambitions of the legislation's architect, Governor Robert La Follette, and his opponents in the Republican party. The highly publicized battles over direct nominations in New York were also unusual, but, as in so many other areas of politics, New York came to be referred to as "typical of the industrial states." The result is that by focusing on a seemingly innovative state and on the largest state, a wholly misleading impression of the debate over the direct primary was created by contemporary reform journalists. That impression has been sustained over the years.

The third reason relates to the part played by V. O. Key, Jr. If Merriam was the founding father of American political science, Key was probably the most insightful analyst of American parties in the twentieth century. Nevertheless, in relation to nomination reform, there was an important respect in which Key developed a misleading argument. In what is probably his greatest work, *Southern Politics*, Key explained how the spread of the direct primary in that region after the early 1890s was associated with the collapse of party competition and the establishment of a new political order.[35] However, later in two books published in the 1950s – *American State Politics* and the fourth edition of *Politics, Parties, and Pressure Groups* – he sought to link southern developments with those in the north. He argued that, just as in the South, where decline in party competition had prompted the rise of the direct primary:

[s]imilarly, in Wisconsin and surrounding states the Republicans ruled without serious challenge. The ties of party – given the recency of the Civil War – made it simpler to advance popular government by introducing the direct primary to permit intraparty competition than to proceed by a realignment of parties.[36]

This is an ingenious argument, and, if it were true, it might explain how elected politicians, under pressure from mass electorates, came to be converted to support for the direct primary. In fact, there is little evidence to

---

[35] V. O. Key, Jr., *Southern Politics*, New York, Alfred A. Knopf, 1949.

[36] V. O. Key, Jr., *American State Politics: An Introduction*, New York, Knopf, 1956, Chapter 4, and *Politics, Parties and Pressure Groups*, Fourth Edition, New York, Thomas Y. Crowell, 1958, p. 412.

substantiate his claim about these midwestern states. Nevertheless, the significant point is that the claim had been made by Key, and his influence in the profession led to it becoming part of the tangle of arguments that were being made about the direct primary. By looking for a way of linking developments in the South, where his analysis may well have been correct, to those in the North, where he was not, Key inadvertently misled generations of scholars.

The fourth reason is that in recent decades political scientists have paid too little attention to the work of contemporary political historians. Reacting against the views of the previous generations of (Progressive) historians, such as George Mowry, and others, such as Richard Hofstadter, who helped to propagate the view that reformers had ruined the parties, these historians have provided evidence that points in a very different direction.[37] Their research suggests that parties were far from being the victims of antiparty reformers; the evidence indicates a much greater degree of control by the parties over reform than political scientists, such as Austin Ranney, usually provide for. For example, Abrams's explanation of the crucial part played by Robert Luce and Joseph Walker in the adoption of the direct primary in Massachusetts, Reynolds's account of primary reform in New Jersey, and Pegram's analysis of the same reform in Illinois all cast doubt on the view that antipartism was a crucial factor there.[38] Especially for the states achieving statehood before 1840, it is far from evident that studies by historians of individual states support the view that the primary was the product of antipartism. In part, this book attempts to build on the work of these historians, and to show its relevance in the broader context of American politics.

5. North and South

The focus of the study is on the American north, or more accurately, the non-South. This restriction is necessary because the adoption of direct nominations in the South had very different origins from those elsewhere in the United States. In the eleven states of the Confederacy, two-party competition had only been evident briefly between the late 1830s and the early

---

[37] Of their many works, see especially Richard Hofstadter, *The Age of Reform: From Bryan to FDR*, London, Jonathan Cape, 1962, and George Mowry, *The Era of Theodore Roosevelt, 1900–12*, London, Hamish Hamilton, 1958.

[38] Richard M. Abrams, *Conservatism in a Progressive Age*, pp. 179–84 and 239–43; John F. Reynolds, *Testing Democracy: Electoral Behavior and Progressive Reform in New Jersey, 1880–1920*, Chapel Hill and London, University of North Carolina Press, 1988, p. 130; Thomas R. Pegram, *Partisans and Progressives: Private Interest and Public Policy in Illinois, 1870–1922*, Urbana and Chicago, University of Illinois Press, 1992, pp. 166–81.

1850s, and again in the decade or so after the Civil War, when restrictions on electoral participation by "rebel" voters made it possible for Republicans to win statewide elections. In the twenty years after Reconstruction, the Democrats dominated politics at a statewide level, although within each state there were still some areas of Republican support. From the 1890s a variety of devices were introduced to limit black participation in elections, and each of these states saw the collapse not just of the Republican parties there, but, more important, of *any* viable alternative to Democratic candidates. The relation of the direct primary to these developments is a matter of academic dispute. The long dominant view – deriving from the ideas of V. O. Key and the historian C. Vann Woodward – held that primaries helped to sustain and legitimate this new political order.[39] Thus, writing in 2001, Jewell and Morehouse claim that:

[T]he major purpose and effect of the primaries in southern states was to guarantee Democratic control of southern politics. Democratic leaders believed that public primaries would "legitimate the nominees, settle intraparty differences before the general election and greatly reduce the power of opposition voters" (Kousser, 1974, 4). The Democrats were concerned about opposition from both Republican candidates and third parties and about the possibility that such challengers would seek support from black voters.[40]

An opposing view of the direct primary in the South is that, in at least some states, its purpose was not so much that of facilitating Democratic control through the restriction of black participation, though it did do that, but of broadening the base of the white electorate. For example, Kirwan argued that this was why the Democratic State Executive Committee in Mississippi had adopted the direct primary in 1903:

... an additional hurdle was placed between the Negro and the franchise ... [and] ... In this respect the primary law was a move away from democracy. In another sense, however, the primary law was the most democratic measure which the voters had yet obtained. Henceforth in election of state officials choice rested not with a small group acting through the medium of the state convention, but with the mass of voters in the state. If thousands of white men were barred from the franchise, yet those who could actually had a voice in the selection of officials. Furthermore, the control of [white politicians from] the black counties over the nominating process was effectively broken.[41]

---

[39] On Woodward, see especially C. Vann Woodward, *The Strange Career of Jim Crow*, Third Edition, New York, Oxford University Press, 1974.

[40] Malcolm E. Jewell and Sarah M. Morehouse, *Political Parties and Elections in American States*, Washington, D.C., CQ Press, 2001, p. 101; J. Morgan Kousser, *The Shaping of Southern Politics: Suffrage Restrictions and the Establishment of the One-Party South, 1880–1910*, New Haven, Conn., Yale University Press, 1974.

[41] Albert D. Kirwan, *Revolt of the Rednecks: Mississippi Politics, 1876–1925*, New York, Harper and Row, 1951, p. 131.

However, whichever account of the rise of the direct primary in the South is accepted, the central point is that the southern states had very different political systems to those in the north, and in the early 1890s the latter were far from being on the verge of a collapse into partyless politics. In the north, whatever attracted proponents of the direct primary to that device, it could not have been a response to the kind of political restructuring seen in the South. It is with respect to the north that the interesting question, of why party politicians should have allowed the adoption of a mechanism that eventually would undermine party control, has to be addressed. Consequently, in this study, the South is considered only insofar as its experience may be relevant to that in the north.

Of course, the influence of the southern experience was not confined just to the eleven states of the Confederacy. Aspects of party politics in the border states, especially in the more rural states, such as Kentucky, continued to reflect the legacy of the division over slavery and the Civil War. However, political conflict in these states did not dissolve into one-partyism, nor was the role of African Americans in the polity a central factor in the rise of direct nominations in the parties. For that reason, it is appropriate to consider them alongside the other northern states.

With the partial exception of the border states, the northern polities into which the direct primary was introduced were white and male. Although African American migration to the north was to increase greatly during the first two decades of the twentieth century, the relatively small number of black Americans in most of these states at the beginning of the century meant that they played virtually no role in the advent of direct nominations. To white politicians they were neither rivals nor potential coalition partners of any significance. Similarly, and in spite of their numbers, women were not an important part of formal political institutions; only a few western states had enfranchised women by the early twentieth century. In just four states did women's suffrage precede the adoption of direct nominations for most public offices (Colorado, Idaho, Utah, and Wyoming). Although, as is seen in Chapter 8, women were a significant factor in preventing the repeal of direct primaries in the 1920s, they were not at the time of their introduction.

6. Institutionalization of the Parties

The evidence that emerges in the succeeding chapters is that in much of the American north, the proposed introduction of the direct primary either did not generate much political conflict, or, if there were major disputes, these were not on the basis usually posited – namely, reformers-versus-parties. Party politicians usually cooperated in the passage of primary laws; indeed, if the laws were to be passed at all, the cooperation of some of them was essential, for, even in the Progressive era, it was still party politicians who acted as gatekeepers to the legislative process. What was actually occurring was a process that began as *institutionalization*; that is the replacement of informal modes of organizing party politics by rule-governed procedures. More formally, institutionalized organization may be defined as it was by Nelson Polsby in his classic study of that process in the U.S. Congress; it has:

three major characteristics: (1) it is relatively well-bounded, that is to say, differentiated from its environment. Its members are easily identifiable, it is relatively difficult to become a member, and its leaders are recruited principally from within the organization. (2) The organization is relatively complex, that is, its functions are internally separated on some regular and explicit basis, its parts are not wholly interchangeable, and for at least some important purposes, its parts are interdependent. There is a division of labor in which roles are specified, and there are widely shared expectations about the performance of roles. There are regularized patterns of recruitment to roles, and of movement from role to role. (3) Finally, the organization tends to use universalistic rather than particularistic criteria, and automatic rather than discretionary methods for conducting its internal business. Precedents and rules are followed; merit systems replace favoritism and nepotism; and impersonal codes supplant personal preferences as prescriptions for behavior.[42]

The pressure for party institutionalization came from changes in American society. The parties had developed originally in the 1830s in an America that consisted of small towns and rural hinterlands; it was a face-to-face society in which informal constraints were largely sufficient to regulate the conduct of politics – in spite of the highly competitive nature of that politics.

However, in the decades after the emergence of mass party politics in the 1830s, the social base of America changed radically. The population became much larger, more urbanized, and far more heterogeneous. A style of politics that worked relatively well in the 1830s was working much less well in the new circumstances. The adverse consequences of relying on informal practices, that were now less effective in facilitating control of the political system, affected not just those members of the middle class who might be attracted to overturning the party order, but, more important, party politicians themselves. To take one example: The main source of split-ticket voting in the early 1880s was the inability of county parties to control party officials in particular wards or districts; disputed nominations could create rival candidacies, or ward leaders might cut their own deals unless candidates paid them to stay loyal. At the local level, one of the main causes of this turbulence was the ballot. Parties issued their own ballot papers, but it was the established practice that the names of alternative candidates could be pasted onto that ballot. It was a way of operating that maximized the

---

[42] Nelson W. Polsby, "The Institutionalization of the U.S. House of Representatives," *American Political Science Review*, 62(1968), p. 145.

opportunity for disorder when the informal constraints were absent; the result was a much higher level of split-ticket voting than would have been expected in a society that was so partisan and in which there were only two major parties. For that reason, many party politicians came to accept that older practices had to be changed somehow; that could only be done through introducing formal rules and regulations to replace the mores, conventions, and informal procedures on which the Jacksonian party democracy had been founded.

Parties do not institutionalize just because, in some sense, it is necessary for the political system to work efficiently, or even to work at all. They institutionalize because a sufficient number of politicians within those parties come to understand that their own interests are affected by present arrangements. Of course, there may be disagreements about where those interests lie, or how their interests may be affected by particular reforms, so that institutionalization may well be accompanied by conflict. Moreover, institutionalization can generate unforeseen outcomes – whether beneficial or otherwise – to the interests of those who supported particular reforms. Institutionalization in a democracy is not something that happens to politicians, it is something they do; its results may or may not solve the problems that gave rise to the pressure for it, and its unintended consequences may or may not create new problems, and pressures for further change. In fact, as will become apparent in this study, one of the notable features of late-nineteenth-century institutionalization in the American parties is that the very success of the early reform, the Australian Ballot, affected adversely the context in which decisions about the later reform, the direct primary, were taken.

The direct primary, then, was not an isolated reform that happened to be enacted when parties were sufficiently weak that their opponents could overcome them ("heroically"). It was a reform that had its origins in changes in American society that, by the 1880s, were starting to pose severe problems for party politicians. The efforts by those politicians to devise procedures and regulations for dealing with them culminated in a reform that, much later, many politicians wished had not been enacted and which they tried to repeal. The direct primary was to have many consequences for the conduct of party politics – its most important long-term consequence being to reduce the role of party in American politics. Yet it is wholly misleading to deduce from those adverse consequences, and from the opposition of politicians in the 1920s to the direct primary, that its introduction must have been imposed on the parties, and have been opposed by them. As will be seen, the truth was less dramatic, in that the direct primary's introduction did not usually involve a pitched battle between antiparty reformers and party leaders, but much more complex assessments of where personal and party interests might lie. However, the background context in which all these calculations were being made, and which drove nomination reform forward, was one in which the older Jacksonian model of party politics was no longer working well, so that there were good reasons for modifying it.

However, if the start of the process of nomination reform can be understood as one of party institutionalization, this takes us only so far in explaining why it was the direct primary that came to be adopted. Thus, institutionalization does help to explain why, throughout the 1890s, partisan-controlled state legislatures were enacting laws to regulate how candidates should be selected. It cannot explain, though, why it was the direct primary, and not some other device, that was introduced in the next two decades. As is seen in subsequent chapters, part of that explanation lies within the parties themselves. Use of the direct primary had been increasing on a voluntary basis in a number of rural counties in the nineteenth century, and by the 1890s it was the only widely deployed alternative to the caucus-convention system. Moreover, not only did some party elites become convinced that the direct primary might strengthen the parties, but others saw that their own careers could be advanced by its adoption. Nevertheless, these were not the only factors accounting for its rise.

Party institutionalization took place in a context in which party elites were constrained in two respects in terms of what they would do. First, public attitudes to parties had long valued extensive public participation in the parties, and for their introduction to be successful reforms probably had to conform with those expectations. The direct primary was one that could do so. Second, from the second half of the 1890s onward, reformers – including those of an antiparty persuasion – started to concentrate their attention not on the evident complexities of the problems arising from the nominating system, but on a single supposed "solution" to it – the direct primary. By focusing on the direct primary, they made it more likely that extensive experiments with direct nominations would be tried by state governments than would have been attempted had debate remained focused on the problems of the nominating system. Consequently, the account presented in this book is one that does accord a role both to political values and to antiparty reformers in explaining the direct primary's introduction. However, it is a more restricted role than is usually accorded to either of them.

While the conventional interpretation sees the values of reformers as conflicting with those of party elites, the point being made here is that the crucial value – that parties should be forums for mass participation – was one that was partially shared by a wide range of political actors. No one believed that participation in the parties should be restricted to just a few – whether that few be ideological adherents, or selected on some other basis. There was disagreement as to who should be let in – many antiparty reformers would have wanted to exclude the uneducated – but all subscribed to an ideal of a relatively highly participatory party. That this view of parties was widely shared in the broader society as well, was important in shaping how reform might proceed.

As for the antiparty reformers, there is no doubt that their part in focusing attention on the direct primary itself helped, from about 1897 onward, to create a privileged position in public debate for that particular way of conducting candidate selection. However, it is only in a limited sense that these reformers could be said to have set the political agenda. They did not invent the direct primary – its use was increasing anyway. Moreover, arguably there were no feasible alternatives to the direct primary or some slight modification of the status quo. By focusing on this "solution," those who wished to weaken parties could scarcely have been said to have shifted the political agenda in a way that was very different from how it would have been set in their absence. That they made a contribution to the process is important, but the rather restricted nature of their role is also apparent.

Moreover, if the argument presented here is that the direct primary arose out of particular problems internal to the parties, this does not mean that this reform can be treated completely in isolation from other reforms. In the long term, the significance of the adoption of the direct primary was to be affected greatly by the results of another aspect of late-nineteenth-century institutionalization. The Jacksonian democracy placed parties at the center of American society, and it facilitated that by the intertwining of party and government. Not only did the huge population expansion prompt institutionalization in the parties, it also created demands on governments to do far more by way of social regulation than had been required earlier. The patronage-centred Jacksonian politics, based as it was on informal arrangements and personal contacts, was increasingly less able to cope with the new demands of an urbanizing society. Over a period of forty years, from about 1880 to 1920, the main elements of the divorce between party and government were put in place. New budgeting arrangements in local government, civil service rules that applied to the employment of at least some appointed public officials, and a number of other reforms led to the gradual replacement of the older, informal, relationships.[43] As the interpenetration of party and government was dissolving, so this aspect of institutionalization increased the relative importance of the role of candidate selection for the parties; deprived of their "marriage" to government, America's parties now depended far more on their nominating role if they were to exercise control over individual politicians. By the 1960s, when changes in electoral technology made it more possible for candidates to seek office independently of their parties, their exposed position

---

[43] See Martin J. Schiesl, *The Politics of Efficiency: Municipal Administration and Reform in America, 1880–1920*, Berkeley, University of California Press, 1977; C. K. Yearley, *The Money Machines: The Breakdown and Reform of Government and Party Finance in the North, 1860–1920*, Albany, State University of New York, 1920.

became all too evident. The direct primary then enabled America's parties to complete a move down a very different trajectory from their European counterparts.

7. Organization of the Book

This book is divided into three sections. The first section, consisting of Chapters 2, 3, and 4, is concerned with how the direct primary came to be introduced. It examines various aspects of the legislation relevant to the direct primary that was enacted between the late nineteenth century and 1915. The second section comprises Chapters 5, 6, and 7, and it considers different explanations of why the direct primary should have been introduced so widely – and within only a few years. The third section, containing just one chapter (8), is concerned with the aftermath and consequences of the pre-1916 reforms, while the concluding chapter returns to the theme of party institutionalization as an explanation for the direct primary.

Section A

Chapter 2 considers the reform that preceded direct nominations, but which was so important for that later reform, the Australian Ballot. It shows how at the very end of the 1880s and the beginning of the 1890s, most states enacted laws requiring the use of an official ballot, in place of the older party-ballots. This reform was prompted by concerns within them about the consequences for the major parties – in particular their inability to control party officials at the ward level – of retaining a ballot that facilitated "treachery" among their own supporters. Moreover, it is shown that, although antiparty reformers initially secured the introduction of a type of official ballot that tended to weaken party control, during the 1890s many states changed their form of ballot to ones that favored party interests. Even during the Progressive era, the parties' grip on the type of ballot used was not much reduced. The Australian Ballot demonstrates that, faced by the need for reform, the parties were more than capable of protecting their own interests when it was clear where those interests lay.

Chapter 3 examines how parties became subjected to extensive state regulation at the end of the nineteenth century, and why legal controls were needed to effect reforms. Until the 1880s there was relatively little state regulation of party procedures, and many state parties themselves did not have formal rules. From the late 1880s onward, there was a spate of such state regulation, with an increasingly large number of statutes regulating how candidates could be nominated. It is shown that these reforms were aimed at codifying the older, caucus-convention, system of nomination, and state regulation was the mechanism used because the decentralized nature of the parties meant that it was only by that means that effective formal procedures could be introduced. Consequently, the point of such regulation was not to "punish the parties for their misdeeds," as is often alleged. The process of regulation was boosted by the perceived success of the Australian Ballot reform, but unlike ballot reform, no simple solution to the problems posed by the passing of the "face-to-face" society was apparent with candidate selection. It was for this reason that a now forgotten national conference was convened in 1898 to discuss nomination reform – a conference attended by both traditional reformers and "regular" party politicians. The later sections of the chapter examine why the structure of American parties necessitated far more state regulation of them than was the case for parties in other democracies. It is also shown that the Supreme Court has generally protected a party's control of its internal affairs – usually rejecting claims that parties can be regulated to further other political objectives.

The reforms discussed in Chapter 3 were directed mainly at problems emerging in urban America. However, during the last decades of the nineteenth century, parties in rural counties were increasingly adopting a form of nomination that had first been used in Crawford County, Pennsylvania, in the early 1840s. The "Crawford County System" was a direct primary, but by the end of the 1890s its use had spread well beyond that county. It was employed in some counties in about one-third of all states by then, although the caucus-convention system still prevailed in the vast majority of counties. The spread of the Crawford County System forms the subject of Chapter 4. It is shown that, for the first time in the 1890s, the system was used in a major urban area, Cleveland, Ohio, but that the adverse consequences apparent there convinced even the "good government" reformers in the city that the direct primary was not a satisfactory solution. Nevertheless, the Cleveland experience had very little effect in stemming the appeal of the direct primary. By 1899, the first northern state (Minnesota) to mandate its use in one of its counties did so, and, beginning with Wisconsin in 1903, states started to require its use for nearly all offices within their boundaries. By 1915 all but three states required direct nominations for some offices, and most of them required it for all offices. At first it was eastern states that were more likely to experiment with the direct primary, but from 1907 insurgent Republicanism in many western states facilitated its rapid adoption there.

Section B

The three chapters in this section are each concerned with different kinds of explanation to account for the introduction of the direct primary by so many states. Chapter 5 examines the argument that the direct primary was mainly a dispute between urban reformers, who wanted to change state nominating procedures as a way of further reforming city government, and the urban-based parties that wished to retain the older form of nominating procedures. To test this claim, the chapter examines how primary legislation came to be introduced in the states that contained the five largest cities in 1900 (Massachusetts, Pennsylvania, Missouri, Illinois, and New York). If the direct primary had really involved such a conflict, then it would surely be most evident in these states. In fact, only in New York was there a fight over primary legislation that in any way resembles that account. In the four other states what happened was very different from the New York experience. Far from being typical, New York was exceptional, largely because the greater relative size of its major city gave urban politicians there much more clout in the state legislature than they had elsewhere. The central point is that in most states neither antiparty reformers nor the urban machines had enough representation in state legislatures to be the crucial actors in legislating for nomination reform.

Chapter 6 analyzes the possible effects of party competition on nomination reforms. It shows both that the change in party competition after the 1890s is often misunderstood, and that there is no evidence to support the argument that it was the absence of interparty competition that prompted the introduction of the direct primary in the north. Rather, it was competition between parties that tended to prompt primary legislation, largely because nomination reform was an issue to which mass electorates appeared to respond positively. However, in two New England states, Connecticut and Rhode Island, the Republican parties resisted successfully the direct primary as part of a strategy of consolidating their own political base, reducing the influence of "non-Yankee" voters, and keeping the Democrats at bay.

Chapter 7 provides an alternative explanation to the ones usually advanced to account for the introduction of direct nominations. It examines the constraints imposed by the widespread view that parties should be participatory, and how the direct primary came to be regarded as an appropriate device in spite of clear indications, including evidence from Cleveland, that it was a highly flawed reform. It is argued here that party elites were under pressure "to do something" because of the unsatisfactory performance of the older nominating system under changed circumstances, but that there were few alternatives to the direct primary, given the need to provide for high levels of participation in the parties. The real contribution of the antiparty reformers was that, by focusing on the direct primary so much since the later 1890s, they narrowed the range of options embraced by the public debate. These reformers lacked the political power to impose the direct primary on state legislatures, but, in the absence of any serious alternatives, the reform they had championed came to be seen as the "only game in town."

Section C
Chapter 8 is concerned with what happened after 1915. It explores the reaction against the direct primary in the 1920s and the attempts to repeal

it. It shows also that much party control over party nominations remained, with the exception of the occasional state like California where specific conditions had greatly weakened party power. However, the main impact of the primary was evident only in the 1960s when new campaign technologies provided a much greater incentive for candidates to divorce themselves from their parties. The chapter also considers briefly the relationship between the direct primary and the (indirect) presidential primary, showing, in part, how the patterns of their adoption in the different regions varied.

In the concluding chapter, it is argued that the direct primary should not be understood as an external factor that changed the course of American party development. To the contrary, the decentralization of America's parties meant that there were really no alternatives, other than some variation on the status quo, to direct nominations. Moreover, once states had started experimenting with the direct primary, there would always be incentives for the politically ambitious to extend their use if this would likely boost their own career prospects. The incentive for doing just that would have increased anyway in the 1960s, with the advent of television, even if the growth of direct primaries had somehow been curtailed in the Progressive era. Far from having the direct primary imposed on them, America's parties were operating throughout their history in an institutional framework in which it was always likely that they would change their systems of nomination to something that provided for greater candidate autonomy.

A

HOW THE DIRECT PRIMARY AROSE

The Catalytic Effect of Ballot Reform

The years between 1885 and 1915 saw the introduction of a number of reforms with which the introduction of the direct primary is sometimes bracketed. They include the direct election of U.S. Senators, the initiative referendum, and recall elections. However, only one of the various reforms is crucial to an understanding of how and why direct primaries were introduced, and that is the adoption of the Australian Ballot. There are two reasons why ballot reform should have been so important for the later debate about nomination reform. First, the switch from ballots administered by parties to ballots that were distributed and regulated by the states had direct consequences for the process of nominating candidates. Second, the apparent success of the Australian Ballot – as far as both party elites and antiparty reformers were concerned – helped to create expectations about political reform that would frame the context in which reform of the nominating system was discussed. However, in explaining why the direct primary was introduced, ballot reform is significant for another reason, one that forms the subject of this chapter. It demonstrates how successfully the parties were able to defend their interests in enacting reforms when their own interests could be identified clearly. As becomes evident in later chapters, in many respects it was much less obvious in the case of nomination reform where the interests of the parties lay, and that was to produce very different results in terms of future party development.

1. The Adoption of the Australian Ballot

By the early 1880s the Australian Ballot, as it came to be known in the United States, had been adopted for elections not only in Australia but also in several European countries, including Britain, Belgium, Luxembourg, and Italy. The essential elements of this system were that the ballot paper was printed by the state, and not by the candidates or parties, it was available only at the place of balloting and at the time of voting, and a ballot paper could not legally be removed from the balloting place. The point of the last requirement was to prevent a practice known as the "Tasmanian dodge."[1]

Secrecy was an important feature of the Australian ballot, and, indeed, in Britain the procedure that was adopted in 1872 was known simply as the secret ballot. However, secrecy was ensured not merely by having a ballot box into which ballots could be placed without revealing their contents, but more especially by the fact that ballots were uniform in design and could be acquired only at the time of voting. (Indeed in some states, such as Massachusetts, there were already laws by the 1880s regulating the use of boxes in balloting, as a measure to prevent ballot stuffing and other forms of fraud.[2]) The real significance of the Australian Ballot was that it was an official (or state) ballot as opposed to an unofficial ballot.

Before 1888 no state in the United States used the Australian system of balloting, but in that year Kentucky enacted legislation that applied only to the city of Louisville, while Massachusetts passed a comprehensive law that applied statewide. By 1891, thirty-one of the thirty-three nonsouthern states had adopted some variant of the Australian Ballot law, and by 1893 the two remaining states (Iowa and Kansas) had followed suit. Thereafter, the type of ballot used was the subject of considerable change by non-southern state legislatures in the thirty years or so after its adoption; a total of forty-six changes of ballot type (involving twenty-six states and territories) were made between the Australian Ballot's first adoption (in 1888) and 1917 (See Table 2.1).

2. Informal Procedures and the Problems of Scale

To understand why American ballot reform proceeded so quickly, it is necessary to outline first the nature of the American party system that had been established in the 1830s and that had so firmly taken root throughout the country by the 1860s. Five aspects of it are crucial in explaining the later adoption of the Australian ballot:

1. the parties operated in a face-to-face society, which was primarily rural and with an homogeneous electorate, at least in rural areas;
2. the society was highly partisan;

---

[1] This involved a person who controlled the votes of a number of others arranging for one of them to go to the balloting place supposedly to vote but in practice to acquire a ballot that would then be used by the next "client"; that "client" would take that ballot, as filled out by the "patron," to the poll and use it in voting, having first acquired another blank ballot that would be used subsequently by the next "client." For the loss of one vote at the beginning of the process, a patron could thereby ensure that his people would vote exactly as he wished them to.

[2] L. E. Fredman, *The Australian Ballot: The Story of An American Reform*, East Lansing, Michigan State University Press, 1968, p. 38.

TABLE 2.1. *Changes in Type of Official Ballot by Nonsouthern States, 1888–1917*

	States Making Changes		Number of Changes
1888–1891	Minnesota Missouri	Washington Wisconsin	4
1892–1900	California (2) Colorado Kentucky Missouri Montana Nebraska (2) New Hampshire New York	North Dakota (2) Pennsylvania South Dakota Utah Vermont Washington Wyoming	18
1901–1910	California Connecticut Idaho Iowa Kansas Maryland	Montana Nebraska Oklahoma (2) Pennsylvania Rhode Island Washington	13
1911–1917	California Colorado Kansas Montana	New Jersey New York South Dakota Wyoming	8
Total number of changes of ballot type, 1888–1917			43

3. a large number of public offices were elective, with short terms of office, so that there were elections at least once a year in most communities;
4. within states and even within counties, parties were highly decentralized;[3] and

---

[3] Even in the large cities from the 1860s to the 1890s, and in spite of the reputation of the parties there being "machines," the reality was more often that of competing local leaders, rather than leaders who were well integrated into a tightly disciplined hierarchy. New York City, which sometimes gave the appearance of being slightly more hierarchical than many cities, was not; Tammany Hall had serious challengers within the Democratic party until the end of the 1880s. In Shefter's words, "a system of rampant factionalism" was then replaced by one in which Tammany was able "to exercise reliable discipline over the city's Democratic party." Martin Shefter, "The Electoral Foundations of the Political

5. elections were won mainly by a party mobilizing its own partisans, rather than converting its opponents' supporters or by mobilizing the small number of uncommitted voters.

Only the first of these factors was to change radically in the decades following the 1860s, and thereby generate problems for the system of balloting, but once these problems emerged, the other four factors were an important element affecting what would come to be regarded as an acceptable solution to these problems.

In a "face-to-face" society, most citizens knew most other citizens, or at least knew who they were. Consequently, politics could largely be organized on an informal basis – that is without formal, or legally binding, rules. For example, if everyone in a community knew who was entitled to vote, it was unnecessary to construct a list of eligible voters; nor could there be any possibility of impersonation of voters in that type of community. One of the ways in which informality still persisted in 1880 was in the form of the ballot, but the rapidly expanding population, especially in urban areas, was creating problems for the informal system on a scale that had not existed earlier; it came under pressure in these areas.

In the early years of the American Republic voting at elections had often been by voice, but by the mid-nineteenth century the ballot was used virtually everywhere.[4] Typically, parties supplied the ballots – they gave a ballot to the voter who intended to vote for them, either in advance of the election or near the polling place on the day of the election, and the voter then took it along to the ballot box. The public nature of this action was reinforced by the fact that each of the major parties normally used differently colored paper for their ballots.[5] For the parties these arrangements

Machine in New York City, 1884–1897," in Joel H. Silbey, Allan G. Bogue, and William H. Flanigan (eds.), *The History of American Electoral Behavior*, Princeton, N.J., Princeton University Press, 1978, p. 293. Elsewhere, in cities like Chicago and Philadelphia, ward bosses displayed even more of the quasi-autonomy of the political oligopolist than the characteristics usually associated with functionaries in a system of line management; it was not until the twentieth century that more centralized parties emerged in most of these cities. On Chicago, see Kenneth Finegold, *Experts and Politicians: Reform Challenges to Machine Politics in New York, Cleveland, and Chicago*, Princeton, N.J. Princeton University Press, 1995; on Philadelphia, see Peter McCaffery, *When Bosses Ruled Philadelphia: The Emergence of the Republican Machine, 1867–1933*, University Park, Pennsylvania State University Press, 1993.

[4] A ballot was "one or several pieces of paper which contained the names of the candidates and the designation of the offices, and which were used by the electors in voting." Eldon Cobb Evans, *A History of the Australian Ballot in the United States*, Chicago, University of Chicago Press, 1917, p. 6.

[5] The public nature of the ballot reflected the more general mid-nineteenth-century American value that "the sacred civic act was not a private exercise of conscience or the individual practice of intellect but, in the words of the Loco-Focos, 'speechifying and resolutions at political meetings'." Politics was to be conducted in the public gaze. Mary P. Ryan, *Civic Wars: Democracy and Public Life in the American City During the Nineteenth Century*, Berkeley, University of California Press, 1997, p. 96.

had the advantage of enabling them to keep tabs on their voters, while at the same time it helped the illiterate voter to have confidence that he was actually voting for the candidates of the party for which he intended to vote.

The problems associated with "increasing scale" in American democracy had started to become evident in a few places even before the Civil War. Thus, New York had to introduce voter registration requirements as early as 1859, and other states did so later.[6] The problem with the party ballot was that in places other than small and stable communities it permitted various forms of abuse. For example, it was quite easy to imitate the other party's ballot. If the voter did not know the person who was handing him the ballot, it was possible to give him one that looked like his party's ballot but which actually contained the names of some candidates, or perhaps many candidates, of the opposition party. The illiterate voter could well be at the mercy of such practices, but even diligent and literate voters might fall victim to them. In addition, smaller communities had tended to provide safeguards against the unrestricted sale of votes or the intimidation of voters. The need to preserve social harmony in such places meant that there tended to be conventions about the limits of inducement that could be offered to, or pressure put on, voters; it was a rough and ready system, and it would not have satisfied the standards of some reformers of later generations, but the excesses of the parties were generally kept in check. However, the expansion of the cities was creating large areas within them in which these conventions did not apply, and could not be applied, and the public nature of balloting was seen widely to be providing extensive opportunities for fraud and intimidation.

One response to this was an attempt to standardize the ballot, and between 1867 and the early 1880s ten northern states (plus four in the South) enacted laws specifying the color of the paper and the type of ink to be used on the ballot – Maine having already passed such legislation as early as 1831. In five states there was also legislation in this period to regulate the size of the ballot paper. The purpose of these regulations was to make for a less public ballot – to make it more difficult for anyone to tell how a voter had voted. Parties found it easy to evade such regulation and often colluded in doing so – in Ohio the Democrats started to use a cream-white shade on their ballot, in reacting to an 1868 law requiring the ballot to be printed on white paper, while the Republicans then went for a very white ballot.[7]

It might appear from this last point that the interests of the parties lay in the maintenance of the status quo, but the situation facing them was actually much more complex than this. In the first place, being associated with massive vote fraud and intimidation did not play well, even among many of their own supporters, in a polity founded on democratic norms.

[6] Fredman, *The Australian Ballot*, p. 23.
[7] Evans, *A History of the Australian Ballot in the United States*, p. 8.

Consequently, bosses could, and did, provoke opposition within their own parties. For example, the Tweed ring in New York City, which had its power base in Tammany Hall, had been smashed by the efforts not of Republican politicians but of Democrats – most notably Samuel Tilden, who went on to become his party's presidential nominee in 1876. Some practices were always overlooked, quite conveniently, by party elites, but others could not be by politicians following a path of enlightened self-interest in the electoral market. Second, the most dubious practices were often found in the major urban areas, and intraparty conflict and rivalries made party elites outside these areas only too willing to constrain their own parties within them. Nor were the urban party leaders usually in a position to "call the tune" on their own; in 1880 the population of "outstate" areas was usually greater than those of urban areas, and, even in those states that did reapportion their legislatures regularly, there was a lag between population growth and the fair representation of cities. The U.S. Census defined an urban area as one containing more than five thousand people, and even with this liberal definition, only four states had more than 50 percent of their population living in urban areas in 1880 – Massachusetts, New Jersey, New York, and Rhode Island. In general, therefore, it was difficult for urban party elites to prevail in any conflict with their rural colleagues.

Finally, existing balloting arrangements created serious problems of party management. Although this was a highly partisan era, widespread ticket-splitting was actually practiced. Reynolds and McCormick's data for New Jersey and New York are illuminating in this regard. For example, in Essex County, New Jersey in elections in the 1880s, typically between 4 and 9 percent of Democratic voters failed to support the entire party ticket; in New York, and especially in New York City, ticket-splitting was even greater. In Manhattan in the 1880s Republican ticket-splitters never accounted for less than a quarter of all Republicans, and often much more – in 1884, 63.5 percent of all those who supported at least one Republican candidate failed to support the whole ticket.[8] Most of the ticket-splitting occurred low down the ticket, and resulted not from weak partisanship, but from the activities of a whole variety of local politicos who found their interests temporarily diverging from those of other levels of their party. The decentralization of America's parties meant that county parties could undermine the electoral strategies of their state parties and, more especially, party officials at the district and ward levels could similarly frustrate the county party organizations. In addition, party freelancers, operating on behalf of candidates who had failed to gain the official nomination, might well be distributing ballots that looked like party ballots – except that for one office

[8] John F. Reynolds and Richard L. McCormick, "Outlawing 'Treachery': Split Tickets and Ballot Laws in New York and New Jersey, 1880–1910," *Journal of American History*, 72(1986), p. 842.

the name of a different candidate had been substituted. Altogether, this meant that parties rarely controlled the process of ballot distribution as much as they would wish to.

Decentralization of the parties produced serious problems of coordination, particularly given the informal nature of much party work, including the nomination of candidates. Consequently, factionalism in a county party could produce "bolters" who would nominate their own candidates for some offices and run their own campaigns, but who would seek to show they were allied to those higher up a party ticket. "Bolting" occurred frequently, because, as Reynolds and McCormick observe, there were "a multiplicity of local customs and understandings concerning the rotation and division of offices among localities, factions, or ethnic groups."[9] Disputes over their implementation in particular nominations might produce a "bolt" from a nominating caucus and the holding of a rival one, and this was more likely to occur in communities where the opposition party was weak. Furthermore, given the reliance on informal procedures – on customs and conventions, rather than rules – it could often be unclear who really could be said to be the official nominees.

It was not even necessary for "bolters" to have the resources to produce a complete ballot of their own – many did not. Without their vote becoming invalid, voters were permitted to strike out the names of candidates on the ballot for whom they did not wish to vote, and they could substitute the names of alternative persons for whom they did wish to vote – by sticking on what was called a "paster" to the relevant part of the ballot. The supporters of "bolters" would supply the appropriate "pasters" to voters before they got to the polling place – "printing and distributing pasters was one way for an individual to present himself to voters despite the opposition of the party."[10]

However, disorder came about not just through the actions of competing factions and of bolting candidates. The ability of a district captain to "knife" particular candidates was a resource that could be used by him for extracting campaign contributions from those who might fall victim to it. As Bass notes of New York:

Since "trading" and "knifing" were so easy, candidates were forced to take precautions against these acts of treachery. Each district leader and captain had to be paid for his services rendered in distributing the ballot. This payment was also regarded as a premium on an anti-knifing insurance policy.[11]

The result of all this was that by the 1880s the attitude of even urban party elites to the existing party ballot was often complex. On the one hand,

---

[9] Reynolds and McCormick, "Outlawing 'Treachery'," p. 845.
[10] *Ibid.*
[11] Herbert J. Bass, *"I am a Democrat: The Political Career of David Bennett Hill*, Syracuse, Syracuse University Press, 1961, p. 97.

to the extent that it gave them the opportunity to keep tabs on the behavior of "their" voters, they were supporters of it, and might be presumed to be in favor of its retention. But, on the other hand, to the extent that it made life easy for "bolters," they would wish to reform it – in order to provide for greater order in the electoral market. Like all would-be oligopolists they wanted stability, and, despite the highly partisan character of the nineteenth-century American electorate, order was often missing. This lack of order could be costly indeed, especially given the close margins of victory that were typical in the nineteenth century – both nationally and in most states. The most notorious example of an absence of party discipline occurred in 1888. Incumbent Democratic president Grover Cleveland won a plurality of votes in the country as a whole, and would have won in the Electoral College had he carried his home state of New York. He had won New York in 1884 but lost it by 12,787 votes in 1888. Yet at the same time the Democratic state governor, David Hill, won reelection by 17,740 votes, and in New York City ran ahead of Cleveland by about 11,000 votes. At the time there were widespread allegations that Tammany Hall had done a deal with some New York City Republicans, and that "in the eighth district, for example, Republicans peddlers had been distributing Tammany's congressional and county tickets."[12] Not surprisingly, then, when the idea of an official, nonparty, ballot started to be discussed in the early-to-mid 1880s party elites would be likely supporters, providing a version of it could be found that would not weaken their links to their own voters.

There was one final consideration that might have weighed with party elites in their attitude to the party ballot – expense. One of the advantages that the Australian Ballot would have is that it would transfer a significant election expense from the parties to government. Just how important a reason for action it was in the 1880s is difficult to say, but interestingly it was cited by a reformer, John Milholland, a decade later – in January 1898. In his opening address to the National Conference on Practical Reform of Primary Elections, Milholland read out a letter of support for the Conference's aims from the governor of New York, Frank Black. Milholland noted that Black "prides himself upon his adherence to machine men and methods, and yet I hold in my hand a statement bearing the signature of Frank S. Black, expressing the fullest sympathy with the movement and the assurance of his co-operation in the furtherance of its ends."[13] Black noted that his audience might find this kind of support for reform from practical politicians surprising, but he then explained to them:

---

[12] Fredman, *The Australian Ballot*, p. 29.
[13] *Proceedings of the National Conference on Practical Reform of Primary Elections*, New York City, January 20 and 21, 1898, p. 12.

Well, it should not, for I make the assertion without fear of successful contradiction, that the Civil Service Reform and the Australian Ballot law owe more to the efforts of the practical politicians than has ever yet been acknowledged. The best politicians are in favor of genuine Civil Service reform, because it is their only salvation from the clamor of insatiable constituents. They favored the Australian Ballot law because it meant a tremendous saving of their money on Election Day.

Certainly it is plausible to argue that the reduction in campaign expenditures made possible by the Australian Ballot may have played some role in the support of party elites for it, though Milholland's explanation is probably an oversimplification. In particular, it ignores the fact that disorder was debilitating to the parties, expense was not. However, Milholland's speech is also interesting because it reinforces the key point about late-nineteenth-century political reform, that even party politicians who were dependent on machines could have reasons for pursuing it. While reformers at the time did tend to propagate what Reynolds and McCormick call the "standard account" of how the Australian Ballot was adopted (that "the struggle . . . pitted nonpartisan reformers against partisan stalwarts"), not all of them did so, and Milholland is one example of a reformer trying to put the record straight.[14]

3. Reformers' Promotion of the Australian Ballot

The argument thus far is that party elites were likely to be receptive to ballot reforms that would preserve party control over the electorate while removing the causes of party disorder. Nevertheless, and not surprisingly for a device previously unknown in America, the initial proposals for ballot reform came from those on the fringes of the parties, and by those who might even be hostile to disciplined parties. The Australian Ballot appears to have been advocated first by the Philadelphia Civil Service Reform Association in 1882, and then, among others, by Henry George.[15] Rather quickly, by the mid-1880s, the issue could be said to have got onto the political agenda; writing in the *North American Review* in 1886 Allen Thorndike Rice, for example, could note, "During the recent elections, very frequent reference was made by candidates of different parties to what was termed the 'Australian system' of voting."[16] He then proceeded to inform his readers how the system operated. Since there were more would-be reformers living in Massachusetts and New York than elsewhere, these states became the center of agitation for the official ballot. However, Michigan was actually the first state in which a legislator introduced

---

[14] Reynolds and McCormick, "Outlawing 'Treachery'," p. 836.
[15] Evans, *A History of the Australian Ballot in the United States*, p. 18.
[16] Allen Thorndike Rice, "Recent Reforms in Balloting," *North American Review*, 143(1886), pp. 632–3.

bills to require its use, although neither the 1885 nor the 1887 bills passed. In both cases the authors of the proposed legislation could be regarded as being toward the fringes of the two-party system. The proponent of the 1885 bill was only twenty-five years old and had been elected on the Greenback as well as the Democratic ticket, while the 1887 bill was introduced by a state senator who was linked to the Knights of Labor and the labor press.[17]

There is little evidence that the early propagandists for the Australian Ballot were in much contact, if any, with each other. To the contrary, years later one of the central figures, Richard Henry Dana III of Massachusetts, said of the efforts to promote the Australian Ballot in New York, "None of us had ever heard of the New York bill while we were drafting our measures."[18]

Some of the leading early proponents of the official ballot were not merely reformist in some general way but also quite explicitly antiparty. Or, rather, it might be more generous perhaps to describe them as having a highly instrumental view of parties. This was the case with William Mills Ivins in New York, and also, more significantly, with Dana in Massachusetts. It was Dana's legislation that was enacted in 1888, and his importance in ballot reform extends well beyond Massachusetts because that legislation served as a model in a number of other states in the years immediately following. Dana's political career appears almost to be a parody of a certain kind of late-nineteenth-century reformer. He became part of the Mugwump bolt from the Republican party when James Blaine was nominated as the party's presidential candidate in 1884, and he voted for Grover Cleveland that year. He remained a Republican until 1886 when he supported fellow Mugwump John Foster Andrew who was now running as the Democratic candidate for Governor. In 1888 Dana was backing an Independent in a congressional race, while, later, in 1890, after voting for a Democratic governor, he ran for mayor of Cambridge as a Republican.[19]

Dana was precisely the kind of party hopper whom most partisans would have regarded either with suspicion or as a political lightweight. Yet he was largely responsible for drafting the legislation that was enacted in 1888, which, significantly, passed with relatively large majorities in both chambers.[20] What made it possible for Dana to be so influential among both Republicans and Democrats was, first, that there was considerable grass-

---

[17] Fredman, *The Australian Ballot*, p. 35.

[18] Dana Family Papers, Massachusetts Historical Society. ("Sir William Vernon Harcourt and the Australian Ballot," draft of a 1925 chapter intended for an autobiography; Dana Family I, Richard Henry Dana III, Box 46, p. 98.)

[19] Geoffrey Blodgett, *The Gentle Reformers: Massachusetts Democrats in the Cleveland Era*, Cambridge, Mass., Harvard University Press, 1966, p. 26.

[20] It passed 18–10 in the Senate and 121–41 in the House.

roots support for electoral reform, as evidenced by petitions to the state assembly. (As is seen in subsequent chapters, especially Chapter 7, public attitudes were also important in limiting how politicians could respond to problems in candidate selection.) Second, it was a matter that was not defined by the parties as adversely affecting their interests. Finally, the chair of the relevant committee in the Senate was a reformer and a fellow member of a reform club to which Dana belonged. Dana's party hopping was arguably less significant among politicos than the fact that he had drafted a successful civil service reform law in the state five years earlier.[21] On a matter that was actually quite consensual at the time in his state, Dana and his allies could guide legislation down the path they wanted.

It was at this point that party elites started to intervene far more actively and to shape Australian Ballot legislation in the direction they wanted, and in a direction that antipartisan reformers did not wish to go. In particular, they devised other types of ballot that were likely to better preserve party control over their voters. They took a mechanism that originally provided them with some undoubted advantages, but at the cost of possibly weaker control over their own voters, and converted it into one that removed most of that cost. While they may have initiated the move toward an official ballot, antiparty reformers, like Dana, were to be marginalized as party elites took the reform in a very different direction from the one the former had intended.

4. Variants of the Australian Ballot in the United States

During the period between 1888 and 1917 five types of official ballot were used in the United States, four of which were much more conducive to party control than the other one.

(i) *Pure Office Block (POB)*
The ballot introduced in both Louisville and statewide in Massachusetts in 1888 is usually known as the Office-Block or Office Group Ballot (which I call here Pure Office Block [POB]). The names of all candidates for a particular office are listed under the title of that office, and the ballot lists sequentially all the offices to be contested at the particular election. In the states that came to employ this method a voter who wished to vote in the election for every office would have to make his way through the entire ballot, checking off the names of the candidates he supported. Typically in the nonsouthern states the parties nominating a given candidate were listed after his name, but eleven counties in Maryland followed a practice used in parts of the South of not showing party designations, this being a practice designed to reduce the impact of black voters.

---

[21] Fredman, *The Australian Ballot*, p. 38.

(ii) Office Block Ballot with Straight Ticket Provision (OBSTP)

This type was first introduced in 1889 by Montana and by Minnesota, although in the latter the law applied only to cities with populations of more than ten thousand. This ballot is arranged on POB lines, but it provides a simple method for voting a straight ticket if the voter wishes to; usually all that is required under OBSTP is the marking of a box at the head of the ballot, thus saving the voter the time required in marking a cross against the name of every single candidate of his party. (Later, when voting machines were introduced, a single lever could be pulled for straight ticket voting.)

(iii) Pure Party Column (PPC)

The Pure Party Column type of ballot (PPC) also made its first appearance in 1889, in Indiana, and very rapidly it was to become the most widely used ballot of all. Each of the parties has a separate column on the ballot paper, and under each party heading are listed all its candidates for office. However, straight ticket voting is made even easier by placing a box at the head of each column that can be used by those wanting to vote a straight ticket, and who do not want to wade through the list of candidates marking a cross against each of them.

(iv) Party Column without Box (PCB)

A few states used a type of ballot similar to the PPC, but dispensed with the box at the head of the columns that facilitated easy straight ticket voting. The PCB was first used in Missouri cities with populations of more than five thousand in 1889.

(v) "Shoestring" Ballot

The "shoestring" ballot, popularly known by this name because of its thin appearance, was also known sometimes as a compromise law, at least by those reformers who refused to accept that it was a version of the Australian Ballot at all. In its most advanced form, as in New York from 1891 to 1895, it was unquestionably an official ballot, in that it was printed by the state and was made available only at polling places. It was arranged like a PPC ballot but each of the parties' candidates were listed on separate ballot papers, hence the thin appearance of the ballot. Consequently, the "shoestring" ballot was not a "blanket" ballot as were the POB, OBSTP, PPC, or PCB forms, and it was for that reason that many reformers refused to accept that it was really a version of the Australian Ballot. The voter would be given a ballot for each of the parties, as well as one blank ballot that simply listed the names of the offices; the latter was designed for voters who wished to ticket-split. The voter could use only one of them when voting. A rather similar arrangement was used in Missouri after 1897, a state that was unique in that, having adopted a "blanket" ballot, it then abandoned it.

However, the two other states that used a form of "shoestring" ballot, Connecticut (1889–1909) and New Jersey (1890–1911), had arrangements that might more properly be regarded as compromises between the original Australian form of ballot and the older, unofficial ballots. In Connecticut, the parties continued to print their own ballots, which they gave to voters, although the paper was supplied by the state and the form of the ballot was also specified. Moreover, voting had to be conducted in secret at voting booths and the votes placed in envelopes supplied by the state and available only at the booths. New Jersey differed in that the ballots were printed by the state, but as in Connecticut they could be distributed before polling began. In both states, therefore, the parties were still involved in the balloting process although their role was much restricted by comparison with the older, unofficial balloting system.

5. The Positions of Reformers and Parties in Relation to the Types of Ballot Used

There was no question of which form of ballot was favoured by those who either wished to weaken the role of parties in the American democracy or who were indifferent to the claims of parties. This was the POB. Antiparty reformers had two main objections to other types of "official" ballot.

First, any system that facilitated straight ticket voting discouraged independent political action in support of candidates who were not running for a major party. It also made it more difficult for those of independent spirit who had received a party nomination to attract voters from outside that party. An instance of this objection being made to a particular ballot law (in this case a rather odd modification of the PPC) is that of Charles C. Binney who said of the rival POB, which the Pennsylvania 1891 ballot law had failed to adopt:

The most narrow partisan and the most thorough freelance must each do precisely the same amount of work. There is no inducement to vote for one man rather than another to save trouble, nor any risk of voting for any man without being aware of it.[22]

This kind of view was still the position of a small minority at the end of the 1880s, although, interestingly, it was not regarded even by a party hopper like Richard Dana as the main objection to OBSTP, PPC, PCB, and "shoestring" ballots. At that time, Dana was more concerned about alleged voter dependence on party leaders than the ease of independence. In a letter to the *Nation* in early 1890, he noted:

The real evils of this method are more fundamental. It deprives the system substantially of its secrecy. A voter who votes a straight party ticket has to be in the

[22] Charles C. Binney, "The Merits and Defects of the Pennsylvania Ballot Law of 1891," *Annals of the American Academy of Political and Social Science*, 2(1891–2), p. 761.

marking compartment but a few seconds, while one who votes independently, even as to one candidate, has to stay in the compartment one or two minutes. Now the question usually is, not which party a man belongs to, but whether he is going to vote "straight" or to scratch (for example) Gov. Hill on the Democratic ticket or some particular candidate on the Republican ticket. This the party workers can ascertain under the party-column system almost as well as under the old system of party ballots.[23]

The point Dana was making was that party organizations would still retain control over certain voters because "treachery" in the form of split ticket voting was detectable through the ability of the former to know how long the latter had spent in the voting booth.

The "shoestring" ballot contained an additional feature that Dana and others found objectionable, and that made it the least attractive ballot type for this kind of reformer. Because there had to be a blank ballot for those who wanted to ticket-split, the practice of "pasting" was retained, and its availability provided the potential for further control over voters by party organization leaders:

. . . as there has to be on the official ballot a blank column in which any voter may paste names, it is only necessary to furnish each voter a blanket paster with the names of the party candidates or any combination that may be got up by a trade, and this the voter is quickly to paste on to this blank space, and pass through the compartment.[24]

While reformers like Dana objected most to the "shoestring" ballot, they approved wholeheartedly of only one type of ballot (the POB). This continued to be Dana's line. In 1911 he published a pamphlet defending this system against its opponents, while in 1925, in a chapter for his intended autobiography, he noted of the 1888 Massachusetts bill, ". . . several states afterwards adopted the party column and single cross system [i.e., all the other types of ballot], to the great disadvantage of independent voting, of secrecy and of accurate 'counting'."[25] Nevertheless, despite this hostility to other types of ballot, most of those who identified themselves as "independent" reformers still approved even of "shoestring" ballots as significant improvements on the wholly party ballot. Reynolds and McCormick provide evidence of this in two of the states that introduced the "shoestring" ballot:

The *Newark Evening News*, New Jersey's foremost independent newspaper, praised the state's law for incorporating "all the best features" of the Australian ballot system. The *Century Magazine* [a mugwumpish paper] declared, "The State of New York has now the most thoroughly reformed electoral system of all States in the Union. . . . The new ballot law, though the outcome of a compromise, is really an excellent measure."[26]

[23] *Nation*, February 6, 1890. [24] *Nation*, February 6, 1890.
[25] Dana, "Sir William Vernon Harcourt," p. 98.
[26] Reynolds and McCormick, "Outlawing 'Treachery'," p. 851.

The result of this was that between most party elites, on the one side, and the antiparty reformers, on the other, there were both shared and conflicting interests. Both sides saw an official ballot as providing distinct advantages over partisan ballots – but they differed with respect to what they regarded as being advantages. In turn, that meant that they had completely opposing views as to which type of ballot was preferable: party elites generally wanted anything but the POB, while the reformers wanted only that type. Given that structure of preferences, it is not surprising that legislatures in most states moved so quickly to enact *some* form of Australian Ballot legislation; within three years, thirty of the thirty-three states had an official ballot, and in most cases this was achieved without that much controversy. Furthermore, the fact that the POB was the "first in the field" meant that, initially, the antiparty reformers did very well, with many states simply copying the Massachusetts model. These two points are now considered in greater detail.

6. The Weakness of Opposition to the Australian Ballot

While opposition among party elites to the official ballot was not sufficiently great to hold up legislation in most cases, there were some who opposed it. Generally, the opponents were to be found in the larger urban areas, but by no means all urban politicos were opponents. Moreover, rural and small town dominance among the electorates of most states meant that it could be imposed on urban areas irrespective of the views of their legislators, and, indeed, in some states (Kentucky, Minnesota, and Missouri), it was imposed on urban areas before it was used statewide. New York is interesting because it was exceptional. The Australian Ballot was highly controversial there, and largely this was the result of the much greater power that urban parties had in a state that was both urbanized, and, unlike Maryland, for example, did not have a state legislature that was seriously malapportioned in favour of rural areas. The upshot of this was that the Australian Ballot became the subject of interparty competition in a way that it did not elsewhere.

Legislation to enact an official ballot was first introduced in New York in 1888 by a Republican Senator. It had the backing of reformist elements in both parties and was passed by both chambers. Democratic Governor David Hill then vetoed it, and although he was able to produce a number of plausible reasons for opposing it, it is clear that his motive in doing so was the fear of party disadvantage. He believed that its provisions would prevent the party in New York City mobilizing its full voting strength, because of difficulties in ensuring that the illiterate voted in the way in which they intended; in an era of closely contest elections this would endanger his own political future and that of his party. Hill's denunciation of the measure had two related consequences for him. First, it exposed the division within the Democratic party between its large machines, especially Tammany Hall, and the other elements in the party. As Bass notes, "By stressing Hill's opposition to electoral reform, the Republicans weakened Hill position with non-machine members, and cost him some support."[27] Second, given the popularity of electoral reform within the electorate, it enabled the Republicans to consolidate around it and use it as a stick with which to beat the Democrats. An originally nonpartisan issue, which produced divisions in both parties, emerged into a partisan one.

Hill's strategy now was to emphasize his support for measures designed to deal with corrupt electoral practices while opposing vehemently the official ballot. In 1889 the Republicans reintroduced an Australian Ballot bill, but this time the legislation would have provided for a blanket ballot, something that the 1888 measure would not have. This was even more difficult for Hill to swallow, and in its passage through the assembly it became a straight party measure. The result was that not a single Democrat voted for the legislation and Hill duly vetoed it.[28] By 1890, though, it was clear that Hill had underestimated the popularity of the official ballot, and that his optimal strategy was to work toward a version of the ballot that would largely preserve the ability of the Democrats to mobilize the immigrant vote in New York City. The popularity of the official ballot is highly significant, because in most states – and certainly in Massachusetts as well as in New York – politicians had to operate in an environment in which public opinion constrained them on this matter. Even in this rather strongly partisan society it was far from being the case that all opinions were shaped by partisan attitudes or values.[29] The official ballot was popular simply because it seemed to provide for fairness; it was perfectly consistent for someone to be both a strong partisan and a supporter of enforceable electoral rules. Many voters appear to have been both, and there is little evidence that such views on the ballot reflected an underlying antipartisanship.

Hill outmaneuvered the Republicans by suggesting that he would accept the official ballot providing his previously declared constitutional objections to it were not upheld in a referral to the Court of Appeal for an informal opinion. With this out of the way, Hill was able to present himself as having been a supporter of "real" electoral reform all along, and a bill acceptable to a majority of Democrats and Republican legislators could be constructed and passed.

With Democrat involvement in the process, the result was the shoestring ballot. The urban party organizations, including Tammany Hall, could most

---

[27] Bass, "*I am a Democrat*," p. 116.   [28] Bass, *ibid.* p. 134.

[29] The argument that other institutions, including churches, were important in shaping nineteenth-century American political values has been argued by Glenn C. Altschuler and Stuart M. Blumin, *Rude Republic: Americans and their Politics in the 19th Century*, Princeton, N.J., Princeton University Press, 2000.

easily live with this type of ballot because it would help to deal with "treachery" in the party and at the same time not make it too difficult to keep the ethnic vote predominantly Democratic. Conversely, for upstate Democratic politicos and for many Republicans, the official ballot seemed to provide a way of introducing some order into a system without endangering the interests of parties. The shoestring ballot was not the system most favored by all, but it was acceptable to a broad range of opinion.

However, the shoestring ballot was not a common solution – only Connecticut, New Jersey, and New York employed it initially, and only Missouri and New Mexico adopted it later. It tended to emerge in states where particularly tightly organized county organizations could fear the loss of control over voters through the use of a blanket ballot, and were able, in effect, to veto any moves toward such a ballot. But there were many other states in which the parties were highly organized, as in Indiana, where party elites believed that party interests were sufficiently well protected through the use of a particular form of blanket ballot, most usually the PPC.

7. Success and Failure for the Antiparty Reformers

With its relatively open politics, and a tradition of political response to moderate reform proposals, Massachusetts was the ideal state in which someone like Dana could operate. The very success of that legislation led to it being copied elsewhere, and that meant the system supported by the antipartisan reformers (the POB) made significant advances, far ahead of any public support such reformers might have for their own views. In 1888, two states adopted the POB, in 1899 four states had adopted it (44 percent of the total), by 1890 six states (40 percent of the total), and by 1891 eleven states (36 percent of the total). In part, the rapid spread of the POB was helped by outcries about corruption in the 1888 elections; as Perman says of the Australian Ballot after 1888, "If ever there was a reform whose time had come, this seemed to be it."[30] The year 1891 was the high point in the use of the POB, but even before then it was clear that many states were turning not to the POB but to forms of official ballot that better facilitated straight ticket voting. Particularly with the Indiana model, the PPC, it became evident just how best to protect party interests.

A good example of this was in Maryland in 1890. There, the Democratic governor was opposed initially to the Australian Ballot, largely on the grounds that it would tend to disenfranchise the illiterate, who formed an important constituency for the party. After various other proposals failed to attract sufficient support, the Democrats turned to the

---

[30] Michael Perman, *Struggle for Mastery: Disfranchisement in the South, 1888–1908*, Chapel Hill, N.C., and London, University of North Carolina Press, 2001, p. 49.

PPC, which met their requirements and that satisfied most reformers as well. As Argersinger has said of the Maryland experience:

Although labor reformers, mugwumps, conservative businessmen, and political radicals had led the movement for ballot reform, the actual law was shaped and enacted by practical politicians who understood the electorate and how election machinery influenced political outcomes. The law derived from political conflict; not surprisingly, it also reflected it. "In matters of [electoral] legislation," one newspaper later concluded, "the 'professionals' beat the amateurs every day."[31]

Moreover, party interests could be protected even after the passage of the initial official ballot legislation. One of the most important points to emphasize about American ballot laws is just how much legislation was enacted even after the initial adoption of the Australian Ballot. In part, this was because a number of states, such as Kentucky in 1888, began by requiring the use of an official ballot in only some localities; later legislation would be required to extend it statewide. But even in states where "complete" legislation was passed early on, subsequent amendments to that legislation were common. Massachusetts is a case in point. Of the twenty-one years following the passage of the 1888 legislation, seventeen of them saw successful amendments to the legislation introduced. Connecticut provides another example; its legislature met only biennially, but between 1889 and 1909 the only sessions in which ballot legislation was not enacted were those of 1891, 1893, and 1907.[32] More significantly, as mentioned earlier, there was also considerable switching in the type of ballot used by a state.

In discussing this, it is possible to identify four distinct periods – the early years 1888–91, the remainder of the 1890s up to 1900, the decade from 1901 to 1910, and the period from 1911 to 1917 (see Table 2.2).

Not surprisingly, in the early years, there was rather little switching of ballot systems. However, even so, a pattern that was to become more pronounced during the remainder of the 1890s was evident. Four states (Missouri, Washington, Wisconsin, and Minnesota) changed their ballot system in 1891. The first three moved in the direction of party influence over the ballot, with only Minnesota moving in the opposite direction (to the POB).

This trend became even more pronounced during the second period, 1892–1900, which was one of defeat for the POB. Indeed, by 1900 the POB was used in a mere six states – Massachusetts, Minnesota, Nebraska, Nevada, Oregon, and Rhode Island. These years were marked by considerable shifts in the use of official ballots, with a total of eighteen changes being made. However, only two of these switches involved states adopting

[31] Peter H. Argersinger, "From Party Tickets to Secret Ballots: the Evolution of the Electoral Process in Maryland during the Gilded Age," in Argersinger (ed.), *Structure, Process and Party: Essays in American Political History*, Armonk, N.Y., M. E. Sharpe, 1992, p. 140. The newspaper cited is the Baltimore *Sun*, March 8, 1892.

[32] Arthur C. Luddington, *American Ballot Laws 1888–1910*, Albany, N.Y., University of the State of New York, Education Department Bulletin, 1911, pp. 16–19 and 33–6.

TABLE 2.2. *Use of Pure Office Block Ballot (POB) by Nonsouthern States, 1888–1917*

	States using POB Ballot	Total Number of States using POB	Total Number of States using Official Ballots	States using POB as a Percentage of all States using Official Ballots
1891	Kentucky Massachusetts Minnesota Nebraska Nevada New Hampshire Oregon Rhode Island South Dakota Vermont Wyoming	11	30	37
1900	Massachusetts Minnesota Nebraska Nevada Oregon Rhode Island	6	34	18
1910	Maryland Massachusetts Minnesota Nevada Oregon	5	35	14
1917	California Colorado Kansas Maryland Massachusetts Minnesota Nevada New Jersey New York Oregon	10	37	27

the POB. California did so in 1893, though it abandoned it again in 1899. That same year Nebraska moved directly from PPC, which it had adopted as recently as 1897, back to its original POB ballot of 1891. While there was ballot legislation throughout most of this second period, 1897 was a year of particularly high activity, with six states changing their ballot that year. This is a point that is considered again later.

The third period, from 1901 to 1910, was one that involved rather less movement on the form of the ballot than in the 1890s, although eleven states were still making changes in these years. Nevertheless, unlike the preceding decade there was no clear pattern to these shifts. Maryland was the only state to adopt the POB (in 1901). However, that same year Nebraska, made yet another switch, abandoning POB in favour of OBSTP, and in 1905 Rhode Island jettisoned POB for PPC. In 1901 Montana switched from PPC to PCB, with Iowa making the same switch in 1906; yet in 1901 Kansas moved in exactly the opposite direction and in 1903 it was joined by both California and Idaho. Similarly, while Washington dropped OBSTP in 1901, and replaced it with PPC, the contrary switch was made by Pennsylvania two years later. Finally, in 1910 Connecticut abandoned the shoestring ballot that it had adopted in 1889 and started to use the PPC. Thus, despite the fact that nearly one-third of the states had changed their ballot laws in the first decade of the twentieth century, the overall distribution of ballot types was much the same as a decade earlier. What is clear is that there was no marked movement in the direction of the POB. Indeed, one less state was using it in 1910 than in 1900.

Furthermore, the party elites do seem to have got what they wanted in terms of the manageability of mass electorates. As Reynolds and McCormick have shown for New Jersey and New York, ticket-splitting declined in these states in the 1890s – in three of the five New Jersey counties that formed their sample, and in all five of the New York counties they examined, "The average index of split tickets was lower between 1890 and 1902 than it had been between 1880 and 1889."[33] When ticket-splitting started to rise again from 1904 onward, it was of a new kind. It was concentrated in the more visible, high-profile offices, rather than in the lower level offices that had been the centers of voter-management problems twenty years earlier. The political world was changing, and, for various reasons, a new form of political independence among voters was being manifested:

Independent-minded electors, caring less about local party organizations than before, split their tickets to reward or to punish charismatic candidates – for example, William Jennings Bryan, Theodore Roosevelt, Charles Evans Hughes, and William Randolph Hearst – men who stood at the head of their slates and, in a sense, above their parties.[34]

Against such political behavior, the Australian Ballot could not serve as a device preserving the party vote, but, and this is an important point, neither is there any evidence whatsoever to show that it facilitated or encouraged such behavior.

---

[33] Reynolds and McCormick, "Outlawing 'Treachery'," p. 853.   [34] *Ibid.*, p. 856.

In the final period (1911–17), a partial reversal of earlier trends was evident with the POB more popular among the states. In these years, eight states changed their ballot, but in only one instance was this in the direction of party influence over the ballot. Three states (California, Kansas, and New York) dropped the PPC in favor of the POB, while New Jersey also employed it on giving up the "shoestring ballot" in 1911. Colorado switched from OBSTP to POB. The effect of these changes was to double the number of states using POB (from five to ten) by 1917, but even so it was still used in fewer states than in 1891.[35] With thirty-seven nonsouthern states now in the Union, that meant that 73 percent of the states were now using Australian Ballots of a type that favored party control of the electorate, with 27 percent using the POB.

8. Ballot Reform and Interparty Competition

How should this pattern of change be interpreted? One view might be that there was a major Progressive influence on the choice of ballot type after 1911. However, there are a number of serious qualifications and possible objections to such a view. First, any gains at the expense of those who would have defended party interests were modest, given that this was a policy area in which legislative changes had been frequent in the recent past and in which the position of those who wished to weaken parties was clear cut. A net change by five out of the thirty-two states not using the POB previously scarcely represents a revolution. Part of the significance of this last point lies in the fact that the states that did change their ballot were disproportionately likely to be ones in which Progressive influences would be expected to be greater. Whereas only 55 percent of the older states – those occupying territory that acquired statehood before 1840 – changed their original ballot type in the period 1888–1917, 84 percent of the newer states did so (see Table 2.3). It was these newer states in the West, where party penetration of society was lower, that, as Shefter has argued, were most susceptible to Progressive influences.[36] (The significance of region as a variable in explaining nomination reform is considered further in Chapter 4.) The

---

[35] A failure to actually look at the changes in ballot types has led some authors to make claims that are simply not true. For example, Sabato argues, "The incidence of straight party levers began to decline with the onset of the antiboss Progressive Era, and just twenty states retain it today." In fact, in 1891, 61 percent of nonsouthern states used a straight party lever facility or equivalent (that is, OBSTP, PPC or "shoestring" ballots), while in 1917, 62 percent of states did so; at the time he was writing (1988) a mere 40 percent of states used a straight ticket lever, so that the real decline in this facility came *after* the Progressive Era, and not during it. Larry J. Sabato, *The Party's Just Begun*, Glenview, Ill., Scott Foresman, 1988, p. 224.

[36] Martin Shefter, "Regional Receptivity to Reform in the United States," in Shefter, *Political Parties and the State: The American Historical Experience*, Princeton, N.J., Princeton University Press, 1993. I refer to states "occupying territory that acquired statehood before 1840" rather than to "states acquiring statehood before 1840" to take account of the anomalous case of West Virginia.

TABLE 2.3. *Change of Ballot Type, 1888–1917, by Age of State*

	States that Changed their Type of Ballot	States that Did Not Change their Type of Ballot
States occupying territory that attained statehood before 1840	Connecticut Kentucky Maryland Missouri New Hampshire New Jersey New York Pennsylvania Rhode Island Vermont (10)	Delaware Illinois Indiana Maine Massachusetts Michigan Ohio West Virginia (8)
States occupying territory that did not attain statehood until after 1840	California Colorado Idaho Iowa Kansas Minnesota Montana Nebraska North Dakota Oklahoma South Dakota Utah Washington Wisconsin Wyoming (15)	Nevada Oregon (2)

states in which change did occur, therefore, were those that might have been expected to have been more willing to permit the use of the POB.

Second, it can be argued that overall party control of the ballot might have been even greater had it not been for the fact that it was Dana's plan that was the first to be enacted, thereby giving the antipartisan position an initial impetus: three of the states using the POB in 1917 (Massachusetts, Nevada, and Oregon) were among the ten states that had never changed the type of ballot used. It can be argued that, if Indiana had been the first in the field with the PPC, rather than Dana's ballot being the original statewide exemplar, the fate of the POB ballot would have been worse than it actually was.

Third, while the changes from 1911 are not without interest, equally noteworthy is the fact that there was no such trend between 1901 and 1910. The years of complete party dominance on the ballot issue (1891–1910) overlap with the period in which the direct primary was introduced in many states. By the beginning of 1911, the introduction of the direct primary was already well advanced. More than half the states (eighteen) had already enacted what Charles Merriam called "complete" primary laws, that is, laws covering an entire state and most elected offices. In addition, a further six states had direct primary laws that either applied to particular localities, or were optional in nature, or were applied by party officials and not state officials. In other words, more than two-thirds of the states outside the South had legislation providing for some form of direct primary during the period when there was no switching toward the POB. This raises the possibility, at least, that there might have been other factors responsible for the switches after 1911. In fact, such a factor can be identified. To introduce this it is necessary to examine how the interests of Republican and Democratic political elites differed in one important respect.

Although the years after the early 1870s were ones of close competition between the parties, the Democrats on their own often polled fewer votes than the Republicans. Frequently neither party secured a majority of the votes, and in 1892 this was the case in three-quarters of the states, so that the key to success was a party's relations with smaller parties. For the Democrats, fusion – that is "electoral support of a single set of candidates by two or more parties"[37] – was a device that often brought them victory. For the Republicans preventing such fusion was important, and after the adoption of the Australian Ballot it became possible to eliminate fusion by law, by, for example, prohibiting a candidate's name from being listed more than once on an official ballot.[38] Yet, if this was the main battleground for exploiting party advantage, it was not the only one. The form the ballot took could also affect the potential for fusion.

In particular, the opportunity for successful fusion around a few offices, rather than an entire slate, could be affected by whether the POB or a more "party friendly" ballot was used. Any of the latter were likely to work against the interests of a single candidate who hoped to attract support from likely voters for minor parties. Consequently, party advantage pulled Republicans even further toward supporting PPC, OBSTP, PCB, or "shoe-string" ballots; Democrats came under some cross-pressure; despite its evident disadvantages, POB did have one benefit for them compared with other ballots. Almost certainly, party advantage is one factor accounting for the large number of switches (seven in total, and six to the PPC) in 1897.

[37] Peter H. Argersinger, "A Place on the Ballot: Fusion Politics and Antifusion Laws," *American Historical Review*, 85(1980), p. 288.
[38] *Ibid.*, p. 291.

The 1896 election produced the largest gap in the share of the presidential vote obtained by the two main parties in more than twenty years; in 1897, one way of consolidating the advantage of the winning party in a state was to make it more likely that voters would vote a straight ticket, and, for the Republicans, ballot reform in the direction of the PPC especially was a means of doing that.

The connection between the exploitation of party advantage and the ballot can be illustrated by considering elections contested between 1892 and 1912. In these twenty-one years, there were four elections that resulted in significant shifts in voter support nationally – 1894, 1896, 1910, and 1912 – while the remaining elections years generally saw the preservation of the *status quo ante*. Twenty of the thirty-seven changes in ballot systems between 1893 and 1913 were enacted in the year immediately following one of these four elections, while only seventeen were introduced on other occasions. It can be argued that part of the impetus toward POB after 1910 had nothing to do with Progressive influences at all; by 1910 the Democrats were much more competitive than at any point since 1892, and, given the role of fusion in the past, it made sense for them to switch to ballots that increased the potential for fusion. The move from "shoestring" ballots to the POB in New Jersey followed Democratic electoral success in that state, and thus occurred in situations where the seemingly more natural switch, for states with strong parties, from the increasingly outmoded "shoestring" ballot to the PPC, would have provided an advantage to the Republicans.

In New York, too, a switch from the PPC to POB followed the Democratic electoral upsurge in the state after 1910. Significantly, it did not occur under the reform governor, Charles E. Hughes, who championed the POB but who failed to get it "even seriously considered by the legislature."[39] (As is seen in Chapter 5, Hughes's experience with the ballot contrasted with his promotion of the direct primary, where despite his ultimate failure, he was able at least to generate a high-profile confrontation with the legislature.) The 1895 law (and its amendments in 1896) had been pushed through the legislature by a "traditional" Republican governor. The shoestring ballot was abandoned that year in favor of PPC, thereby raising the literacy level required of voters and hurting the Democrats in the process, although it also made independent nominations more difficult.[40] But the PPC also hurt fusion in New York and one way of restoring the balance of party competition, following the years of Republican dominance after 1893, was to tilt the ballot laws slightly in the Democrats' favor.

The upshot of all this is that, once the initial impetus of the Dana-inspired legislation was over, the parties used legislation on the

[39] Richard L. McCormick, *From Realignment to Reform: Political Change in New York State, 1893–1910*, Ithaca, N.Y., and London, Cornell University Press, 1981, p. 243.
[40] See McCormick, *From Realignment to Reform*, pp. 114–18.

official ballot exclusively for their own advantage. They continued to do so right into the period that is known as the Progressive era and, indeed, well beyond that time.[41] Only in the later part of that era is there any evidence at all that the antipartisan reformers were getting what they wanted, but that gain was comparatively small and, at least to some extent, seems to have had more to do with intraparty politics than with any power supposedly possessed by those reformers.

9. Concluding Remarks

Ballot reform was extremely important for nomination reform. The Australian Ballot really did provide a solution to the problem that the parties were facing, even though initially it had been championed by many who were on the fringes of the major parties or even hostile to them. Consequently, its success appeared to demonstrate that there were institutional reforms that could protect the interests of parties just as there were others that could harm those interests. In other words, to many observers it would appear that not only could there be solutions to the parties' difficulties, but there was one that, *ceteris paribus*, would not break the links between parties and voters. There was a potential danger, however. In the case of the Australian Ballot the parties could tell where their interests lay, and in most states party interests predominated in the reform process, with the POB system of nomination remaining one that was used in only a minority of states. Whether party interests would be so clear in other aspects of party institutionalization was a different matter, though.

The catalytic effect of the Australian Ballot was to be evident both with respect to the legal control of the nomination process and in hastening the introduction of the direct primary itself. In relation to the former it seemed to provide evidence that subjecting political activity to legal regulation could lead to the replacement of unsatisfactory practices by ones that were better. However, legislating for nomination reform was to raise far more complex issues than ballot reform had, a point that was recognized by a few commentators at the time; for instance, in a speech to the National Municipal League in 1900 Amos Parker Wilder informed his audience:

Nominating reform is not a concrete achievement to be won at a single stroke like the Australian Ballot. It is not even a well-defined principle universally applicable.[42]

---

[41] For example, writing in 1966, Jack L. Walker noted of Ohio that it had changed the ballot six times in the twentieth century, and on each occasion "the Republican majority tried to gain an advantage for itself," "Ballot Form and Voter Fatigue," *Midwest Journal of Political Science*, 10(1966), p. 448.

[42] Amos Parker Wilder, "Primary Election Laws," *Proceedings of the Milwaukee Conference for Good City Government and 6th Annual Meeting of the National Municipal League*, Philadelphia, National Municipal League, 1900, p. 216.

The apparent success of the Australian Ballot legislation also helped to focus attention on the direct nomination system that had originated in Crawford County, Pennsylvania: Of all the conceivable methods of nominating candidates, this was the one that most resembled an election. Reforms that worked in the one arena might provide the basis for reform in another arena that had many similarities with electoral politics. In this way, ballot reform gave an important impetus to pressures for change in the nomination process that were becoming evident already.

3

Legal Control of Party Activity

One of the most distinctive features of American political parties during the twentieth century was the extent to which party activities had come to be regulated by law. Two aspects of this are especially important in relation to the introduction of the direct primary. In many states more than a decade of extensive regulation of the nomination process usually preceded the introduction of the direct primary. Often the direct primary was the culmination of repeated attempts by legislators to provide for nomination procedures that worked better than the existing ones. Second, in making direct primaries mandatory, state governments turned a process that, unquestionably, had been that of a private association into something resembling a public election; in doing so, inevitably they generated controversies about the nature of American political parties. Were they still private associations, or were they public agencies? This chapter examines how party nomination procedures became subjected to legal control, and why such legal control was necessary in the United States.

1. Candidate Selection in the Nineteenth Century

From the days of the Jacksonian democracy onward, most counties in the United States employed a system of nominating candidates that political scientists later would describe as one involving caucuses and conventions. That is, it was a two-stage process. At the first stage party supporters would select delegates to represent them at a convention – a county convention for county level offices, or a state convention for state level offices, and so on. In its standard form this type of nominating system permitted delegates to a convention to vote for whom they wanted when they attended it; they were bound neither by party rules nor law to do otherwise. The constraints on them were solely those of peer group opinion – what those who had selected them might think should they vote in ways contrary to any indications they had given earlier. In theory, at least, candidates were selected by majority vote of the delegates at the relevant party convention.

However, even in proceeding this far in the discussion a minefield has been entered – in this case one that is partly about terminology, though, as will be seen in Chapter 4, the terminological issues are of significance in understanding the rise of the direct primary. The problem of terminology relates to the initial party meetings – the ones referred to here as "caucuses," and that continue to be called caucuses throughout this book. The fact is that in much of the United States these meetings were not called caucuses at all, but were referred to as "primaries" or "primary elections"!

One of the clearest statements about the names given to initial party meetings is to be found in a now largely forgotten book published in 1897, Frederick W. Dallinger's *Nominations for Elective Office in the United States*, which is still probably the most detailed and thorough study of nineteenth-century party nominations. Dallinger observed that:

> In New England, and in a few of the western states, these primary meetings of party voters are called *caucuses*. In the Middle States, and throughout the greater part of the West, such meetings are known as *primaries*. In Pennsylvania and the South, as well as in the statute books of most of the States outside of New England they are called *primary elections*.[1]

Unfortunately, though, this is not quite the end of the matter. Dallinger himself notes that both in New England and in some of the older western states caucuses "are simply called 'town meetings' of the party voters."[2] His contemporaries, Robert Luce and Daniel Remsen, generally concurred with Dallinger in believing that "caucus" was a New England term. However, Remsen also appears to have believed that "caucus" was a term used in rural areas in some other parts of the country, while "primaries" was a term used mainly in urban localities.[3] Moreover, even in Dallinger's book, there is indirect evidence that either some terms had more than one meaning or, possibly, that their usage was changing. The entry in his Index under "Primary Elections" says merely "see Crawford County System," which was the name by which the direct primary was usually known before 1900. A similar usage of the term "primary election" is also evident in a long, and rather technical, speech delivered in 1898 by Kentucky's former Chief

---

[1] Frederick W. Dallinger, *Nominations for Elective Office in the United States*, New York, Longmans, Green, 1897, p. 53n; emphases in original.

[2] Dallinger, *Nominations for Elective Office in the United States*, p. 53.

[3] Robert Luce observed, " 'Caucus' is a good old Yankee name. Our Western and Southern brethren have forsaken it and substituted 'primary'"; *Proceedings of the Providence Conference for Good Government and the 13th Annual Meeting of the National Municipal League*, 1907, p. 37. Daniel S. Remsen, *Primary Elections: A Study of Methods for Improving the Basis of Party Organization*, New York and London, G.P. Putnam's, 1894, p. 48.

Supervisor of Elections in which he stated that "[T]here are two legitimate ways of selecting party nominees: (1) By conventions, or (2) by primaries."[4] Both here and in the subsequent development of his argument, it is quite clear that he was using both "primaries" and "primary elections" as synonyms for "direct primaries." Despite the unintended impression that it might give of a New England bias to the analysis, therefore, there is a strong case for using the term "caucus" throughout this book in order to avoid ambiguity.

However, in employing the term "caucus" to cover all initial party meetings, it is important not to assume that those meetings actually involved the discussion of the merits of particular candidates by party members – even in those states that used the term "caucus." In most places there was no such discussion at all, and caucuses were nothing more than elections of party candidates. This is a point Dallinger makes on more than one occasion, and it is worth quoting him at length, because this feature, evident in most caucuses, is significant in explaining the subsequent appeal of the direct primary. He argues:

In many of the states . . . the primaries are conducted like elections. There is no opportunity for discussion. They are simply held for the purpose of choosing delegates, the polls being open a certain length of time, as in the case of the regular election.[5]

Later he expands on this point:

In the Middle States and in the South, the party primaries or primary elections, as they are called, normally lack the town-meeting feature of the old New England caucus, namely the discussion in open meeting of the merits of the different persons to be voted for. They are, as their name implies, elections, their sole function being the choice of delegates and members of the various party committees, and, in the smaller cities, the direct nomination of candidates for some municipal offices. The only exception to this rule is to be found in the "Crawford County" Plan, where the party voters nominate the candidates directly, without the intervention of delegate conventions. In either case, however, the primary meetings are nothing more nor less than elections held in the different election districts or voting precincts, and differing from the regular legal election only in the fact that they are confined to the voters of a single party. The polls are kept open during a certain specified time, and the balloting is conducted by officers chosen either in accordance with party rules or the laws of the state.[6]

Dallinger's last point, about state laws regulating ballots at caucuses or direct primaries, refers to a relatively new practice, for it was an aspect of party nominations that had been changing considerably in the decade before

---

[4] Edward J. McDermott, address to *National Conference on Practical Reform of Primary Elections*, New York, January 20, 1898, p. 42.
[5] Dallinger, *Nominations for Elective Office in the United States*, p. 53.
[6] Dallinger, *Nominations for Elective Office in the United States*, p. 56.

he completed his manuscript (1896). This suggests that it is important to raise the question of whether other aspects of party nominations he was describing also constituted recent developments. In particular, it might be asked whether the lack of discussion at caucuses was a lapse from earlier practices or whether these meetings had long been nothing more than elections.

It is certainly the case that in New England discussion had been a feature of party caucuses. It was a practice that had been grafted onto parties from the older tradition of direct democracy, that of town meetings. However, in the urban and (increasingly) suburban counties in that region discussion had been abandoned and by the later decades of the nineteenth century caucuses there were no more than elections. But had the early New England practices been transplanted to other parts of the country? There are good reasons for doubting that emigrants from that region had done so. First, of course, much of the land beyond the Appalachians was also settled by migrants from other parts of the country and from abroad, places where there were no such traditions of deliberation. It is only in those areas – such as upstate New York, northern Ohio, and Michigan – where there was a strong concentration of New England emigrants that formal interaction by party members at caucuses might have developed. Second, however, the relatively small area covered by towns in New England meant that it was possible there to gather a local population together for a meeting; this was often much more difficult in the generally less compact settlements to the west. Third, the Jacksonian revolution, which had least impact in New England, saw the creation of a whole range of elective local and state offices. The caucus-convention system of nominating that the Jacksonians introduced operated in a political environment in which there were a large number of nominations to be made. This made communal discussion on the merits of candidates, let alone any discussion of party principles, difficult, given that there would have to be elections in the case of any office for which more than one person was seeking the nomination. For these three reasons, it is highly likely that the situation Dallinger was describing in the mid-1890s – of most caucuses simply being elections – was one that had persisted in many places since the 1830s. There is little direct evidence to support this claim, but equally there is none that would tend to contradict it, and, significantly, outside New England the criticisms that were made of the nominating system in the 1880s and 1890s do not include the contention that there had been a large-scale switch away from caucuses-as-discussion-groups to caucuses-as-elections.

Having outlined the terminological difficulties, and having explained the point that caucuses were often no more than elections (of convention delegates), it is now necessary to introduce a third complication of nineteenth-century nominations. This is that there were variations on the basic caucus-convention model. As is shown in Chapter 4, by the 1890s some counties in a number of states had started to use the Crawford County Plan, usually within the preceding ten-to-twenty years. Nor should this kind of local experimentation seem surprising. The mainspring of party strength was at the county level and below. County parties had their own customs, and they were free to adopt whatever form of nomination they wished. When existing practices caused difficulties they could change them, though, of course, this required a high level of consensus, since there would always be a bias in favor of retaining the status quo; the power of custom could be great. Yet, providing the new arrangements still made it possible for a county party to send the appropriate number of delegates to a state party convention, it could go its own way. Few state parties had any formal rules even as late as the 1890s, and certainly they did not have rules that required nominations to be made in any particular way at the county level or below.

Thus, while the standard caucus-convention model was the main type of nominating procedure, it was not the only one. Furthermore, in one state – Pennsylvania – there were a whole variety of procedures used by different counties. When delivering a paper on the subject in 1898, Clinton Rogers Woodruff began by observing that "[A]s the laws of Pennsylvania do not prescribe uniformity as a prerequisite of primary rules and regulations we find almost as many systems of primaries as there are counties."[7] He then proceeded to describe the systems of the majority party in a few counties, which he said could be regarded as typical; this involved outlining five different systems, in addition to the standard model which was used, for example, in Philadelphia:

- *Bucks County*. Republicans had a county convention but no proceeding caucuses; any citizen who wished to attend the convention, and who was willing to support the ticket nominated at it, could do so.
- *Erie County*. Republicans operated a model that was usually known as the Clarion County system. This was a complicated system in which each district had only one delegate to the county convention; that delegate reported the name of the winning candidate for each office, and the winner was then credited initially with the number of Republican votes cast in that district at the last election; the Alternative Vote voting system was then applied in nominating candidates, so that the votes of those who supported nonwinning candidates at the district level could still be counted. In essence the County Convention had a purely mechanical procedure function – that of recording votes.
- *Bedford County*. The Republican County Convention had only one delegate per district and that delegate had one vote for each fifty

---

[7] Clinton Rogers Woodruff, address to *National Conference of Practical Reform of Primary Elections*, January 20, 1898, p. 52. Woodruff was Secretary of the National Municipal League and a member of the Pennsylvania state legislature.

Republican votes cast in his district at the preceding general election. The delegate had no discretion in voting at the convention, being required to vote for the candidate who had carried his district caucus for the office in question.

- *Delaware County*. The Republicans here also used a single delegate system. Delegates were required to vote for those candidates for whom they had been instructed so long as their names were before the convention. Only then did they have any discretion.
- *Crawford County*. This was the county in which the direct primary originated in the United States; it had been used there first by the Democrats in 1842.[8]

All of these systems differed from the standard caucus-convention nominating system, in that the latter made no provision for ensuring that the preferences of voters at caucuses were translated into votes at conventions. These other systems did so by different means – the Bucks County system abolished the caucus, the Crawford County Plan abolished the convention and so on – but they were alike in this one, crucial, respect.

These variations at the county level in Pennsylvania resulted not so much from the survival of Jacksonian-era original nominating systems, as from more recent attempts to find solutions to particular problems that had arisen. At least in some counties, there was considerable understanding of how nominating systems worked and efforts had been made to adopt nominating systems that solved those problems. Such was the case in Erie County, which had used the Crawford County Plan before turning to the Clarion County system. According to its state legislator, Colonel E. P. Gould, the direct primary arrangement "did not work."[9] The large votes in the cities of Erie and Corry at the primary meant that they could determine the nomination, but the more reliable Republican vote in general elections was from outside these cities. Under the Clarion County arrangement the Republican voting strength of these areas was given appropriate weight, and, thereby, the Republicans were more likely to make nominations that would ensure success at the general election.

The experimentation with different nominating systems in Erie county shows that in a few places, at least, problems of candidate selection were being met with reform at the local level. The more usual situation, though, was of a growing awareness that the standard caucus-convention nominating system had serious problems, but without knowledge of alternative

---

[8] In fact, at the time of Woodruff's address, it was not known that the Crawford County system was quite as old as this. At the time it was believed that the system dated from about 1860, and it was not until 1935 that Booser discovered that it had been used much earlier; James H. Booser, "Origin of the Direct Primary," *National Municipal Review*, April 1935, pp. 222–3.

[9] *National Conference on Practical Reform of Primaries*, January 20, 1898, p. 54.

models of candidate selection that might replace those that were perceived to be failing. It is necessary now, therefore, to turn to look at what was thought to be wrong with the nominating system.

2. The Problems With the Caucus-Convention System

As was the case with the party ballot, the most conspicuous feature of nineteenth-century party nomination procedures was their informal and decentralized nature. In most counties, nominations were supposed to conform with established customs and recognized conventions; the process was not regulated by state party rules (let alone national party ones) nor was it regulated by law. Even in the mid-1890s, most state parties did not have formal rules governing the conduct of their activities. In 1894 Daniel Remsen published a survey of all state Democratic and Republican parties to discover whether they had formal or printed rules. For the nonsouthern states he was able to obtain information from sixty parties, including at least one in all of the thirty-three nonsouthern states. Of these sixty parties, only twelve (20 percent of the total) had what he described as "printed" or "manuscript" rules – the rest had neither formal rules nor printed rules.[10] That the total was this low as late as the early 1890s gives an indication of just how low it probably was a decade or so earlier.

Furthermore, there was a link between the adoption of state party rules and the level of urbanization in the state. Eight of the twelve parties that had printed or manuscript party rules by 1894 were from the five of the seven most urban states in the country (as measured by 1890 census data) – California (Democrats), Connecticut (Democrats and Republicans), Maryland (Republicans), Massachusetts (Democrats and Republicans), and Pennsylvania (Democrats and Republicans). Of the seven most urban states, only in New Jersey and New York had the state party not adopted such rules. The link between urbanization and the need for state party rules, of course, is that it was in areas of large, concentrated, populations that disputes about the application of established customs and conventions would most likely occur, and it is in those states that pressure for devising ways of resolving them would arise.

Nor are the two other states in which party rules had been adopted by 1894 (Indiana and Kentucky) merely random "outliers." Indiana was, perhaps, the most fiercely competitive state in the Union, and competition had helped to produce extensive and highly complex party institutions.[11] Keeping a party competitive entailed keeping order within it and,

[10] Daniel S. Remsen, *Primary Elections: A Study of Methods for Improving the Basis of Party Organization*, New York and London, G.P. Putnam's Sons, 1894, pp. 38–9.

[11] Philip R. VanderMeer, *The Hoosier Politician: Officeholding and Political Culture in Indiana, 1896–1920*, Urbana and Chicago, University of Illinois Press, 1984, p. 32.

increasingly, that became possible only when there were formal rules that could be invoked in disputes. As for Kentucky, although it was one of the least urbanized states, it had long had problems about the conduct of politics within its one major city, Louisville. As noted in Chapter 2 (Section 1), it was Louisville that was the first city in the country to be subjected to an Australian Ballot law by its state legislature (in 1888). The adoption by some states of party rules, therefore, was more a response to particular needs of party politics rather than a reflection of some general reformist spirit, and, for the most part, American parties remained largely rule-free, even as late as the 1890s.

Disputes about whether customs have been adhered to, and whether existing conventions have been followed, can, and do, arise with any informal practice. Disagreements of this kind surfaced before the Civil War, but the relatively small scale of the society meant that the number of such disagreements did not pose a serious threat to the parties. However, two directly related factors were rapidly changing this. Obviously, one was the growth of large urban areas, areas containing electoral districts with huge numbers of people; the other was the influx of poor, foreign immigrants to these urban areas. Beginning with the mass migration of the Irish in the 1840s, the pattern of immigration to the United States was to change markedly from that evident in the early decades of the nineteenth century. Not only were there many more newcomers, in relation to the size of the native-born population, but there were also greater cultural divisions between the two groups. Most immigrants before the 1840s were Protestant – English, Scots-Irish, and German – while after that date many were Catholics (and later still there were Jews and other religious denominations). Both poverty and also social exclusion practiced by native-born Protestants tended to drive immigrants toward the industrial and commercial centers, and to particular neighborhoods within those cities. With few traditions of democracy in their past, and armed with a need for group solidarity in the face of prejudice and discrimination from native-born Americans, immigrants were to provide the "ground troops" for urban political parties.

Urbanization and mass immigration changed – or, at least, increasingly were thought at the time to be changing – how America's parties operated in four, interconnected, ways. For reasons of brevity, these four changes are discussed under the headings of *participation, logistics, fraud,* and *control.* By the early 1880s, and more vociferously thereafter, the informal system of intraparty relations, and especially of nominating candidates, was being subjected to criticisms that fell under one or more of these headings. What was to make the debate over the next thirty years a complex one was that critics often disagreed as to which problems they believed were the key ones, while even those who had a stake in the status quo found it easier to find allies in deflecting some lines of criticism than they did others.

(i) Participation

Between the late 1820s and the late 1830s, the United States underwent a major transformation. A system of politics that had been based in the early decades of the republic on social deference and rather limited popular participation in politics gave way to "a political nation."[12] This was a world in which most Americans were partisans and in which partisan politics was one of the central arenas of social life. The frequency of elections, a feature of the Jacksonian reforms (noted in Chapter 2), helped to solidify the role of politics as a form of mass, interactive, entertainment. The outward trappings of this, seemingly, highly participatory style of politics – the torchlight parades and so on – persisted well into the late nineteenth century and beyond. But from the 1880s, critics were drawing attention to what they claimed were relatively low levels of participation in the nomination process.

The significance of participation extended well beyond the role it played in public *discussions* of candidate selection. It helped to shape what kinds of reforms of the parties would play well with mass electorates, and, in turn, that constrained the kinds of reforms party elites could contemplate seriously. The reason for this is that mass involvement in the parties had been such a major feature of the Jacksonian democracy. As McGerr noted:

Popular politics involved more than suffrage rights and record turnouts . . . elections in the mid-nineteenth century required the visible endorsement of the people. . . . American politics from roughly the 'thirties to the 'nineties demanded the legitimacy conferred by all classes of the people through parades and rallies and huge turnouts.[13]

This mass involvement of people in electoral politics extended to the nomination process, and high levels of participation in that process were valued widely.

Although early in the public debate about nomination reform participation often appeared a secondary issue, it was a powerful one. Nevertheless, while all paid lip-service to the importance of high levels of participation, some valued it only for instrumental reasons. For example, some reformers with antiparty views believed that having many more people involved in candidate selection would both make fraud less easy and would help reduce the control that party organizations had over the process. Moreover, throughout the period from 1880 to 1915, many reformers – and that includes those with an antiparty orientation – often were not idealists who favored increased political participation *per se*; they favored it to the extent that it might increase the influence of people like themselves or lead to the

---

[12] Joel H. Silbey, *The American Political Nation, 1838–1893*, Stanford, Calif., Stanford University Press, 1991.

[13] Michael E. McGerr, *The Decline of Popular Politics: The American North, 1865–1928*, New York and Oxford, Oxford University Press, 1986, p. 5.

pursuit of policy goals they supported. Thus, for some, a belief that insufficient people participated in the nomination process could even go hand-in-glove with the belief (current in the later 1870s and 1880s) that the franchise should be restricted in municipal elections to those who had a stake in their localities. What was needed was participation by the "right sort of people," and the following passage from the reform weekly *Outlook* (in 1901) is representative of a view common among reformers:

A ballot which automatically excludes the ignorant and indifferent voter, and a direct primary which enables all voters who are not ignorant and indifferent to participate in the nomination of candidates will not constitute a panacea . . . but by decreasing the power of the ignorant and the indifferent, and increasing the power of the intelligent and the interested, much can be done to overthrow the oligarchy.[14]

Of course, this kind of argument about selective participation would play well only in reform circles, and in placing the argument before a wider audience reform politicians had to appeal to a more general argument about the value of participation. In Daniel Remsen's words, the "aim should be to maximize participation."[15] However, here reformers were on strong ground. As we have seen, political participation was a powerful clarion call because the dominant ideology of American politics since the 1830s had been one of mass participation of white males in the political process – through the parties. That ideology was something that both those who wished to weaken parties and those who sought to defend them had to contend, and ultimately that was to shape how change in the selection process would be enacted.

For some – though not all – of those who sought to increase the number of people involved in selecting candidates, there had been a "golden age" that had been lost, at least in most urban areas. According to Wilder:

The town meeting was a caucus beyond reproach and in small homogeneous communities continues an ideal exemplification of the democracy which has made our nation great.[16]

Charles B. Spahr, too, was among many others who saw the rural and small town ideal of democracy as having been corrupted.[17] By contrast, Charles Merriam gave short shrift to the notion that the nominating system had been corrupted by urbanization, primarily in the post–Civil War era. For him, the whole Jacksonian enterprise had been flawed from the beginning: "This experiment in unregulated representative government of the parties

---

[14] *Outlook*, April 13, 1901, p. 839.   [15] Remsen, *Primary Elections*, p. 6.
[16] Wilder, "Primary Election Laws," p. 216.
[17] Charles B. Spahr, "Direct Primaries," *Proceedings of the Rochester Conference for Good City Government, and 7th Annual Meeting of the National Municipal League*, Philadelphia, National Municipal League, 1901, p. 185.

did not begin or continue . . . under wholly favorable auspices."[18] But, irrespective of whether there was substance to the idea of there having been some kind of party "golden age," and the evidence for that is mixed, the idea that parties were properly vehicles for mass participation was widely accepted in American society.[19] That even in the 1890s many Americans were still participating in the parties' election campaigns reinforced the myth of a participatory past.

Furthermore, the expectations of what should be the rate of popular participation in party nominations was extraordinarily high – at least by the standards of the century following. The participation rates that were found wanting included the following. It was estimated that between a fifth and a quarter of the entire electorate attended the Bucks County (Pennsylvania) Republican Convention in 1902.[20] Or again, attendance at Republican caucuses in Minneapolis prior to 1900 could well represent 35 percent of the party's general election vote, although usually not more than that.[21] Moreover, the reformer Ira Cross, someone who had absolutely no reason to exaggerate participation levels, claimed in 1906: "An average of but 39 percent of the voters in San Francisco, 41 percent of those in New York, and 38 percent of those in Cook County, Illinois, take part in nominations."[22]

Not all reformers cited data that indicated such high levels of participation in the nomination process as in these cities and states. Thus, writing in 1917, Arthur Millspaugh described the proportion of "the party membership attending the primaries" in Michigan in the 1890s as "very small"; by this he meant that "the average was probably not more than 20 percent."[23] Earlier, in 1897, F. M. Brooks had complained:

[18] Charles E. Merriam and Louise Overacker, *Primary Elections*, Chicago, University of Chicago Press, 1928, p. 2.

[19] One of the sources of disagreement among scholars concerns the question of what is to count as participation. Those, like Altschuler and Blumin, who claim that participation was lower than is usually acknowledged are probably on stronger ground in relation to the formal involvement by party activists in decision making structures. Their evidence shows that, like most other political communities, those in nineteenth-century America were characterized by the most intense forms of participation being confined to relatively small minorities. However, the more "recreational" aspects of party politics – especially those associated with campaigning – do seem to have attracted far more participants (in marching bands, and so on) and spectators than has been the case in most liberal democracies. See Glenn C. Altschuler and Stuart M. Blumin, *Rude Republic: Americans and their Politics in the 19th Century*, Princeton, N.J., Princeton University Press, 2000, and Michael E. McGerr, *The Decline of Popular Politics: The American North, 1865–1928*, New York, Oxford University Press, 1986.

[20] "Notes: Municipal Government: County Primary Election," *Annals of the American Academy of Political and Social Science*, 20(1902), p. 641.

[21] Frank Maloy Anderson, "The Test of the Minnesota Primary Election System," *Annals of the American Academy of Political and Social Science*, 20(1902), p. 618.

[22] Ira Cross, *Arena*, 35(June 1906), p. 588.

[23] Arthur Chester Millspaugh, *Party Organization and Machinery in Michigan since 1890*, Baltimore, Md., Johns Hopkins University Press, 1917, p. 37.

It is not too much to say that ninety percent of the voters do not participate in the selection of candidates for office. Of the remaining ten percent, at least one-half are office-holders or office-seekers.[24]

The remarkable aspect of his statement is that, even though Brooks's estimate of attendance at caucuses is only about one-third the level of some of the parties just cited, it is still high by the standards of later generations and of other liberal democracies. According to Brooks, one man in twenty with no "career" stake in the nominations was bothering to participate in his party, while a further one in twenty did so because they were seeking office. And still that was not good enough for reformers – much greater participation was being demanded. The old Jacksonian ideal, that citizens should not just vote at general elections but should be involved more generally in political life, continued to inform political debate.

For many reformers, irrespective of whether they really thought there had been a "golden age" of mass participation in party nominations, the main obstacles to greater participation were the party structures in urban areas that discouraged participation.[25] According to them, "party bosses" did not want the intelligent and informed voters to participate, for fear of losing control of their organizations, and they wanted only as many of their own supporters to be involved as was necessary to effect a nomination. On their account, the party boss was an urban phenomenon – he was the product of urbanization and immigration, and he had an incentive to keep participation levels low. Interestingly, they were wrong on both counts. Reform journalists misled their contemporaries and future generations about the links between the urban masses and bossism. In the twentieth century, the most boss-dominated states were to be Connecticut and Rhode Island; to use Buenker's term, they came to be run with an "iron grip" by Republican machines that drew on rural Yankees and business interests, as a way of keeping urban, new-stock masses from power.[26] Furthermore, for "bosses" in urban areas, being able to stimulate a high turnout in the nomination process could be a source of their own power in the party.

(ii) Logistics
One consequence of the rapid growth of urban America was that some practices that were possible in smaller communities had to be abandoned. As

---

[24] F. M. Brooks, "The Nominating Ballot," *Outlook*, December 18, 1897, p. 951.
[25] This was a point made by R. M. Easley, for example: "Experience shows that people will and do go to primaries when they can be assured that their votes will not be thrown into the sewer by corrupt judges and clerks or their heads cracked by drunken bums or political thugs. To secure laws which will remove these obstacles is one of the purposes of this conference." *National Conference on Practical Reform of Primary Elections*, January 20, 1898, p. 93.
[26] John D. Buenker, "The Politics of Resistance: The Rural-based Republican Machines of Connecticut and Rhode Island, *New England Quarterly*, 47(1974), pp. 212–37.

noted earlier, in the larger electoral districts of New England, this meant the loss of the face-to-face discussions that had been characteristic of this region. In 1898 Samuel B. Capen, who was from the suburbs of Boston, lamented:

The old system had some advantages. We met . . . in our Ward in a large hall capable of accommodating a thousand men. We looked each other in the face, we discussed men and measures and the best citizens were in evidence as well as the selfish and corrupt.[27]

In its place was a procedure that was really just an election of delegates, which Capen argued had actually had the effect of depressing interest and participation in the primary stage of nomination. As most of its politicians were inclined to emphasize, Massachusetts was not an especially corrupt state, but, significantly, it was to be an early leader in the legal regulation of the nomination process: the growth of urban populations was posing problems for parties, even in places where boss control was not that excessive.

The extent of the change can be considered by comparing the size of the electorate in the 1840 congressional elections with its size in 1888. (Both were closely fought contests in which an incumbent President was defeated.) In Massachusetts in 1840 between seven thousand and ten thousand people were voting in each district; in 1888 typically between twenty-five thousand and thirty thousand votes were cast in each congressional district. Since the country's population increased by more than threefold between 1840 and 1890, it is scarcely surprising that electoral turnout should reflect this trend.

As the population size of electoral districts grew, so it became less possible to hold meetings to discuss either the selection of candidates or issues. As early as 1875, arguments were being made in support of smaller election precincts.[28] Indeed, in the very largest electoral districts there was actually a problem of providing facilities in which all those who wanted to could vote; polling one thousand men or more took a long time, and there were complaints that the traditional hours set aside for voting were insufficient. The problems of size were compounded when there were even more voters than this, and when the nomination process involved arranging more than mere voting. A critical observer at the Bucks County (Pennsylvania) Republican Convention in 1902, a convention open to all Republicans since there were no preceding caucuses, noted that:

Those who wished to take part in, or to follow the proceedings, were compelled to stand near the platform. . . . It is variously estimated that there were four or five thousand or more . . . in attendance on this convention. The deliberative

---

[27] Samuel B. Capen, Address to *National Conference on Practical Reform of Primary Elections*, January 20, 1898, p. 17.
[28] *New Englander*, 34(1875), pp. 473–87.

proceedings were a mere farce. Neither the chairman nor the secretary was heard by more than a small portion of the assemblage.[29]

Thus, problems of increasing scale provided an impetus for the regulation of hitherto informal procedures. Given that the state parties themselves tended not to be governed by formal or written rules, turning to state law as the means of effecting reform was the obvious alternative. That legal reform rather than internal party reform would be required was recognized by some reformers early on; one of the earliest pamphlets on the subject, written in 1883, spoke of only "effective legal control" as the remedy for the "evils of the caucus system."[30]

Of course, larger and more heterogeneous districts merely exacerbated problems that arose elsewhere, albeit in less serious forms. Even in stable, rural districts, disputes could arise over customary procedures about "whose turn it really was" to be nominated for a particular office, and in extreme cases this could produce "bolting" by the groups who believed that they were losing out. In rural communities these difficulties were not usually frequent enough to warrant moving from an informal system to a rule-governed one. However, in the ethnically diverse cities severe problems of control for the parties were posed in the decades after the Civil War. Furthermore, large electoral districts made various forms of fraud that much easier to practise. Since individuals did not know each other, the self-policing of caucuses could be ineffective, and impersonation of party members made easy. Those from outside the district, those impersonating dead party members, and Democrats participating in Republican caucuses (and vice versa) could all vote at the caucuses in favorable circumstances.

(iii) Fraud

It is impossible to read any book or academic article on American political parties in the second half of the nineteenth century without reference being made, in many cases frequently, to fraud and corruption. In commencing discussion on what is actually a complex subject, it is important to recognize that there was electoral corruption and it was increasing. In addition to the causes just cited, there were two further, and interconnected, reasons why the situation seemed to contemporaries to be worse in the 1880s than in the 1850s.

The first reason is that the rewards for controlling large cities were that much greater than for controlling smaller cities or rural areas. The contracts that local governments issued to private companies for performing basic public services were highly valuable, and that helped to make public

---

[29] "Notes: Municipal Government: County Primary Election," *Annals of the American Academy of Political and Social Science*, 20(1902), p. 641.

[30] Frederick W. Whitridge, *Caucus System* (Economic Tracts No. VIII), New York, Society for Political Education, 1883, p. 26.

officeholding much more lucrative. Thus, in explaining why abuse of the caucus system was primarily an urban, and not a rural, issue, Frederick Dallinger listed the absence of "lucrative offices" in rural areas as one of the four explanations for it. (The other reasons were (i) that everyone knew each other in rural areas, (ii) that there was a small number of voters in rural electoral districts, and hence no problems of disorder, and (iii) the absence of "excitable foreign elements.")[31]

Second, there was much more money in post–Civil War politics than there had been prewar. For example, although the voting population was increasing rapidly in this period, the increase in presidential election campaign expenditures outpaced it; using estimates constructed by Alexander, it seems that in presidential elections spending had been about 3¢ per voter in 1860, but it was 22¢ per voter in 1876, 27¢ in 1884, and 29¢ in 1896.[32] Money could be, and was, directed toward internal control of the parties, as much as toward general election campaigns, and undoubtedly inducements and bribes were offered in exchange for votes at some party conventions.

Yet, the many claims about fraud and corruption that were to be found in the pages of journals such as *Nation* and *Outlook*, and in the *Proceedings of the National Municipal League* must be treated with considerable caution. The language of American politics, certainly since the Jacksonian era, and arguably before as well, was both far more vitriolic than it was to be in the twentieth century, and it also was rife with such claims about "fraud" and "corruption."[33] Money was used regularly by Democrats and Republicans alike in ways that would invoke criticism were it to occur today, but which were part of normal politics then:

. . . both sides produced money. Some of it went to buy voters. A dollar (sometimes as much as five, in a close race) thrust into one hand and a printed ballot pressed into the other could be depended on in ways that a real secret ballot never could. Voters whose loyalty was never in doubt still might expect payment, say, "two dollars for time lost in going to the polls." Some of the payoffs were just tokens of gratitude, like the yellow tickets Democrats once passed out in downtown Philadelphia, inscribed, "Good for a drink." Altogether, contemporaries estimated

---

[31] Dallinger, *Nominations for Elective Office in the United States*, p. 96.

[32] Herbert E. Alexander, *Financing Politics*, Washington, D.C., Congressional Quarterly Press, 1976, p. 20.

[33] How corrupt nineteenth-century politics was has been a matter of some dispute among political historians. Those who are skeptical of nineteenth-century claims about how widespread corruption was include Paul Kleppner and Stephen C. Baker, "The Impact of Voter Registration Requirements on Electoral Turnout, 1900–16," paper presented at the 1979 Annual Meeting of the American Political Science Association, and Howard W. Allen and Kay Warren Allen, "Vote Fraud and Data Validity," in Jerome M. Clubb, William H. Flanigan, and Nancy H. Zingale (eds.), *Analyzing Electoral History: A Guide to the Study of American Voting Behaviour*, Beverly Hills, Calif., Sage, 1981. For an opposing view, see Peter H. Argersinger, "New Perspectives on Electoral Fraud in the Gilded Age," *Political Science Quarterly*, 100(1985–6), pp. 669–87.

that one New Hampshire voter in ten expected payment, and a later historian put the total in New Jersey at one-third or more.[34]

Money was similarly used in contesting party nominations, and here, too, the offering of inducements to act in a particular way in politics was widespread. It was the "losers" who resorted to allegations of corruption: Those who had lost an election, or who had failed to get a party nomination, or who had failed to get a patronage position would cry "corruption" in much the same way that soccer supporters scream at hard tackles made by the opposing team. As noted in Chapter 1, Stampp observed of politics in 1857, "The spoils system was not without its critics, but they were always most plentiful among the members of a defeated party," and both before and after 1857 many allegations of corruption were made by those who had played the political game and then been disappointed by the results.[35]

By the 1890s, attitudes were changing. In part, this may have been a response to an increased cost in campaigning for party nominations by the end of the century. For example, Millspaugh argued that in Michigan in 1900 and 1902 more money was spent on primaries and conventions than ever before; he cited three counties in which each of the three candidates spent $10,000 in all of the counties.[36] Then again, the legitimacy of the spoils system was being questioned more widely than by a small group of reformers, as was both the giving of money to voters and also such practices as the rapid naturalization of aliens by partisan judges in the run-up to an election. Nevertheless, what had been striking about the earlier period of American democracy was how well it worked in spite of the widespread use of methods that later generations would regard as unacceptable. For example, an interesting point about patronage appointees is just how competent and dedicated many of them probably were; it is, perhaps, significant that Lord Bryce in his much cited late-nineteenth-century study of the American polity was not critical of their performance.[37]

Nevertheless, by the 1890s there was a growing demand for greater and more complex public services and for greater local regulation of key economic actors; in these circumstances the issue of how well, and how efficiently, a service was delivered, came into the public domain because the potential tension between preferment and competence was revealed. Moreover, not only were key interest groups, particularly business groups, wanting more efficient delivery of service from public employees – such as those in the U.S. Post Office – but the growth in public employment also

[34] Mark Wahlgren Summers, *Rum, Romanism and Rebellion: The Making of a President, 1884*, Chapel Hill, University of North Carolina Press, 2000, p. 14.

[35] Kenneth M. Stampp, *America in 1857*, New York, Oxford University Press, 1990, p. 73.

[36] Millspaugh, *Party Organization and Machinery*, p. 39.

[37] C. K. Yearley, *The Money Machines: The Breakdown and Reform of Governmental and Party Finance in the North 1860–1920*, Albany, State University of New York Press, 1970, pp. 101–2.

was making it more difficult for elected politicians to control those they appointed. The result was an increasing division within parties between, on the one hand, elected executives (the president and state governors) and legislators (in Congress and in the states) and, on the other, lower level party functionaries. Especially in the most populous states, the former group were supporting the introduction of merit-based systems of public employment.[38]

As public support for the system of preferment started to wane, so the language of "fraud" and "corruption" became a more valuable tool to use against those party elites who appeared to oppose reform. Long-accepted practices started to lose their legitimacy as the spoils system struggled to deal effectively with the new demands of urban populations. In their battle for control of the parties, reformers found this language even more useful than it had been earlier. But that does not mean that their verdicts on how parties conducted their nomination procedures should be accepted at face value.

For all the hyperbole about "fraud," the real dispute between the urban machines and their opponents was about control, and not fraud. This was a point made by Walter J. Branson (of the University of Pennsylvania) in 1899 in an article about nominations in Philadelphia. Branson was no friend of machines, but he pointed out that fraud was largely conducted between rival professional politicians. According to Branson, it was not fraud that was keeping out the independent-minded middle-classes; rather, "[T]he true explanation of 'machine rule' will be found, not in the corrupt practices which are occasionally resorted to, but in the superior effectiveness of organized action."[39] The real significance of urbanization is that it made it possible to mobilize large numbers of supporters, and through the organization of them control the nomination process. Consequently, as Branson noted, "Without organizing in a similar manner and resorting to the same methods, disinterested citizens are powerless to offer effective opposition."[40] This brings the discussion directly to the subject of control.

(iv) Control

The caucus-convention system advantaged in three ways those who were organized and who had control of political resources. First, at the ward or district level, it was possible in some places for particular professional politicians to select the delegations they wanted. Second, because there was no method of preventing delegates from doing what they wanted, once they were selected, it was possible for such politicians to provide delegates with

---

[38] See Ronald N. Johnson and Gary D. Libecap, "Patronage to Merit and Control of the Federal Government Labor Force," *Explorations in Economic History* 31(1994), 91–119.

[39] Walter J. Branson, "The Philadelphia Nominating System," *Annals of the American Academy of Political and Social Science*, 14(1899), p. 26.

[40] Branson, "The Philadelphia Nominating System," p. 30.

inducements in return for their support at the convention. Finally, those who were organized were usually able to run conventions in the way that they wanted, if necessary, thereby negating challenges from any opponents. Often this advantage resulted from the need to simplify proceedings. For example, even in a relatively "open" state such as Massachusetts, decisions about nominations might be taken not in the convention itself but by small committees, which in theory were responsible to the convention but that, in practice, were controlled by party professionals. Dallinger, for example, said of the Massachusetts Democrats, "In some cases even where a candidate is nominated for the governorship, the question of the nomination of candidates for minor offices on the State ticket is referred by the State convention to a committee, which reports a list of candidates to the convention."[41]

A good example of how professional politicians could operate in a caucus-convention system was provided by William Flewellyn Saunders, Secretary of the Board of Election Commissioners in St. Louis in the late 1890s. Saunders gave an account of how nominations worked in both Kansas City and St. Louis during the mid-1870s. He refers to the practices he describes as "frauds," although it is clear from his description that they amount to little more than the inherent advantage of organization in a decentralized and informal process. Saunders wrote:

. . . the central or managing committees of both parties made nominations, and candidates spent little or no time going through the form of standing before the people for nominating votes. Each party had a Central Committee composed of one member from each ward. When there were delegates to be sent to a city convention which was to choose a mayor and other officers, the Central Committee met and called the convention and fixed the date for the selection of the delegates in the wards. Then the member of the Central Committee for that ward consulted a few chums or candidates and decided on the delegates he wanted to send to the convention. His slate was invariably elected. The committeeman treated the voters of the ward with the scantiest pretense of fairness, even when they were entirely unorganized in opposition. His delegates would be chosen in a place selected by himself, presided over by himself, the tellers of the ballot chosen by himself, and packed by his friends in advance of the time announced for the meeting. If there was opposition to him in the ward, and he feared that his mass meeting might be captured, he would resort to tricks that were bolder.[42]

Saunders does not say what these "tricks" actually were, but the entire account would have been grist to Branson's mill; it is a good example of how the organized would always outmaneuver the unorganized. Fraud, as such, was usually unnecessary.

---

[41] Dallinger, *Nominations for Elective Office in the United States*, p. 68.
[42] William Flewellyn Saunders, address to the *National Conference on Practical Reform of Primary Elections*, January 21, 1898, p. 142.

Saunders then proceeded to describe how, beginning in 1875, legislation had been passed in Missouri to deal with the unsatisfactory consequences of previously informal systems of candidate selection. He argued that even in the late 1890s the problems had not been solved but the situation was rather better than it had been. But who was responsible for reforms, and who opposed them? The traditional picture is one of independent reformers taking on party machines and defeating them. But Missouri was an especially partisan state in a nation that was highly partisan. Political independence was a weak movement in Missouri; for example, although the Liberal Republican defection of 1872 had begun in that state, the Mugwump bolt of 1884 had few adherents in the midwest. However, their putative opponents, "political bosses" in St. Louis and Kansas City, also could not dominate state politics on their own. Even in 1890, only 32 percent of the state's population lived in cities with populations of more than five thousand – rural and small town legislators controlled the state. It was legislators representing these sorts of places who were responsible for enacting a flurry of laws on party nominations in the 1890s; like most states, by 1898 Missouri had passed several pieces of legislation relating to party nominations – in its case in 1875, 1889, 1891, 1893, and 1897.

The fact is that control of the nominating process was important for a wide range of party politicians, and how they viewed it would likely depend on the particular circumstances in their state and at a given time. Consider a hypothetical Democratic legislator from a smaller city in Missouri. Democratic bosses in Missouri and Kansas City had their uses – they could get the vote out and help to win statewide offices for the party and also carry it for the Democrats in presidential elections. However, any publicity for some of their methods would not sell well with his own supporters. Indeed, even in urban areas these methods would not be acceptable to some voters and most parties had to present the public appearance of being committed to open and fair methods of nomination. This point is evident in a speech by Edward Lauterbach; Lauterbach was a close associate of New York Republican "boss" Thomas Platt, and had been Chairman of the New York Republican County Committee. He argued, ". . . I say, as a party man, that it is the true interest of each party to make honest straight primaries the possibility, and to render it impossible, if possible, to accomplish any result by fraud."[43]

To return to the situation facing the hypothetical Missouri Democratic legislator: the greater the relative size of the urban parties within the state Democratic party, the more difficult it might be for nonurban Democrats to get their nominees for state office selected. This was less of a problem to the Missourian, than it was for someone from rural New York where

[43] Edward Lauterbach, address to *National Conference on Practical Reform of Primary Elections*, January 21, 1898, p. 114.

urban areas in the state were relatively larger, and, hence, more important in state parties. Nevertheless, ambivalence to their big-city allies was still a core feature in the attitudes of rural and smaller city politicians. Party mattered to them and, when reform proposals produced a cleavage on party lines, usually they would vote with their party. As was seen in Chapter 2, ballot reform in New York developed a highly partisan character and, when it did, legislators tended to vote with their party. In relation to nomination reform, this ambivalence of rural legislators to political practices in large cities was to have three consequences for debates in state legislatures.

First, some legislation related only to urban areas. Rural and small town areas were often more than content with their own procedures, and there was a disinclination to change them so that, when possible, these areas might be excluded from legislation.[44] (Illinois' legislation of 1898 placed the expense of holding caucuses on the public purse and provided nearly all the safeguards of general elections, but while it was mandatory for Chicago, it was merely optional for the rest of the state.[45]) Second, even when local exclusions were not possible, the recognition that the practices of city parties were both embarrassing and also potentially threatened the balance of power within a state party, could prompt legislation. However, whether a particular nonurban legislator supported or opposed statewide legislation would depend, for example, on how seriously he viewed the nomination problems in the cities and how much he was opposed to tampering with arrangements that worked well in his own district. Consequently, support for reforms often cut across party lines, and could produce complex divisions within a party. Third, as was seen in connection with David Hill's handling of the Australian Ballot issue in New York, the logic of party competition meant that the politics of legislation at times could move from being an essentially bipartisan matter to a partisan one. How legislation was handled as it was being passed, and how the parties perceived their short term advantage being affected by it, were among the factors influencing this.

(v) The Interconnections of the Four Factors

It should be apparent that the four factors that have been identified – participation, logistics, fraud, and control – were linked to each other in a variety of ways. By the time that most of the original Australian Ballot legislation was being enacted (1888–91), the situation could broadly be summarized as follows:

– there was a growing awareness among state politicians that the older, informal procedures for nominating candidates were seriously flawed in the larger, urban electoral districts; the changing scale of American society required change in party nominating procedures.

---

[44] This is a point noted by Spahr, "Direct Primaries," p. 185.
[45] *Outlook*, February 19, 1898, p. 455.

- any proposed changes would have to recognize the importance of the myth of mass participation in the parties.
- although its prevalence was exaggerated, fraud and corruption in the nomination had increased, especially in urban areas.
- any changes in procedures would affect the distribution of influence in parties, and this would be fiercely contested by all those affected.
- how individual politicians would perceive how their interests were affected was a complicated matter, and would depend on the particular context.
- given the decentralization of the parties, statewide reform could only be achieved by legislation; the state parties were not in a position to oversee and direct control of particular county parties.

In response to the changed circumstances, state legislatures had been active in passing legislation even before 1888. The list of laws relating to legislation on nominations complied by Merriam and Overacker shows that between 1866 and the end of 1887 fifteen states had enacted legislation. Many of the larger states (including New York, New Jersey, and Ohio) had done so in several years during this period. However, this was but a trickle compared with the flood of legislation that was to be enacted in the years following. Much of the legislation was aimed at preventing blatant fraud (such as disturbance of primary meetings), but a number of states passed laws regulating how and when caucuses could be held. In some states, including New York, this involved quite detailed regulations specifying the size of the polling place, the hours of polling, and much else.[46] Significantly, most of these laws were enacted long before "regular" parties in some states were being challenged by "insurgents" who wished to reform parties, in order to break the power of entrenched interests.

Consequently, even while the Democratic and Republican parties were at the height of their power, there was a move throughout much of the country to regulate by law how the parties made their nominations. While some later writers, including Charles Merriam, derided the scope of the early legislation by comparison with what was to come later, the more appropriate observation, perhaps, is that it is interesting that it happened at all. Far from being hostile to change, and having to have it imposed on them, American state legislators – men who usually were close to the heart of their parties' organizations – were passing laws that were to transform the informal basis of party politics.

3. The Impact of the Australian Ballot

Although measures to control the parties' procedures for candidate selection via legislation were already underway by the time the first Australian

[46] Merriam and Overacker, *Primary Elections*, pp. 7–20.

Ballot laws were introduced in 1888, the adoption of official ballots had a huge impact on the future development of that legislation. It did so in three main ways.

One effect was on reformers – both those, like a majority of ex-Mugwumps, who wished to rein in the power of the parties, and those like Josiah Quincy who saw strong parties as essential for American democracy.[47] In part, the Australian Ballot encouraged reformers because it demonstrated that it was possible to enact legislation that would modify practices of which reformers disapproved. However, it was also a spur to action, for there were those who believed (correctly) that one of the main consequences of that legislation had been to strengthen party organization control over the nomination process. This was a line taken by the Buffalo reformer William H. Hotchkiss, who observed in 1898 that during the previous four or five years there had developed a "concentration of party power in the hands of a few – a concentration which is the outgrowth of the Australian ballot system."[48] Thus, the effect of the Australian Ballot legislation was not to dampen reforming zeal but to intensify it and target it directly at the party nominating system.

The second effect was on those party elites who could not be classified as enthusiastic reformers. They tended to perceive the official ballot legislation as a success. It had eradicated the problems facing the parties in the 1880s and yet party control over mass electorates had not been threatened. It demonstrated that a successful transition from an informal system of party activity to one in which some activities were rule-governed was possible.

Finally, and equally important, official ballot legislation actually led state legislatures to address the issue of the role of parties in the nomination of candidates. This point was made by the Democratic Mayor of Boston, Josiah Quincy:

. . . this question of caucus reform has arisen directly and logically out of the adoption of the Australian Ballot. . . . I think that today . . . most of us, at least, see that it [the Australian Ballot] logically involves, leads to, and requires, first, the recognition, and second, the regulation of the political party, or of the convention, or of the caucus; it was the right of any citizen, or any number of citizens, to print a

---

[47] Although he had been a Mugwump, Quincy became a Democrat partisan. Much to the annoyance of his former allies, he was involved in the distribution of patronage in the 1889–93 Cleveland administration. As Mayor of Boston in the 1890s, ". . . his complete commitment to the Democratic party reflected a belief that the political party was not merely an unfortunate expedient but a crucial instrument of social progress." Geoffrey Blodgett, *The Gentle Reformers: Massachusetts Democrats in the Cleveland Era*, Cambridge, Mass., Harvard University Press, 1966, p. 246.

[48] William H. Hotchkiss, address to *National Conference on Practical Reform of Primary Elections*, January 21, 1898, p. 131.

ballot and to present any nominations which he or they saw fit at the polls. But under the Australian Ballot system it is different; the State is obliged to recognize the existence of the political party and of political machinery; and the recognition of this inevitably and logically leads up to the regulation of the practices of political parties, of their conventions and of their caucuses.[49]

The reason for this so-called logical connection was that in nearly all states Australian Ballot legislation gave a privileged position to the two large parties in the nomination of candidates. This was recognized at the time. The political scientist Charles C. Binney noted in 1892 that:

... the fact that political parties have long been regarded as the possible nominating bodies except in unusual cases, has influenced even legislation. Under nearly all American ballot reform laws the officers of conventions or other constituted authorities of parties (in most laws, those of a certain numerical strength only) may execute and file what are usually distinctively known as "certificates of nomination," while for nominations made by parties less fully developed or by voters acting outside of recognized party organizations a much larger number of persons must sign "nomination papers," as they are usually called.[50]

But why did the partes have to be privileged in this way? In an obvious respect, it was not "logical" at all: Britain had introduced an official ballot in 1872, but no special privileges were thereby accorded to parties. In fact, nearly one hundred years passed before the party affiliation of a candidate was printed on the ballot in Britain. In the United States, the length of the ballot meant that electoral confusion would have been the likely result of a form of ballot from which party labels were absent. Not only would northern partisan state legislators not have countenanced such a reform, but there were few antiparty reformers who would have gone this far in reducing the parties' role. Parties were needed to bring order to the ballot, and that was why the major parties' nominations were treated differently from other nominations under Australian Ballot legislation. However, once this step had been taken, it was evident that disputes would arise as to who were the official nominees of a party. For example, in Michigan in 1891 a court case arose out of a split party convention, producing precisely this problem.[51] Thus, courts (and then state legislators) were forced to decide on matters such as which institution, or group of people within an institution, had the power to make party nominations. Once they had been drawn into dispute resolution of this kind, it was always likely that state legislators would then try to establish rules that would make it less likely

[49] Josiah Quincy, address to the *National Conference on Practical Reform of Primary Elections*, January 21, 1898, p. 103.
[50] Charles C. Binney, "The Merits and Defects of the Pennsylvania Ballot Law of 1891," *Annals of the American Academy of Political and Social Science*, 2(1891–2), p. 756.
[51] Millspaugh, *Party Organization and Machinery*, p. 20.

that disputes would arise. While this was not exactly "logical," in the way Quincy indicated, he was correct in arguing that state control of party nominations did arise "directly" out of ballot reform.

Consequently, even if there had not been a preexisting movement for legal reform of the caucuses, the Australian Ballot legislation inevitably would have drawn state legislatures into this area in the 1890s. In fact, that legislation served to reinforce the drive toward such reform. Or, as Merriam and Overacker put it: "It was an easy step from permitting the two great parties to have their candidates placed upon the ballot . . . to requiring that these nominations should have been made only in accordance with such rules and regulations as might be deemed necessary." [52]

Acting as a catalyst, the Australian Ballot contributed to a large amount of legislation relating to candidate selection being passed by the states in the years following the introduction of the official ballot. By 1896, about two-thirds (22) of the nonsouthern states had special laws regulating party nominations – that is, apart from the provisions contained in Australian Ballot legislation. [53] Four years later every state except Vermont had passed some kind of legislation, and in the larger states many different kinds of laws had been enacted. While in states containing large urban areas special legislation was directed toward those counties in which party nominations might be especially problematic, there also were many laws covering an entire state. Among the reforms enacted were the transference of the financial costs of holding caucuses to the state, requiring the use of ballots in caucuses, the formal enrollment of party voters by the state, requiring caucuses to be held on particular dates, and the strengthening of laws on fraudulent practices. The laws that were enacted in the 1890s were not just blanket proposals designed to demonstrate good intentions on the part of legislators. Much of the legislation in these years was detailed and intricate. Writing in 1905, Deming and Trowbridge said, of New York in the period 1882–98, that there the "tendency, already strongly manifested toward a more minute regulation of the internal organization of political parties, increases with each succeeding change in the law." [54] Such laws were passed by partisan-controlled state legislatures at a time when parties were still at the height of their powers; they were not imposed on the parties by either antiparty reformers or anyone else, but were an attempt by partisans to solve problems they themselves faced.

Yet for all the activity, the context was very different from that surrounding the adoption of the Australian Ballot. With the latter, there were

---

[52] Merriam and Overacker, *Primary Elections*, p. 25.
[53] Dallinger, *Nominations for Elective Office*, p. 174.
[54] Horace E. Deming and Lawrence W. Trowbridge, "Primary Legislation in New York, 1882–1898," *Proceedings of the New York Conference for Good Government and the 11th Annual Meeting of the National Municipal League, 1905*, p. 317.

clear models of reform that could be followed to remove the problems that had become evident early on. Nomination reform was different. In the early 1890s, there was no Massachusetts model, nor an Indiana model, that could be copied. For all the legislation being enacted, dissatisfaction among politicians remained. This was scarcely surprising, given the complexities of the problems in candidate selection they were seeking to address. Thus, by about 1897, party elites in many states were beginning to question whether their counterparts elsewhere had been more successful in their approach to legislation. There was now widespread interest in learning how procedures that were being used particularly at the county level in other states might work or be adapted at home. There was a clear need for exchange of information, and early in 1898 a national conference was organized to do just that. That this conference took place indicates that an important turning point was being reached in nomination reform, despite all the legislative activity in the preceding years.

4. The 1898 National Conference

The National Conference on Practical Reform of Primary Elections was important not for anything that it did but because of the light that it sheds on how reform on party nominations was proceeding at the time. It had no *direct* practical consequences, and, because of this, Charles Merriam did not even bother to mention it in his classic work, *Primary Elections*. But then, as noted earlier, he was not interested in asking how and why direct primary elections came to be adopted so widely; he seems to have believed that he knew the answer to that already, and he did not bother to look at an event that he would have regarded as peripheral to the onward march of state legislation on primaries. Today the conference has been forgotten by those who write about American political parties. However, there are a number of interesting aspects of it – not least, who bothered to attend it and who wrote to the organizers expressing their support for it. The breadth of support for it shows that it was not simply a platform for those who wished to dismantle parties.

Perhaps the most important features of this conference, therefore, were that it happened at all – for there had been no similar conference in relation to ballot reform – and that so many prominent politicians gave their backing to it. It was needed because it was far from clear that current efforts at legislating for reform of the caucus-convention system were producing the kinds of results that had been evident at an early stage with ballot reform. That there was such a conference is evidence of the extent of the problems inherent in nomination reform.

The conference was held in New York City over two days in January 1898. At first glance, the list of those who called for, and attended it, looks like that of the "usual suspects" among late-nineteenth-century political reformers. Carl Schurz was there, as were Edwin L. Godkin, William M. Ivins, Richard Dana, Frank J. Goodnow, Oscar Straus, and ex-Congressman Robert La Follette. But a closer inspection reveals a rather different picture. The sponsors were not just from the Boston–New York axis that had formed the basis of the Mugwump revolt in 1884. They came from twenty-two states across the country (of which three were in the South), and they included a number of elected politicians. Both the mayor and ex-mayor of New York were among the signatories calling for the conference, but so, too, were the mayors of Boston, Baltimore, Buffalo, Milwaukee, San Francisco, Des Moines, and Toledo. The mayors of Boston and New Orleans both delivered major speeches, as did Edward Lauterbach, "Boss" Platt's close political associate. Not only did party "regulars" think it important to be heard, therefore, but the theme of Lauterbach's speech was the importance of reform in party nominations for the continued strength of the parties. He even drew applause for his peroration that concluded, "if the party of the right is strengthened the national cause of Americanism is strengthened."[55] He differed from most speakers in not discussing the direct primary as a cure for the problems of the nomination system, but it was a speech that demonstrated what the legislative record in New York also showed – namely, that nomination reform was not an issue that the parties were trying to keep off the agenda. As *Outlook* commented immediately after the Conference, Lauterbach ". . . admitted that a more open primary, guarded by law against fraud on the part of those in charge, must now receive the support of the Republican machine in this State."[56]

Another speaker was Roy O. West who, thirty years later, would serve briefly in the Coolidge Cabinet. In 1898 he was a close associate of the Chicago "regular" politician, Charles Deneen, who within a decade would be governor of Illinois. Like Lauterbach, West would have been an unlikely participant at a gathering of antiparty reformers – had the National Conference been such a gathering, we can be sure that neither of them (nor quite a few others) would have been there.

Further evidence of the breadth of concern on the issue of candidate selection is revealed in the list of people who had sent letters to the conference organizers expressing their support for it. Extracts from their letters were read out at the conference, and it is doubtful that these politicians would have bothered to write unless the issue was of political significance in their state. They included the governors of thirteen states – Colorado, Connecticut, Illinois, Indiana, Iowa, Kansas, Maryland, Massachusetts, Michigan, Nebraska, New York, Washington, and Wisconsin – as well as the ex-governors of Illinois and Missouri, the mayors of Chattanooga,

---

[55] Edward Lauterbach, address to *National Conference on Practical Reform of Primary Elections*, January 21, 1898, p. 116.
[56] *Outlook*, January 29, 1898, p. 266.

Denver, and East St. Louis, and members of the National Committees of both parties. That the entire thrust of the conference had been to build bridges between reformers generally outside the parties and party elites was summed up by its secretary, Ralph M. Easley, in his introduction to the published proceedings:

There was . . . a general recognition of the utility and necessity of party organization. The President, Hon. Oscar L. Straus, voiced the sentiment of the conference when he said: "I understand that the object of this conference is not to break down parties, but to strengthen parties and to make them representative of the people instead of mere cliques. We recognize the necessity of parties in a free government."[57]

Some of the formal addresses to the conference were fulminations against the evils of party nominations at that time. Most were not, though. There were a number of detailed expositions of how certain reformed procedures worked in a given state, and these were followed by general discussions in which the participants questioned the speakers about particular aspects of the procedures they had described. It became clear from this that procedures tried in one state would not necessarily be wholly acceptable in another, and this would have prevented the emergence of any formal recommendations at the conference's conclusion. In any case, however, it was evident that there would have been a more fundamental division of opinion that would have prevented anything approaching a unanimous recommendation. A number of speakers, including those such as Josiah Quincy, who were fervent partisans, came out in support of the direct primary. Quincy observed: "I think there is a strong sentiment in the city of Boston in favor of giving that system a trial; that sentiment exists in both political parties, and many of the practical politicians sympathize with it and are disposed to favor the movement."[58] But there were those, like Edward Lauterbach, who stood firm by a reformed caucus-convention system, and any attempt to push through a recommendation in favor of the direct primary would simply have undermined the rest of the conference's work. Furthermore, the conference was read a speech by an officer of the Municipal Association of Cleveland that was highly critical of the recent use of the Crawford County Plan in his city.[59] There was little point, therefore, in having a further high profile conference, and although when the proceedings were published it was styled as the *First National Conference on Practical Reform of Primary Elections*, there was no successor to it.

Although some of the schemes discussed at the conference, such as the use of the direct primary in Cleveland, were ones that had not been enacted

---

[57] *First National Conference on Practical Reform of Primary Elections*, pp. 3–4.

[58] Josiah Quincy, address to *National Conference on Practical Reform of Primary Elections*, January 21, 1898, p. 106.

[59] Thomas L. Johnson, speech read by Mr. McDermott, *National Conference on Practical Reform of Primary Elections*, January 21, 1898, pp. 98–102.

in law, most of them had been. Indeed, the working assumption of most of the participants was that nomination reform was a matter for legislation, rather than for the parties themselves. But why? Why was it not simply being left to the parties to sort out?

5. Why Legal Controls Over Parties were Introduced

One way of thinking about the use of legal regulation of parties in the United States is to consider how other types of parties might have handled the kinds of problems that were evident in America by the early 1890s. In doing so, it may be possible to uncover what is really distinctive about the American parties. For this exercise two very different types of party will be considered – the caucus-cadre parties of Third Republic France and the mass-membership parties of post–1945 Europe.

Like the Democratic and Republican parties, the caucus-cadre parties in France drew their organizational strength from the local level. At the parliamentary level parties were little more than labels used by relatively independent politicians whose power base in a particular locality prevented them from being subject to much control by those who, from the outside, appeared to be the nominal leaders of the party nationally. The decentralization of the parties in the two countries at that time is a feature they share and which makes for a marked difference with, say, European social democratic parties in the twentieth century. But the kinds of problems that were arising in late nineteenth century American parties – claims that insufficient numbers of people were participating in party nominations, claims that party leaders were manipulating conventions to prevent the nomination of candidates party members really wanted, and claims that local parties now contained too many people, so that informal controls could not work – simply would not have arisen in a party such as the French Radicals. There are several reasons why they would not have arisen.

First, despite facing universal manhood suffrage in the Third Republic, French parties had little use for large numbers of activists or workers. Parties were vehicles for electing candidates to one major level of office – the National Assembly – and were usually little more than the "personal" organizations of local politicians such as mayors or would-be mayors. Elections were also relatively infrequent. By contrast, in the United States, many offices were filled by election, thanks partly to the Jacksonian reforms of the 1830s, and elections were held frequently because terms of office were usually short. American parties needed party activists because of the sheer scale of party work; in a French party they were unnecessary, and arguably an encumbrance. Even by comparison with other federal systems, such as Canada, where there were several different layers of public office, the United States stands out in the use to which it put a standing army of party activists. Late-nineteenth-century Canadian politics could be run with very small numbers of activists, even though there were both provincial and federal elections to contest.

Second, in France those dissatisfied with their lack of influence, or whatever, could always move to another party or possibly start working for another local politician who was nominally of the same party. Not only did the Third Republic have a multiparty system, but also the looseness of the party groupings even at the national level meant that "exit" and not "voice" was the obvious strategy for the disgruntled.[60] Although small parties, such as the Greenbacks and the Prohibitionists, had an important role in contesting nineteenth-century American elections, because of the narrow margin of victory for many offices, they were not really alternatives to the two main parties. In Summers's words, they were "sideshow" parties.[61] They were weak financially, because they did not control sufficient public offices to generate anything like the regular income that the major parties did, and often they received financial donations from one of these parties during elections, as a way of helping to splinter further the vote of their opponents.[62] The weakness of third parties made "voice" in America a far more worthwhile option than in the parties of the Third Republic. Furthermore, while legislative parties lacked the discipline of their counterparts in, say, Britain or Canada, they were not mere collections of individual politicians.[63] Party mattered, and "exit" from the Democratic party to work on behalf of just one Democratic politician was not really a solution for the disaffected. One hundred years later, of course, it was much more of a solution for that problem, but in the earlier period individual politicians were tied to each other by complex and extensive party organizations and networks.

Finally, the lack of leverage of French party elites over each other – in the National Assembly or elsewhere – meant that there was no incentive for intervening in the "bailiwick" of one set of politicians who appeared to be experiencing trouble with some of their activists. There were relatively few resources that outsiders could supply to influence the resolution of the conflict, and little long-term benefit, if any, from interfering in others' territory. However, what was happening in, say, St. Louis, did matter to politicians from other parts of Missouri; a highly corrupt party organization in a major city could be an electoral liability for the party statewide, just as a

---

[60] Albert O. Hirschman, *Exit, Voice and Loyalty*, Cambridge, Mass., Harvard University Press, 1970.

[61] Mark Wahlgren Summers, *Rum, Romanism and Rebellion: The Making of a President, 1884*, Chapel Hill and London, University of North Carolina Press, 2000, p. 223.

[62] Alan Ware, "North America: The Early Years," in Peter Burnell and Alan Ware (eds.), *Funding Democratization*, Manchester, Manchester University Press, 1998, p. 34.

[63] Distinct party ideologies were expressed during presidential elections, for example; see John Gerring, *Party Ideologies in America, 1828–1996*, Cambridge, Cambridge University Press, 1998.

highly centralized organization in such a city could affect the potential for coalition building, within the party, for elected state offices. This point should not be exaggerated, however. By comparison with the more centralized parties in Britain, say, what happened lower down in American politics had less impact on higher levels of the party, and the incentive for the latter to intervene (leaving aside the opportunity for intervention) was that much less.

That there was at least some incentive to intervene was a feature that the nineteenth-century American parties, nevertheless, shared with the post–1945 European social democrats. For the latter, activist disturbance within a party was important because the parties needed activists for electoral work – they were their most significant resource in the immediate postwar period – and scandal in one area tended to reflect badly on the party as a whole. This is not to say that mass membership parties would always try to keep their parties "clean"; often it could be easier to let matters rest if little press attention was devoted to it. For example, in the 1980s and early 1990s the British Labour party preferred not to intervene in many parts of urban Scotland, in spite of the questionable activities of local parties there. However, mass membership parties did have an incentive not to let widespread public complaints go uninvestigated, and the real difference between these types of parties and the American parties was that the former were much more centralized. Rules could be devised at the national level and they could be enforced through national intervention in local party affairs. By contrast, even at the local level in the United States, there was insufficient centralization for anything like that to be attempted.

Nevertheless, the really significant point about the decentralization of the American parties is not that they had started out life as decentralized parties. Parties that begin as relatively decentralized institutions may come to face changed conditions in which they have a strong incentive to become much more centralized; for example, this was the case with the French parties (after 1962) under the directly elected presidency established in the Fifth Republic. However, between their founding as popular institutions in the 1830s and the end of the nineteenth century, there had been no pressures whatsoever on American parties toward centralization at the state level. State governments continued to provide relatively few services, and the absence of centralizing tendencies in governmental functions within states meant that the incentives facing politicians at different levels did not change. Consequently, state parties remained primarily arenas in which county parties operated, so that imposing any kind of discipline on particular county parties could generate little support within a party; county parties valued their autonomy, and "clean" county organizations would not have contemplated surrendering any of that autonomy even if a strengthened state party could then have had the authority to intervene in certain aspects of the affairs of "tainted" county organizations. The ethos of localism remained strong. Moreover, county party organizations could scarcely be expected to police themselves effectively; or, rather, those organizations that were most in need of policing were the ones that were least likely to do it.

Consequently, from very early on it became apparent that the only effective way of regulating how parties were to conduct their affairs was through the law. The fact that there was no other means of controlling parties was recognized widely, including by those who were at the heart of the "regular" parties. For example, in his address to the National Conference in 1898, Edward Lauterbach discussed many aspects of the legal regulation of parties. He did not dispute the right of the state to regulate parties; rather, he assumed that it was the duty of the state to do so, and he even argued that "since 1860 down to the present time, year in and year out, efforts have been made to keep pace with party demands for protection of primaries and for protection of party organizations."[64] That there should be legal regulation was not disputed by most party elites; all that was disputed was what the limits of such regulation might be and what the best forms of regulation were.

That is why one of the conventional interpretations of this era – emphasizing the role of anti-party reformers – is so misleading. On that interpretation, law was a stick used to beat unwilling parties into reform, and resort had to be made to the law because other methods had failed. Thus, Ranney quotes Richard Hofstadter on the Progressive view of political action:

First the citizen must reclaim the power that he himself had abdicated, refashioning where necessary the instruments of government. Then – since the Yankee found the solution to everything in laws – he must see that the proper remedial laws be passed and that existing laws be enforced.

Ranney uses this quotation in support of his argument that legal regulation was pushed for by Progressives, and that from the mid-1890s, "state after state was conquered by forces" supporting the statutory regulation of parties.[65] But this is to miss the point that there had been considerable regulation of parties before the beginning of that decade, and also the further point that the right of the state to regulate parties was a matter on which there was scarcely any disagreement.

Of course, the move to legal regulation was still a major change for American parties; in Epstein's analysis it constituted a move toward treating parties as public utilities.[66] However, it is important that this supposed

---

[64] Edward Lauterbach, address to *National Conference on Practical Reform of Primary Elections*, January 21, 1898, p. 114.

[65] Austin Ranney, *Curing the Mischiefs of Faction*, Berkeley, University of California Press, 1975, p. 80; the passage from Hofstadter is Richard Hofstadter, *The Age of Reform*, New York, Vintage Books, 1955, p. 202.

[66] Leon D. Epstein, *Political Parties in the American Mold*, Madison, University of Wisconsin Press, 1986, Chapter 6.

transformation from private association to public utility is placed in context. Writers like Ranney, who speak of parties being "stripped of their private character and subjected to legal regulation" tend to both exaggerate the separation between private and public in the American political tradition, and also to underestimate the ability of the state to regulate private associations in the nineteenth century.

From the colonial period until the early decades of the nineteenth century it had been common for institutions to be founded as a result of joint effort between public and private sources, so that the distinction between public institutions and private ones was blurred. Even after the crucial decision in the *Dartmouth College* case (1819), the older corporations did not have "their character as wholly private institutions" resolved finally until decades later.[67] Nevertheless, while the *Dartmouth College* case was a landmark in facilitating the rise of autonomy for nonprofit organizations in the United States, it did not place such organizations beyond the realm of state regulation. It did not undercut what Brock refers to as "the deep roots in Anglo-American law" of the "principle that private property could be regulated when this was demanded by the public interest, or expropriated when it was required for public use."[68] Brock himself has provided compelling evidence of just how much regulation by the states was initiated and enacted in the period from the end of the Civil War until 1900. He argues that "old powers were greatly extended and new agencies came into being," and his review of state and federal court cases leads him to the conclusion that "far too much prominence has been given to the few cases in which state statutes were invalidated and far too little to the widening stream of judicial approval for more and more advances in the regulation of social and economic life."[69]

Thus, it is a caricature of nineteenth-century American political ideas to suggest that there was widespread acceptance that bodies that were private associations should be left to get on with their affairs without any state interference. In this regard, it is worth referring to remarks made by Dallinger. He noted that "a political party is a voluntary association." As such an association, it had the right to manage its own affairs but management had to be "within certain reasonable limits"; this meant that the state should enact laws to "insure the honest and orderly conduct of all caucuses and primaries."[70] Far from making a case that parties had been,

---

[67] Peter Dobkin Hall, *The Organization of American Culture, 1700–1900: Private Institutions, Elites and the Origins of American Nationality*, New York, New York University Press, 1984, p. 112.

[68] William R. Brock, *Investigation and Responsibility: Public Responsibility in the United States, 1865–1900*, Cambridge, Cambridge University Press, 1984, p. 58.

[69] Brock, *Investigation and Responsibility*, pp. 61 and 86.

[70] Frederick W. Dallinger, *Nominations for Elective Office in the United States*, New York, Longmans, Green, 1897, p. 146.

or could be, subjected to greater state regulation than other private bodies, Dallinger is arguing here that parties are just like all other private associations in that, when necessary and within limits, they could be subjected to state regulation. He had noted already that "the people are beginning to see that political parties should be recognized as quasi-public organizations," but this did not mean that they, or other associations subjected to regulation, lost their private character.[71] Being "private" was wholly compatible with being "quasi-public."

Some commentators, especially the most extreme of the antipartisan reformers, did take the view that being subjected to legislation altered the private character of parties. For example, John R. Commons was one reformer who believed that parties were no longer "private concerns."[72] For reasons of political propaganda, he wanted to claim that there was something special about parties – that "the individual citizen has practically no voice in government except through these party organizations." But not only was this not true – increasingly there were many other means of having a "voice" – but the type of legal control to which parties were being subjected was not wholly dissimilar to that which many other kinds of private activity were being subjected after the Civil War.

If the retort to this argument is that most private associations in America were not actually brought under legal regulation in the way that parties came to be, then two points can be emphasized. The first is that Brock's analysis has exposed just how much regulation there was of supposedly private bodies in the last thirty-five years of the nineteenth century; regulation was not invented by "Progressives" between the mid-1890s and 1920, for that period merely saw the extension of a principle that had long been accepted and had been put into practice in many areas of economic and social life already. Second, while many private associations remained unregulated, these were ones that tended to involve far fewer people than did the political parties. Private dining clubs, for example, were not likely to be subjected to legislation directed specifically at them because their activities rebounded on the lives of so few people. In contrast, since the 1830s the American parties had witnessed the participation of millions of people. For that reason it was much more likely that legislation might be necessary. What was different about parties was not that they controlled

---

[71] Dallinger, *Nominations for Elective Office in the United States*, pp. 143–4.

[72] John R. Commons, address to the *National Conference on Practical Reform of Primary Elections*, p. 22. However, some political scientists, including Leon E. Aylsworth, took up this argument about the change of status. He talked of laws "transforming the political party from a voluntary, extralegal association into a public one, whose essential organization and government are defined by law and subjected to legal control," "Primary Elections," *American Political Science Review*, (3)1908, p. 418. Such a view has been revived at various times by political scientists, its most comprehensive recent restatement being that of Leon Epstein, *Political Parties in the American Mold*.

access to government, but that it was an arena of activity affecting large numbers of people and for which self-regulation was difficult.

6. Did Legal Control Turn Parties Into Public Utilities?

Even for the years after 1903–15 – that is, after most states had mandated the use of the direct primary – there is one important sense in which it is not accurate to describe the parties as having become "public utilities," useful though that notion is in some ways. This point is worth making because it might be argued that, by subjecting parties to legal regulation, late-nineteenth-century party elites placed them in a position in which, later, they could be regulated for the benefit of the wider polity.

We may begin by accepting Epstein's characterization of a "public utility" as "an agency performing a service in which the public has a special interest sufficient to justify governmental regulatory control"; using this definition, it is far from evident that, with one important exception, either state legislatures or courts have required parties to conduct their affairs in ways other than they would choose to.[73] Moreover, that single exception originates in the distinctive politics of the South, rather than the North. Beginning with *Nixon v. Herndon* (1927), the Supreme Court did start to restrict party autonomy in relation to "white primaries." Petterson is surely correct in arguing that "[T]he importance of the white primary cases lies in the precedent and powers they established for constitutional intervention in the electoral process."[74] However, subsequently it is with respect only to participation by racial minorities, and not some other criteria, that the Court has removed party autonomy. Generally, parties have remained free to control most areas of their activities; legislation in the 1890s and 1900s, therefore, had not removed parties from the category of private association, and thereby made them subject to the dictates of the public interest. Indeed, in the last thirty years of the twentieth century, Supreme Court decisions actually have confirmed the right of parties to run their own affairs, through the concept of freedom of association being applied to parties.[75]

There have been a number of cases in which rights of association within a party have been affirmed. *Cousins v. Wigoda* (1975) allowed the national Democratic party the right to decide how delegates to its own National Convention should be selected. Then, in *Republican Party of Connecticut v. Tashjian* (1984), the Court upheld the right of a party to decide whether

---

[73] Epstein, *Political Parties in the American Mold*, p. 157.

[74] Paul R. Petterson, "Partisan Autonomy or State Regulatory Authority? The Court as Mediator," in David K. Ryden (ed.), *The U.S. Supreme Court and the Electoral Process*, Washington, D.C., Georgetown University Press, 2000, p. 113.

[75] Petterson, "Partisan Autonomy or State Regulatory Authority?," p. 113.

to adopt open primary rules, and in *Eu v. San Francisco County Democratic Central Committee* (1989) it maintained the right of a party to set its own rules. More recently still, in 2000, in *California Democratic Party v. Jones*, the Court struck down an initiative referendum that had converted the state's primaries into "blanket" primaries. It rejected the idea that parties could have their rules changed by law, against the wishes of their officials, for the purpose of increasing electoral participation.[76]

The one case that might be thought exceptional is *Morse v. Virginia Republican Party* (1996). Significantly, it was a case that was decided 5–4, with two separate majority opinions and three separate dissents. In their decision, the justices denied that a state party had the right, as a private organization, to make a charge of persons attending party conventions. However, the central point about *Morse* is that it was a case in which rights of association, on the one side, and the protection of participation by racial minorities, on the other, converged. The preclearance provisions of Section 5 of the Voting Rights Act of 1965 applied to Virginia, so that "[T]he particular dilemma at issue – between voting rights protection and party freedom of association – ultimately is a question of representation, a tension between the representation of political parties and the representation of African Americans and other victims of discrimination."[77] *Morse* was a case that brought about legal regulation of certain party activities because what was at stake could be shown to involve restrictions on participation by racial minorities. The justices' decision constrained parties because of that element in the case.

Consequently, it is what the southern Democratic parties did in the 1890s, not what the northern parties did at that time in subjecting themselves to legal control, that was to lead to some judicial constraints on their activities much later. Merely bringing their own procedures under the protection of law had not constituted a Faustian bargain in which parties would be treated by courts very differently from other private associations.

How does this experience compare with that in other countries? Of the liberal democracies, the United States is unusual in the extent of state regulation of parties; a number of countries, including those in Scandinavia, have passed laws specifically applying to parties, and some countries, including Germany, have legal requirements covering how candidates can be

---

[76] See Bruce Cain, "Party Rights and Public Wrongs – The Court's Stand Against Proposition 198," *Public Affairs Report*, Vol. 41, No. 4, September 2000, pp. 5–6. The California case is interesting partly because twenty years earlier the Court did not review a case decided in Washington's state supreme court that upheld a challenge to the blanket primary law there (*Heavey v. Chapman*). On *Heavey v. Chapman*, see Leon D. Epstein, *Political Parties in the American Mold*, Madison, University of Wisconsin Press, 1986, p. 193.

[77] Petterson, "Partisan Autonomy or State Regulatory Authority," p. 120.

nominated.[78] However, there can be no questioning the conventional judgement that such regulation is that much more extensive in the United States than elsewhere. It has been argued here, though, that the reason for this lay in the inability of the parties to subject themselves to internal party rules in the nineteenth century because they remained so decentralized. Furthermore, their being brought under state law did not represent a form of special treatment as private associations, for many areas of social and economic life had already become subject to legislation.

However, submitting themselves to legal control in the way that they did had a profound effect on how the American parties could conduct their affairs. Here the contrast with European countries such as Germany is instructive. In Germany, the 1967 law does require that the "highest governing body in every party and party subunit is the party conference, which must convene at least once every two years."[79] However, it is largely left up to the parties how they conform with these requirements – for example, as to whether all members, or merely their representatives, have voting rights. Thus, for example, the state is not responsible for compiling party membership lists, specifying rules for nominating candidates, or conducting the selection process of these candidates – all of which are done in the United States.

The key difference between the United States and Germany is not that courts in the former are "trigger happy" in wanting to restrict party autonomy; to the contrary, as we have seen, the Supreme Court has tended to preserve most aspects of the right to associate within a party. Rather, the difference lies in the fact that in the United States the parties have the equivalent of an agent – the state – that actually carries out some of their activities for them. Because of that, disputes that would otherwise be resolved internally require recourse to the law, and that is a much more inflexible form of conflict resolution. Necessarily external regulation tends to lack the facility of "muddying the issues" that is of so much importance to managing conflict within an organization. Within the Basic Law and specific legislation, German parties retain great flexibility in running their own affairs; without breaking the law there are many ways of managing affairs and manipulating agendas so as to provide for smooth intraparty relations. For example, in these sorts of conditions parties can remove from their ranks members whose involvement is incompatible with party interests and principles.

[78] The constitution requires that parties "conform to democratic principles." However, eighteen years elapsed after the adoption of the country's Basic Law in 1949 before the German parliament passed legislation to regulate parties. By then, of course, party practices in the Federal Republic had become well established; see Susan E. Scarrow, *Parties and their Members: Organizing for Victory in Britain and Germany*, Oxford, Oxford University Press, 1996, pp. 53–4.

[79] Scarrow, *Parties and their Members*, p. 53.

Because there was no alternative to making nomination activities subject to state law at the end of the nineteenth century, the decentralized American parties had to give up much of the flexibility that they had enjoyed earlier. External regulation of the parties meant that in future the kinds of compromises made earlier – balancing tickets, excluding the "treacherous" from party affairs and so on – would be much more difficult, if not impossible, to effect. Internal regulation of an organization – however comprehensive and complex – is much less constraining on it than external regulation that involves the blind application of rules. If late-nineteenth- and early-twentieth-century party institutionalization was the functional equivalent of American parties becoming mass membership parties, it was a solution that made them much more rigid forms of association, in which control of their political environment was now more difficult.

7. Concluding Remarks

Between the early 1880s and the late 1890s, party nominations shifted from being a matter that was run largely on an informal basis to one that operated, in most states, within a system of party rules and, more especially, state law. These rules and laws were still changing, however, as no single reform seemed capable of dealing with the problems the caucus-convention nominating system threw up. In particular, there was a dilemma that was central to that system – how to provide for conventions that still facilitated debate, and yet also were forums into which the views expressed at caucuses could flow directly.

It was in the period between caucus meetings and voting in the convention that the influence of those who were organized could be effective. Indeed, if there were to be balanced tickets, if traditional voting groups were to be given their due in nominations, if unelectable candidates were to be weeded out, that was when they had to be effective. Of course, this also provided opportunities for simply disregarding opinions expressed in caucuses, and not just setting them aside in the electoral interests of the party as a whole. Therein lay a dilemma. Conventions could be subjected to legal control, with delegates being required by law to vote for particular candidates, thereby operating in the way that, say, the Bedford County system did in Pennsylvania, but then they would become merely mechanical devices for counting votes. Ticket balancing, for example, would be impossible. How could conventions be regulated and yet retain the advantages that parties provided in the electoral process? How could they be subject to control and be conventions (that is, decision-making bodies) in anything other than name only? If they were answerable at all, these questions were likely to prove very difficult to answer. Part of the attraction of the Crawford County Plan was to be that, in abolishing conventions, such questions did not have to be addressed. In spite of the evident problems it would pose, some of which had been exposed already in Cleveland and elsewhere, it was this plan that was to emerge between 1898 and 1901 as the one that would be adopted.

4

The Spread of Direct Nominations

The transformation in the nominating process evident in most American states between the 1880s and 1915 was characterized by two developments that began quite separately and then converged. One was discussed in the last chapter: the switch from informal procedures to legal control of the process. The other was the replacement of party caucuses and conventions by direct party elections as the means of selecting candidates. The first development did not entail the second, and, in theory at least, one might have happened without the other. Legal control of candidate selection did not require the use of elections; while the use of elections would have necessitated a move away from wholly informal procedures, logically there was no reason why such elections could not have been conducted under party rules rather controlled by state law. (Indeed, this was practiced in some states.) However, it was the convergence of the two developments that was to create the distinctively American nominating system of the early-to-mid-twentieth century.

This last point is important because one of the reasons that the rise of the direct primary has been misunderstood is that often the two developments are conflated. For example, Austin Ranney has claimed that "[S]trictly speaking, a direct primary is a system in which political parties are required by law to choose their candidates through state-administered elections in which any legally qualified person must be allowed to vote."[1] Now it is true that the expression, "direct primary," seems to have been used relatively little until the early twentieth century, by which time many reformers had linked the demand for a direct vote to the legal regulation of nominations. (It should be noted, though, that "direct primary" was used quite regularly in the columns of the journal *Outlook* from at least January

---

[1] Austin Ranney, *Curing the Mischiefs of Faction*, Berkeley, University of California Press, 1975, p. 121.

1898, and quite possibly earlier.[2]) Nevertheless, previously expressions such as "direct voting plan"[3] and "direct nominations"[4] had been used widely to refer to party-administered elections, such as the one used in South Carolina in the 1890s. Moreover, when "direct primary" did become a widely used expression, there was no question of it being confined just to state-administered elections. This is clear from the following passage from a 1903 article in the *Nation*:

> One striking feature of the movement for direct primaries is the rapidity with which it is spreading. Many of the Southern States have long observed the principle, though the element of official regulation, which is basic in the systems adopted by the Northern States, has been for the most part lacking in the South.[5]

Nevertheless, the main problem with Ranney's stipulative definition of "direct primary" is not its lack of correspondence with how the term was employed when it came into use. Rather, the problem is that it tends to obscure the fact that the model that became the dominant one, the legally regulated direct nomination, involved a fusion of two quite different strands of change in American parties. It tends to add weight to the view, propagated by Progressives such as Charles Merriam, that public opinion was pushing for greater "popular control," that politicians were continually looking for ways of meeting this demand, and that eventually a suitable vehicle, the state-administered direct primary, was found.[6] The process was actually rather less rational than this sort of account suggests, involving the marriage (arguably, not altogether a happy one) in the 1890s of two hitherto parallel procedural changes. In the last chapter, it was shown how legal regulation spread rapidly during the 1890s. This chapter is concerned with the second development and it consequences – the rise of intraparty elections as the dominant method of selecting candidates and the subsequent merger of the two types of reform.

However, before turning to see how direct nominations arose and then spread, it is necessary to be precise about what is being claimed in stating

---

[2] *Outlook*, January 29, 1898, pp. 261–2, September 17, 1898, p. 156, October 28, 1899, p. 475, February 17, 1900, p. 378, and August 4, 1900, p. 761.

[3] Amos Parker Wilder, "Primary Election Laws," *Proceedings of the Milwaukee Conference for Good City Government and 6th Annual Meeting of the National Municipal League*, Philadelphia, National Municipal League, 1900, p. 222.

[4] Daniel Remsen, *Primary Elections: A Study of Methods for Improving the Basis of Party Organization*, New York and London, G.P. Putnam's Sons, 1894, Chapter 12 (title).

[5] *Nation*, 2 July 1903, pp. 5–6.

[6] According to Merriam and Overacker, the direct primary "was part of that broad tendency in the direction of popular control of all agencies of politics which wrote the initiative, the referendum and the recall upon the statute books of many of our states. In many directions there was manifest a democratic sentiment which was reaching out for new ways by which more direct responsibility of the governor to the governed could be secured." Charles E. Merriam and Louis Overacker, *Primary Elections*, Chicago, University of Chicago Press, 1928, pp. 60–1.

that the rise of the direct primary was a parallel change to that of the expansion of legal control of parties. It has to be admitted that, as early as 1880, there were those who advocated both legally controlling party nominations and also requiring that parties use direct elections.[7] For example, D. C. McMillan published a book that year that, among other proposals, advocated such a plan. Furthermore, in 1881 a New York state legislator, Erastus Brooks, apparently introduced a bill to put it into effect.[8] Other adherents to the view were evident between then and the early-to-mid-1890s, but they had little or no impact on the adoption of the direct primary in various counties in that period, and their influence on the subjection of American party nominations to state laws was also relatively small. Consequently, they were not the originators of the transformation of party nominations, in the way that the Wright brothers could be thought of, indirectly, as the originators of transatlantic flight. Rather, they were more like Leonardo da Vinci, who appears to have had various ideas about how manned flight might be possible but who did not contribute directly to it realization. The key actors were not to be these kinds of visionaries, but instead party elites in the 1890s who were facing a serious practical problem. Legal reform of the existing nominating system was not producing the kinds of results that the official ballot had, and alternative means of dealing with the problem of nomination had to be sought. In doing so, they turned to a device that had been gaining in popularity in some parts of rural America during the previous few decades, the so-called Crawford County System.

1. The Rising Popularity of the Crawford County System

Direct elections for nominating candidates were first agreed by the Democratic party in Crawford County, Pennsylvania, in 1842.[9] They were used in that county throughout the rest of the 19th century; and certainly by the early 1880s the term "Crawford County System" (or "Method" or "Plan") was used both in Pennsylvania and elsewhere to refer to the direct nomination of candidates by election.[10] Thereafter, and until the term "direct primary" became a commonplace, between about 1900 and 1903, "Crawford County System" was often used as a synonym for direct nominations.[11] The original decision to introduce this method was taken at a mass meeting of Democrats in 1842. Two years later the Democrats in Greene County, Pennsylvania, also adopted it.[12]

---

[7] Frederick W. Whitridge, *Caucus System* (Economic Tracts No. VIII), New York, Society for Political Education, 1883, pp. 24–5.

[8] Whitridge, *Caucus System*, pp. 24–5.

[9] James H. Booser, "Origin of the Direct Primary," *National Municipal Review*, April 1935, p. 232.

[10] Whitridge, *Caucus System*, p. 25.   [11] Booser, "Origin of the Direct Primary," p. 222.

[12] Booser, "Origin of the Direct Primary," p. 222.

There is no evidence of Whigs in Crawford County ever using the system, but in June 1860, only six years after the first Republican party gathering, the Republicans in Crawford County decided to adopt direct nominations. The decision was taken at a county convention, and adopted in 1861 by the party's county committee. It appears that the rules then introduced, and used for subsequent nominations, were submitted to the county party's voters – but not until 1876.[13] Other counties in Pennsylvania experimented with the system – including Erie County, which, as was seen in Chapter 3, abandoned it subsequently in favor of the Clarion County system,[14] and the city of Philadelphia used it briefly in 1882–3.[15] The Philadelphia experiment is interesting because it is the only instance before the 1890s of the direct primary being deployed in a major urban area.

Mapping the spread of direct nominations after their first appearance in Crawford County is not easy. Few original documents survived, so that even writers in the 1890s or early twentieth century could be unsure as to exactly when direct primaries had been introduced. The result is confusion on the subject. Thus, writing in 1901, Ernest Hempstead claimed that Columbiana County in eastern Ohio had employed the Crawford County System for "nearly half a century"; if true, this would have been worthy of more attention than Hempstead gives it, because it suggests that its adoption there preceded its use by Republicans in Crawford County. The significance of that point is that Hempstead, who like others of his generation did not know of its earlier use by Democrats in Crawford and Greene counties, also believed that the Republicans of Crawford County were the originators of direct nominations.[16] Presumably Hempstead intended to suggest the 1860s, and not the 1850s, as the starting date in Columbiana, but, of course, no one can be certain of this. The absence of satisfactory documentation at the county level of parties meant that commentators like Hempstead could not be sure of how direct nominations had developed and spread. The same problem faces contemporary analysts. Consequently, rather than attempting the impossible task of tracing the spread of direct nominations on a step-by-step basis, it is more sensible to begin with the slightly more solid evidence that is available – namely how far direct nominations had spread by the mid-1890s.

Fortunately, for an initial survey, there is a reasonably good source available for the later period – the seemingly meticulous Frederick Dallinger, whose book was completed in July 1896. Dallinger described the Crawford

---

[13] Ernest A. Hempstead, "Forty Years of Direct Primaries," *Michigan Political Science Association Publications*, March 1905, pp. 31–54.

[14] *National Conference on Practical Reform of Primaries*, p. 54.

[15] Ernest A. Hempstead, "The Crawford County or Direct Primary System", *Proceedings of the Rochester Conference for Good Government and the 7th Annual Meeting of the National Municipal League*, Philadelphia, National Municipal League, 1901, p. 199.

[16] Hempstead, "The Crawford County or Direct Primary System," p. 201.

County System as being found "in a number of states," and in a footnote he cited twelve states – five in the South (Alabama, Arkansas, Mississippi, South Carolina, and Tennessee) and seven nonsouthern states (California, Indiana, Kentucky, Maryland, Missouri, Ohio, and Pennsylvania). However, he was careful to emphasize that in all of these states, "the convention system appears to be the general rule, the system of primary elections being in operation occasionally or in but a few counties." He illustrated this general comment by noting that in Maryland direct elections were used in only three of the twenty-four counties, that in Tennessee it was used only for congressional elections, although in Arkansas it was the principal method except for candidates "to be voted by people of the entire state." Moreover, he observed that the system was not used to any appreciable extent in any district larger than that of a county, and South Carolina was the only state to employ the system in anything larger than a congressional district.[17]

Dallinger had no reason to exaggerate the growth of direct nominations – he was rather skeptical about their potential – and, rather than overstating their deployment, almost certainly he understated it because other sources reveal evidence of their use elsewhere. Thus, in 1899 it was reported that the Republicans of Jackson County, Kansas, had employed direct nominations since 1877, while the same article also noted that in Missouri "the system seems to have been long established in many of the rural counties."[18] Dallinger's list also omits Georgia, which had adopted direct nominations for local offices by the mid-1890s. Consequently, if Kansas and Georgia are added to Dallinger's list, it is evident that fourteen of the forty-five states in 1896 (or more than 30 percent of all states) used direct nominations in some form or in some places.

Not surprisingly, it is possible to detect a quite distinct regional concentration to the early use of direct nominations. The three Pennsylvania counties that employed the Crawford County System – Crawford, Erie, and Greene – are all in the westernmost part of the state, and Columbiana County, Ohio, is on the border with Pennsylvania. It would be surprising, if some of the early migration of the system had not been to nearby counties. However, by the 1890s the system had also started to appear in very different regions – though it was not used in the extreme northeast of the country. In 1901, Charles B. Spahr described this expansion of direct nominations: "North and South, different counties without consultation with each other began to adopt different systems of direct primaries."[19]

[17] Dallinger, *Nominations for Elective Office in the United States*, p. 128.
[18] *Outlook*, October 28, 1899, p. 475.
[19] Charles B. Spahr, "Direct Primaries," *Proceedings of the Rochester Conference for Good City Government and 7th Annual Meeting of the National Municipal League*, Philadelphia, National Municipal League, 1901, p. 186.

Altogether, this suggests a very different picture from the one outlined by, for example, Austin Ranney. Writing in 1975, Ranney claimed that before La Follette began his campaign for the direct primary in 1897, the Crawford County practice was followed only "in a few other localities."[20] But this view is difficult to sustain in light of the evidence just presented. Direct nominations were still not a common practice but they were far from being an oddity. Furthermore, they were not an ancient procedure that happened to have survived in some places, but were a form of candidate selection that had been growing in popularity; in Ohio, for example, there had been a move to direct nominations in many counties since the early-to-mid-1880s. In other words, by the time legislation on party nominations was increasing rapidly, so, too, had there been a strong growth in the use of direct nominations.[21]

In relation to the situation of the mid-1890s – the one Dallinger was describing in 1896 – it is worth drawing attention to four aspects. Each is then discussed briefly below:

1. nearly all the counties that had started to use direct elections were rural counties, and, in the case of the northern states they were states that lay to the west of Pennsylvania;
2. from the early 1890s there was a marked move to the use of direct nominations in the South;
3. from 1890 direct nominations started to be used by a party in a major urban area – the Republicans in Cleveland (Ohio) adopting it – thereby moving the direct nomination out of its rural heartland.
4. 1890 also witnessed the first legislation, this time in Kentucky, that brought direct nominations within the embrace of state law.

2. The Rural and Midwestern Base of Direct Elections

The push to regulate party nominations through state law in the 1890s was prompted, in part, by problems that were evident primarily, although by no means exclusively, in urban areas. By contrast, the growth in use of direct elections occurred initially in rural areas. The point about its origins in rural counties was well made by Charles B. Spahr, who argued in 1901 that in the North "the movement [for direct nominations] first began to attract the attention of political writers when it emerged from rural districts fifteen years ago."[22] But, from the 1880s onward, what was prompting rural areas west of the Appalachians to start to change their nominating system? Spahr's argument, and it was one that seems highly plausible, is that the key factor was that in the west it was the county that was the main unit of

[20] Ranney, *Curing the Mischiefs of Faction*, p. 121.
[21] Wilder, "Primary Election Laws," p. 224.   [22] Spahr, "Direct Primaries," p. 188.

political organization. By contrast, in the northeastern states it was the township that formed the basis for party nominations and party organization. Because of their greater size "little knots of men" (in Spahr's words) were coming to dictate nominations, and the result was the nomination of candidates who were "odious."[23]

The direct election was seen as a solution to the problem of larger political units. Even Dallinger, who was not especially enthusiastic about direct nominations, observed that they made it easier to defeat "combinations."[24] However, they had another possible advantage. Where the township was the main unit, it was more possible under the caucus-convention system, that, even if consensus on a slate of candidates could not be reached within the party, those who opposed particular nominees would find the latter's nomination at least acceptable. Strings may have been pulled to secure a nomination, but in smaller units it was much easier to see how they had been pulled than it was in larger units, and the legitimacy of the entire process was much less likely to be called into question, therefore. When the county was the unit, people were less likely to know each other, and suspicions both of how nominations had been obtained, and also of the "character" of those nominated would be that much greater.

It appears that in most cases the county parties that adopted direct nomination procedures tended to stick with them. The one known exception was in Pennsylvania, where a number of different nominating systems were in use by the 1890s, and, as has been seen, here there was at least one instance (Erie County) of the Crawford County system being adopted and subsequently abandoned. Overall, though, by the mid-1890s there were clear signs of a major shift in how candidates were nominated in several regions of the United States; however, even those, like Dallinger, who were aware of this trend did not regard it as a revolutionary one. Why not? There are three related reasons why it was perceived as little more than politics as usual.

First, the regions in which it had been adopted were ones in which caucuses had always been nothing more than elections anyway. In the midwest and West (as well as in the South) party caucuses had simply been ballots – they lacked the "face-to-face" discussions of rural New England. Direct nominations could thus be seen more as a means of streamlining the process by which votes got translated into the nomination of candidates, rather than as a major transformation in the way in which parties conducted their business.

Second, its adoption had generally been confined to the level of the county. As noted earlier, there were very few instances of it being used in a political unit as large as a congressional district – the district that included

---

[23] Spahr, "Direct Primaries," p. 186.
[24] Dallinger, *Nominations for Elective Office*, p. 128.

Crawford County had started using it only in 1887 – with South Carolina being the sole state using it in units larger than this.

Third, it was evident that there were difficulties with direct nominations that would probably preclude them from providing a generalized solution to nomination problems. Dallinger himself saw the arrangements as complicated and involving greater expense. Furthermore, he noted that the "real nomination will be transferred from open primaries to secret conclaves"; in other words, the real decisions about who would run (and who would be persuaded not to) would be taken outside the public arena.[25] Interestingly, he also quoted (in a footnote) an article in the *Nation* in which a writer had said of a California county that the direct vote tended to pit town against town for the nomination, and also facilitated the nomination of the "worst elements of the party."[26] This was an argument that was to become prominent a few years later among opponents of the direct primary, and it is significant that it had been aired already. But the central point is that, irrespective of any advantages it might have, the Crawford County system was known to have unwanted consequences, and for this reason it would not have appeared to a dispassionate observer in 1895 or 1896 – such as Dallinger – as a reform that would sweep the country.

3. The Impact of the Southern Experience

The South was primarily rural, and it had a tradition of holding party caucuses that were no more than elections of delegates to conventions. To this extent, it was just like those northern counties in which direct nominations were being introduced. In part, therefore, similar factors to those in the North contributed to the early growth of direct nominations in the South. However, beginning in about 1890, very different forces further propelled that region away from the caucus-convention system.

Party politics was different in the South in several key respects. In essence it was a one-party region. The post–Civil War electoral base of the Republican party depended on the federal government enforcing the civic and political rights of the black population there. The running down of Reconstruction policies, and their final abandonment in 1876, both made it far more difficult for black southerners to be effective in electoral politics and also eliminated most of the incentive for at least some white southerners to seek power and rewards through the Republican party. Not only were the Democrats now dominant, but also for some years after Reconstruction many southern states were run by a patrician class in a way that the northern states were not. These factors contributed to radically divergent outcomes in the South from those in the West to the electoral

---

[25] Dallinger, *Nominations for Elective Office*, p. 128.
[26] Dallinger, *Nominations for Elective Office*, p. 129fn.

revolt by farmers at the end of the 1880s. In the West, the Democratic Party fought off the farmers' challenge, and the latter moved on to form a People's Party. Organized in the Southern Alliance, however, agricultural interests in that region "captured the Democratic state conventions, wrote their demands into the state platforms, and in the election of 1890 won control of eight legislatures."[27]

Capturing the party prompted consolidation. Beginning with South Carolina in 1890, Democratic parties throughout the region started to move over to direct nominations. On some accounts, this constituted an assertion of power by insurgents – a successful attempt to prevent a return to the more closed politics practiced by the patricians; since there was only one party, the nomination stage was absolutely critical and if patrician power of nomination was ended so would their control of local and state politics cease. However, it was also the case that party-controlled direct nominations were a means of further excluding black people from electoral politics. By making the Democratic primaries fully into elections, elections from which black participation was expressly prohibited, they could become the "real" election, in place of the general election, and in doing this make it even more difficult for dissident white movements seeking to unite with black supporters to become established.

The downgrading of the general election in this way made it virtually impossible for black interests to be heard in the electoral arena. Not only could black voters simply be excluded from a party-controlled primary election – there was no need for literacy tests, poll taxes, or whatever in this arena – but by transforming the party nomination into an election it could acquire the legitimacy and status of an election. Moreover, there was a sense in which southern primaries were a democratic device – they did tend to broaden political influence *within* the white communities. Consequently, even northern reformers would sometimes focus on the democratic credentials of the direct primary in the South, rather than on their role in political exclusion. A typical example is an article in *Outlook* in 1903, which noted:

Today in the South it is only primaries that the voters do attend. The regular elections are foregone conclusions, and relatively few voters go to the polls. It is only through the direct primaries that popular government at the South remains a reality. This fact perhaps accounts for the more rapid growth of the reform at the South than at the North.[28]

This passage from *Outlook* illustrates a key theme that recurs in political speeches and writing from the mid-1890s: The direct primary (albeit

---

[27] Harold U. Faulkner, *Politics, Reform and Expansion, 1890–1900*, London, Hamish Hamilton, 1959, p. 114.
[28] *Outlook*, October 3, 1903, p. 237.

usually only a party-administered primary) was working in the South and this was held up by reformers as evidence of its value for the rest of the country. Thus, in 1900 an article had commended La Follette's proposals for Wisconsin on the following lines:

This is substantially the plan which has worked so well in nominating state officers in South Carolina and Georgia and in nominating local officers in many parts of the West and South.[29]

Earlier, in a speech in 1898, Charles B. Spahr had drawn similarly on the South Carolina experience in a positive vein:

... whatever may be said about Senator Tillman, he was unable to elect his man under his system. He tried to make the primaries accept Governor Evans as a candidate. If he had the legislature to do the work, it would have put Governor Evans in but it was submitted to the whole people and Tillman's man was defeated.[30]

Consequently, often the South was seen as providing evidence of the impact of direct nominations – even party-administered ones – from which the rest of the country could learn.

Nevertheless, the catalytic effect of the South on the move toward direct nominations in the nonsouthern states should not be overstated. Not all writers were convinced that the South did provide a blueprint for the North. In 1899, Walter Branson noted that the direct vote was "possibly well adapted to the conditions of some southern states, where a relatively small upper class still maintains political leadership," but he argued that it was "radically ill-suited to the more democratic conditions of the north, especially of the great cities."[31] Ernst Christopher Meyer was even more forthright that primaries were a source of political exclusion; he cited a South Carolina party rule that any black person applying to vote in a Democratic primary had to produce written statements from "ten reputable white men" who swore that the would-be voter had cast his ballot for General Hampton in 1876 and had voted the Democratic ticket continuously since then.[32] However, whether favorable or unfavorable, arguments about the impact on the South had only an indirect effect on the debate in the North; even favorable reporting of direct elections in the South probably did no more than contribute to a climate in which the case for the direct primary could be aired. In doing so, though, it may well have had some effect for five or six years after the mid-1890s in helping direct elections

[29] *Outlook*, August 4, 1900, p. 761.
[30] Charles B. Spahr, speech at the *National Conference on Practical Reform of Primary Elections*, New York, January 21, 1898, p. 92.
[31] Walter J. Branson, "Tendencies in Primary Legislation," *Annals of the American Academy of Political and Social Science*, 13(1899), p. 357
[32] This is quoted in an article in *World's Work*, August 1903, pp. 3715–16.

to become understood as a possible "solution" to the thorny problem of candidate selection.

4. Direct Nominations Move to the City: Cleveland

While elements of the southern experience with direct nominations could be used by their advocates to bolster support for the procedure, there was a very different message coming from the first experience of direct nominations in a large urban area. As has been seen already, with the exception of a short-lived early "experiment" in Philadelphia, direct nominations had not been deployed in large cities before the 1890s. That Cleveland was the first major city to experience direct nominations is not surprising: it was in a state in which a number of county parties had been switching to direct elections during the previous decade. In 1890 the Republican party of Cuyahoga County decided to follow suit. The result was widely regarded as a failure. In many respects the best summary of this was provided by Thomas L. Johnson, a lawyer and municipal reformer in Cleveland, although – interestingly – not the politician of the same name who, as mayor of Cleveland, was to become one of the great urban reformers of the early twentieth century.[33] (The more famous Tom Johnson was an advocate of the direct primary.) In a paper that was read for him to the National Conference on Practical Reform of Primary Elections (he was unexpectedly unable to come to New York), Johnson provided a damning and perceptive account of the limitations of direct elections in urban areas. As he put it, in its trial in a city such as Cleveland "the Crawford County Plan is a positive failure in securing the nomination of acceptable candidates."[34] Moreover, that the Plan had been a failure in Cleveland was not just Johnson's personal view. The president of the Cleveland Municipal Association, of which Johnson was an officer, also wrote to the Secretary of the National Conference on behalf of the association stating that the opinion of Cleveland's "best citizens is that we should go back to the convention plan."[35]

Johnson's criticisms of the working of the Crawford County system in Cleveland are interesting, partly because so many of them were to be repeated throughout the twentieth century as indictments of the direct primary. Only one of his criticisms was directed at the specific form that the primary had taken in Cleveland; this is important because, as will be seen shortly, advocates of the direct primary tended to respond to the

[33] I am grateful to a number of people for helping me track down the identity of the Thomas Johnson who informed the 1898 conference, thereby avoiding the mistake of assuming he was the famous Tom Johnson. In particular, I wish to thank Kenneth Finegold, John J. Grabowski, and David C. Hammack.

[34] *National Conference on Practical Reform of Primary Elections*, p. 99.

[35] Communication from H. A. Garfield to Ralph M. Easley, and read by Easley to the *National Conference on Practical Reform of Primary Elections*, p. 92.

Cleveland failure as if it merely reflected the inadequacy of the particular scheme used there. They ignored the more general issues to which Johnson drew attention.

Johnson's first point was that in a large county hardly any voters were in a position to judge the ability of particular candidates. In country areas, the voter could get to know the candidate during the election campaign, and would be able to exercise judgment in voting. In heavily populated counties, though, this was not possible, and "the nomination seeker, who can make the most canvass, who uses the largest amount of space for pictures of himself, and wonderful stories of his great love for the common people" was likely to win. In particular, the advantage lay with a candidate whose name was already known to many voters; in Cleveland in the 1890s, of course, this was neither the sports personality nor the television presenter, as it would be one hundred years later, but members of the Police Bench.[36]

Johnson then went on to argue that, far from breaking the power of "political rings or cliques," the Crawford County System made it just as easy as the convention system did for officeholders and their allies to control nominations. His argument was that they chose the candidates they wanted and then used their resources in support of their election. Again, he believed that scale was an important factor here – in less populous counties the power of the politically organized would be relatively less than in major urban areas, and for this reason the impact of the direct primary was different there.

His third argument was that direct nominations tended to generate bitterness and controversy between the candidates. Inevitably this led to attention being focused primarily on the contests for major offices – such as that for mayor – while little notice was paid to contests for minor offices. This reinforced his first point on the lack of voter information about candidates.

He then argued that direct elections provided an opportunity for the expenditure of large amounts of money. He observed that "no candidate can hope to succeed in getting the nomination for any office except by the most liberal use of money in the way of advertising."[37] It is tempting to suggest here that Johnson had seen the future of American politics and saw that it did not work – or, at least, it did not work on wholly democratic lines.

On turning to the quality of candidates brought forth under direct nominations, he observed that far more would-be candidates did come forward, but that many of them were weak and lacking in ability. His view was that candidates were tempted to run because "ready success lies in a vigorous advertising campaign," rather than being the product of ability.

[36] *National Conference on Practical Reform of Primary Elections*, p. 100.
[37] *National Conference on Practical Reform of Primary Elections*, p. 101.

Johnson's final criticism was that there was no system for voter registration in the Cleveland Republican party, and this made fraud possible. Advocates of direct primaries were later to seize on this point as evidence of the weaknesses of the particular system used in the county, and in doing so they were able to evade the far more fundamental weaknesses that had been uncovered. However, even though the president of the Cleveland Municipal Association was attending the conference, as were a number of other civic leaders from the city, there was no discussion there either of the Cleveland experience or more generally of the sorts of points made by Johnson about direct nominations.

Johnson's criticisms were not altogether novel. As noted earlier, in the book he completed in 1896, Dallinger had identified two of the points made by Johnson in 1898 – the expense involved in direct primaries, and the fact that there would be behind-the-scenes decisions over candidacies. The significance of Johnson's remarks should have been that they emanated from a so-called goo-goo, a "good government type" – someone who was an officer with a Municipal Association, and who had had the unusual experience of observing the working of the Crawford County System in a large, urban county. In fact, while his overall conclusion might be noted respectfully, most of Johnson's criticisms, especially those that would be relevant for any major city, were simply ignored. Wilder, for example, having outlined them went on to observe "[T]he shortcomings or even breaking down of legislative attempts of this sort should not be too rashly interpreted as complete failure . . . the principle should not be abandoned merely because its results disappoint."[38]

Another technique for dealing with the awful truths that Cleveland exposed was to deny that the city had really had the kind of reform that was required. Thus, the direct primary advocate, F. M. Brooks, distanced himself from it by claiming: "The Cleveland method is simply the old regulation and discredited primary with all its attendant evils." He admitted that direct elections, together with ballots printed by the Board of Elections and counted by them, all of which were found in Cleveland, were very good measures but, according to him, they were insufficient. What was needed were primaries held on registration days – to maximize participation – and the making of the direct primary mandatory for parties and not optional.[39] This simply missed the whole thrust of Johnson's arguments; high participation rates would do nothing to correct the problems he identified, and all of the problems were found in the party that was using the direct primary rather than in the one that was not. The argument about participation rates came to be used as a trump card in debates about direct primaries, and even Cleveland could provide evidence of the positive effects of direct

[38] Amos Parker Wilder, "Primary Election Laws," pp. 225–6.
[39] *Outlook*, September 24, 1898, pp. 251–2.

nominations. Ira Cross, having taken the perfunctory swipe at the bad design of the Cleveland primary, went on to observe that, nevertheless, popular participation in the nomination process had increased with direct nominations. Under the previous caucus system, only five thousand people took part in nominating Republican candidates for city offices, but in 1893 fourteen thousand Republicans participated and this increased steadily to thirty-one thousand by 1901.[40] Others kept repeating this point: A Citizens Union pamphlet published in New York in 1910 cited the same data for Cleveland in its propaganda for the direct primary in that state. Victory was thereby claimed from the jaws of defeat by proponents of direct nominations.

Consequently, far from acting as a brake on the rush toward the direct primary, the failure in Cleveland seems to have had virtually no impact. The reasons why this might have been so are explored later (in Chapter 7).

5. Statewide Legislation and the Direct Primary: Kentucky

While the Cleveland experience prompted no discussion at the National Conference, a very different response was accorded the paper about the Kentucky legislation of 1890. In an article about the conference a week afterwards, *Outlook* commented on the enthusiasm in the audience for the presentation on this state's system. Kentucky had been an innovator in the regulation of political parties; as was seen in Chapter 2, it was one of the first two states mandating the use of the Australian Ballot (in 1888), and just two years afterwards it passed measures regulating party nominations. Of course, many states were already starting to regulate the nomination process by that time, but the unique feature of Kentucky is that it brought direct nominations within the ambit of the law.

Kentucky had not made direct primaries compulsory for parties, and when caucuses and conventions were employed they were not regulated by law. There were still state conventions for nominating candidates for statewide offices – the argument being that the main problems lay in the cities, not statewide.[41] Moreover, the parties retained considerable power over who could participate in their own primaries – would-be voters could be challenged at the polling booth on the ground that they were not actually supporters of that party. More generally, by 1898 the Kentucky parties had still not lost all of their ability to organize their internal affairs, as the following exchange between a New Yorker, a Mr. Jerome, and the former Chief Supervisor of elections in Kentucky, Edward J. McDermott, illustrates:

---

[40] Ira Cross, "Direct Primaries," *Arena*, June 1906, pp. 587–90.
[41] Address of Edward J. McDermott to the *National Conference on Practical Reform of Primary Elections*, p. 67.

JEROME: "In this city . . . there is a rule of the [party] County Committee . . . that if the vote at any general election shall fall short of the enrolled vote of the party, that district shall be disorganized . . . the courts refused us any redress, as the law did not cover it – that a political party was a power unto itself . . . I would like to know if that is the case under the Kentucky law."

McDERMOTT: "No, it could not be under the Kentucky law."[42]

However, the law was starting to be used in ways that took decisions out of the hands of party officials; for example, the Kentucky law now regulated when a primary election could be held once it had been called.

Part of the interest in the legislation lay in the fact that, as in the case of Cleveland, it had been used in a major urban area, Louisville. In his presentation at the National Conference, McDermott gave an intelligent account of the working of the system, and he provided a number of important criticisms of how it worked.[43] Significantly, though, and with the sole exception of the question of the expense candidates incurred in competing in a direct primary, McDermott did not address the issues raised by Johnson. (He was in a good position to know what they were, since he was the person who was deputed to read out Johnson's speech the following day.) Most especially, questions of whether voters knew anything about candidates for lesser offices, whether cliques could effectively control the nomination, and whether candidates of low quality were elected were not discussed at all by McDermott, nor were they raised by discussants speaking from the floor. However, one point he made in passing, and that could have been linked to one of Johnson's arguments, was that on "whimsical grounds or out of pique" many primary voters did not vote for their party's nominee at the general election. Behavior such as this would throw into doubt the question of voter competence – in much the same way that Johnson argued that voters knew very little about most candidates – but no one picked up on the point. The actual behaviour of urban voters under the direct primary was not a matter that appears to have interested many people at the conference.

Quite how much difference the apparent success of the Kentucky law had on mobilizing opinion may be questioned. Charles B. Spahr, who had attended the National Conference, claimed three years later that it had provided the movement for direct primaries with great impetus.[44] Since the discussion about the Kentucky law had been one of the main focal points of the conference, it is tempting to see the Kentucky experience as, indeed, having some influence. But it would be a mistake to exaggerate that influence. By early 1898, demands for some form of direct primary, usually optional and usually confined to particular counties rather than entire

---

[42] *National Conference on Practical Reform of Primary Elections*, p. 115.
[43] *National Conference on Practical Reform of Primary Elections*, pp. 40–51, 65–7, 70–2.
[44] Spahr, "Direct Primaries," p. 190.

states, were starting to be introduced into other state legislatures. For
example, provisions were attached to bills in Massachusetts in 1896 and
1897 that would have made the Board of Aldermen in Boston subject to a
direct primary. On both occasions it appears as if this measure met with
relatively little opposition, although for other reasons the bills failed to pass.
The marriage between the movement to regulate party nominations and the
movement to adopt direct primaries – the one mainly urban based, the other
originally rural based – was thus commencing in a number of places; it
did not really depend on word spreading of a single successful example of
nomination practice: Kentucky no more brought about the rise of the
direct primary than did the passage later of La Follette's legislation in
Wisconsin (in 1903).

6. The Legally Mandated Direct Primary in Minneapolis, 1899

Robert La Follette is usually credited with having been a major influence
in the rise of the direct primary. However, irrespective of any role played
by his statewide law of 1903, and that is actually much less than is usually
claimed, La Follette's significance before that date was limited; except in
so far as he insisted in pushing for a comprehensive state-administered
law, without waiting for local initiatives or voluntary party-run schemes
to be tested, La Follette was not an innovator and Wisconsin was not an
"advanced" state. By contrast, between the 1890s and 1903 there were
many attempts in a number of other states, some of them wholly successful, to introduce direct nominations. Addressing the National Municipal
League in 1901, Charles B. Spahr claimed that, for three years, bills to
provide for the direct primary had been as numerous "before our state
legislatures as were Australian ballot laws a decade ago."[45] And, in a
book published in 1903, James Albert Woodburn, a professor of American
History and Politics at Indiana University, more modestly described the
direct primary movement as "one of the growing causes in the interest of
better politics."[46]

By 1903, and excluding the case of Wisconsin, various kinds of legislation relating to direct nominations had been passed in Delaware, Maryland,
Massachusetts, Michigan, Minnesota, New Jersey, Ohio, and Oregon. In
addition, bills had been introduced into the state legislatures in Indiana and
Pennsylvania, but failed to be enacted, while there is evidence that the issue
attracted considerable attention in both Missouri and New York but
without attempts at legislation. What is striking about this list is not just
that it includes states that do not appear to have used direct nominations

---

[45] Charles B. Spahr, "Direct Primaries," p. 192.
[46] James Albert Woodburn, *Political Parties and Party Problems in the United States*, New
York and London, G.P. Putnam's Sons, 1903, p. 283.

at all in the mid-1890s, but also that the states now adopting it were not concentrated geographically. From the Atlantic coast of the country there were Delaware, Massachusetts, and New Jersey, from the midwest Minnesota, and, from the west coast, Oregon. Direct nominations were continuing to move outside their original rural heartland in the "old" midwest. In a real sense, support for at least some versions of direct elections was advancing on a broad front.

That advance was occurring at exactly the same time as other legislation on party nominations was growing rapidly, a development examined in Chapter 3. However, it was not just the volume of that legislation that was impressive but also the variety of ways in which parties were now being constrained in relation to how they nominated candidates. One example can illustrate just how much regulation increased in the 1890s. The law passed in Kentucky in 1890, a very advanced one for its time, had left the decision as to whether a nomination was to involve a direct election, and if it was when to call it, in the hands of the parties themselves. Only when a direct election was called did state law apply. By 1899, though, Minnesota was requiring the parties in Hennepin County (which includes the city of Minneapolis) to hold their nominating contests at the same time – a further erosion of the powers of party elites. Nevertheless, as with other changes in party responsibilities, this requirement that primaries be concurrent was not an isolated "leap in the dark" – it had been preceded by the use of voluntary procedures elsewhere; the concurrent primary had already been used on such a basis in Columbus, Ohio, in 1898 and was then employed in mayoral elections in San Francisco in 1899.[47]

This last point is significant because it helps to expose the fallacy of the claim that the road to the direct primary was one of coercion of the parties into using devices that were favored only by antiparty reformers. The fact is that devices such as the concurrent primary could not have been introduced voluntarily by parties if a large proportion of party elites had not been willing to go along with them. But neither, in most cases, could legislation be passed for such measures unless there was a consensus among a wide range of party politicians that they were desirable. The 1899 Minnesota legislation is a good illustration of this, and, for a variety of reasons, it is legislation that especially merits attention.

Minnesota was the first state in the country to require parties in a particular locality to use direct elections. Because of this it gained considerable publicity for the cause of direct elections; when, in 1901, the state legislature extended the legislation, Minnesota had the most comprehensive set of state-administered direct primaries in the United States. Only in 1903 would Wisconsin overtake it, and long before then the general arguments about direct primaries had become well known across the continent.

[47] *Outlook*, September 2, 1899, pp. 8–9.

However, the 1899 legislation for Minneapolis is noteworthy also because it was the third major urban area – after Cleveland and Louisville – to experiment seriously with this form of nomination. Furthermore, it simply did not conform to the Progressive myth, so well expressed in a Citizens Union document of about 1910 that "[N]ever was the convention system abolished in any state without a severe struggle against the special interests intrenched by that system."[48] As subsequently in many other states, there just was not a struggle in Minnesota.

The consensual nature of the 1899 legislation was captured well by a report in 1902 in the *Annals of the American Academy*:

The passage of the law was not due to any very general and insistent demand even in Hennepin County. The old caucus and conventions system had not been marked there by any abuses more flagrant than elsewhere, while the attendance upon the caucuses of the dominant political party had been higher than the average of similar communities in other parts of the country.[49]

The Minnesota law incorporated the point that F. M. Brooks made so much of in relation to the Cleveland practice – namely, that polling should coincide with the registration of voters; in Minneapolis, polling was held on the first of three registration days, this being seven weeks before the election. A voter could declare which party he supported on the day of the election, and could be required to swear on oath that he was indeed a supporter of that party; as noted above, primary elections were held at the same time and voters voted in the same polling booths. The state administered the elections, and not only was it required that all parties nominate their candidates in this way, but failure to win 10 percent of the vote at the preceding general election would preclude a party its place on the ballot. A party that was thereby excluded required the signatures of 10 percent of registered voters to restore its position on the ballot: Independent candidates could get on to the general election ballot, but they had to obtain the signatures of 5 percent of registered voters to do so.

One of the striking features of the law is that it has virtually every characteristic of what would now be regarded as the standard twentieth-century American model of party nominations. This is not a transitional model between the nineteenth- and twentieth-century models of candidate selection; it is the full-blown twentieth-century model. Yet, the only respect in which the 1899 law was innovative was in requiring the use of direct nominations; every other feature had been used elsewhere, often many times and with many variations. However, much of this experimentation

---

[48] "Direct Primary Elections: Why They Should be Adopted in New York," *Citizens Union* pamphlet, no date.

[49] F. M. Anderson, "Communication: The Test of the Minnesota Primary Election System," *Annals of the American Academy of Political and Social Science*, (20)1902, p. 616.

elsewhere had occurred within the preceding decade, and the 1899 law seems to be a political universe away from the framework in which party politics had normally been practiced in the United States up to and including the 1890s. Minnesota is a good illustration of just how much legislation there had been in recent years; the first legislation relating to party nominations was passed in the state in 1887; subsequent measures were enacted in 1889, 1891, 1893, 1895, and 1897.[50] In other words, after 1887 a legislative session did not go by without some addition to the laws on party nominations and by 1899 a completely new framework for selecting party nominees was in place.

The bill was introduced by a Minneapolis member of the state legislature, and he succeeded in persuading other Minneapolis legislators to support it. Seemingly because it was a local measure proposed by representatives of the locality concerned, it attracted absolutely no opposition. It was employed in Minneapolis in 1900 when participation in the primaries was nearly 90 percent of the level of the general election turnout. Since no major problems appeared to have arisen in its use by then, and since it had the apparent advantage of increasing turnout in the nomination process, it was perceived as a success and became law for other counties, although not for all offices in the state, in 1901 – with only fourteen votes in the state House, and twelve votes in the state Senate, cast against its extension.[51] But for the fact that Minnesota's law did not cover every office, the "heroic" struggle by La Follette in Wisconsin – he vetoed a bill passed in 1901 because it did not provide for a statewide direct primary, and his persistence led to the passage of such a law in 1903 – would have been eclipsed. La Follette went for broke at a time when most politicians who were considering adopting the direct primary were more willing to do what they did in Minnesota: trying the Crawford County System out in places, and for offices where it seemed most appropriate, and then extending its deployment. Moreover, it must be remembered that, increasingly, this approach was not that of legislators in wholly rural states but also of those containing major urban areas – such as Boston and Baltimore.

One way of appreciating the likely impact of the Minnesota law on public awareness about nomination reform elsewhere is to look at the relative attention the state received in published material on primary elections. In 1905 the Library of Congress published a bibliography of work on primary elections. Of the forty-four articles cited for the period 1899–1904, twelve are devoted wholly to Minnesota, while three others discuss it in conjunction with other states. Only five are devoted exclusively

---

[50] David F. Simpson, "Primary Legislation in Minnesota," *Proceedings of the New York Conference for Good Government and the 11th Annual Meeting of the National Municipal League*, Philadelphia, National Municipal League, 1905, pp. 329–33.

[51] *Outlook*, March 23, 1901, p. 654, and April 13, 1901, p. 838–9.

to Wisconsin and a further two discuss it along with other states. In fact, there are nearly as many articles on Massachusetts (five in total with three exclusively about the state) as there are on Wisconsin.[52] This evidence is in line with Millspaugh's judgment that, in Michigan, when "public debates and newspaper articles made reference to the experience of other states, it was the Minnesota law [that] was most frequently mentioned."[53] Later, when the Progressive interpretation of what had happened had become established, the direct primary would become associated with La Follette and Wisconsin, but in the first few years of the twentieth century the struggle in Wisconsin was not the main focus of attention.

It is worth taking a brief detour at this point to say something about the later association of the direct primary with La Follette. In part, the responsibility for this lies with Merriam. By so emphasizing "complete" primary laws, that is, laws requiring direct primaries for virtually all offices in a state, Merriam diverted attention away from the earlier experience of direct primaries in rural counties in the South and West, although he himself was well aware of the extent of their use there.[54] Again, while Merriam's analysis did not make La Follette the pivotal actor in the "road to the direct primary," by focusing on the significance of "complete" laws, of which Wisconsin's was the first, of course, he opened the way for later political scientists and historians to make La Follette pivotal. Thus, V. O. Key, while acknowledging that there had been experiments with the direct primary elsewhere, makes no mention of Minneapolis and emphasizes La Follette's role.[55] As has been seen, in Ranney's analysis, this "forgetting" of the pre-Wisconsin developments is taken even further. Possibly, although this can never be demonstrated, it was the fact that La Follette became a major national political figure on moving to the Senate from the state governorship that enabled him later to become so much associated with the rise of the direct primary.

If La Follette can be regarded as reckless in moving to abolish the convention system so quickly, that very charge might also be applied to the behavior of some politicians, like those in Minnesota, who initially appear to have behaved rather more cautiously. Some of the effects of direct primaries could be detected after one election – the increased expense, for example – but others were only likely to become apparent after several elections. Thomas L. Johnson's comments in 1898 were based on six years of experience in Cleveland. By contrast, the Minneapolis experiment was being declared a success after merely one election, and the system was extended

---

[52] Library of Congress, *List of References on Primary Elections*, Washington, D.C., Government Printing Office, 1905.

[53] Arthur Chester Millspaugh, *Party Organization and Machinery in Michigan since 1890*, Baltimore, Md., Johns Hopkins University Press, 1917, p. 73.

[54] Merriam and Overacker, *Primary Elections*, p. 60.

[55] V. O. Key Jr., *Politics, Parties and Pressure Groups*, Fourth Edition, New York, Thomas Y. Crowell, 1958, pp. 411–12.

to other counties; even as this was happening, though, the first mayor of Minneapolis nominated in a direct primary was becoming engulfed in a major scandal. In 1899 the successful candidate for mayor was "Doc" Ames. His administration was so corrupt that by 1902 Ames's brother, the Minneapolis chief of police, was in jail and Ames himself had become a fugitive from justice and was finally arrested in New Hampshire.[56] It might have been expected that, even more than the earlier evidence from Cleveland, the Ames case would have acted as a brake on the rise of the direct primary. Yet, while reform journals like the *Nation* did not choose to rebut the argument that Ames was someone "whom the most brazen of bosses would hardly dare to offer for an elective office," the tide did not turn against the direct primary.[57]

One of main arguments against the Crawford County System and in favor of the caucus-convention system should have been that under the latter the parties had an incentive for cleaning up their own house; after all, as noted in Chapter 2, it was a future Democratic presidential candidate, Samuel Tilden, who had led the assault on the Tweed machine in New York City in the early 1870s. If this check, operating through the politicians themselves, was removed by the direct primary, then the protection against corrupt officials would surely be that much less. Yet, that line of criticism did not produce a major backlash against direct nominations in the wake of the Ames scandal, and supporters of them successfully used a two-pronged defence of it.

First, as with the Cleveland experience, attention was focused on a particular feature of the Minnesota law as the source of the problems. In this case, it was argued that Ames had been able to garner cross-party support in seeking the party nomination, and that this had been the result of the primary being an "open" one. Because voters merely had to state to which party they belonged at registration, although they could be required to swear the point if challenged, it was possible for an individual candidate to "pack" a particular party's primary with personal supporters. The direct primary's supporters maintained that the matter was easily resolved by making the primaries "closed" – that is, restricted to party supporters.[58] (Indeed, Robert Luce noted in 1907 that the Minneapolis fiasco had led to Massachusetts substituting a "closed" primary for an "open" one in its 1903 legislation.[59]) They were able to focus on this point despite the fact that one of the most contentious issues still surrounding the direct

---

[56] Robert Luce addressing the National Municipal League, *Proceedings of the Providence Conference for Good Government and 13th Annual Meeting of the National Municipal League*, Philadelphia, National Municipal League, 1907, p. 40.

[57] *Nation*, October 13, 1904, p. 290.

[58] *Nation*, October 13, 1904, p. 290, and Robert Luce, *Proceedings of the Providence Conference for Good Government*, p. 40.

[59] Robert Luce, *Proceedings of the Providence Conference for Good City Government*, p. 40.

primary was just how primary elections could be restricted to party supporters. In particular, there was no agreement as to how to reconcile a
genuinely "closed" primary with the value placed on maximizing levels of
participation in party nominations. Maximizing "closedness" inevitably
conflicted with maximizing participation, but this point was simply ignored.
As is seen in Chapter 7, making primaries especially "closed" proved to be
impossible.

The second part of the defence of direct nominations was to use an "on
balance" argument – whatever the problems of direct elections, on balance
the advantages outweighed the disadvantages.[60] As the *Nation* put it, it
should be admitted that the direct primary was "neither a failure nor a
panacea."[61] The thrust of the claim was that the direct primary could work
well in some circumstances, and might work better when voters got used
to it. In making such claims, there was little attempt to address two of the
fundamental points raised by Thomas Johnson in 1898 in his evaluation of
the evidence from Cleveland – namely, the quality of potential candidates
actually thrown up by direct nominating systems and the ability of voters
to choose between them. In other words, not unexpectedly, the direct
primary's advocates sought to restrict debate to features of the system
that they could more easily rebut. A good example of this technique was a
Citizens Union pamphlet produced in New York in 1910 at the time of
Governor Hughes's unsuccessful fight for a direct primary law. The
Union identifies six alleged objections to the direct primary, which it then
shows are fallacies: (1) that direct primaries are expensive; (2) that they
undermine representative democracy; (3) that they work against the interests of rural areas; (4) that plurality nominations are unfair; (5) that they
prevent "fusion" and the nonpartisan nomination of judges; and (6) that
they permit the voters of one party to participate in the primaries of
another.[62]

Obviously, this raises the question of why some of the fundamental issues
relating to the direct primary – issues that had been identified in public by
the late 1890s – failed to influence the switch toward the direct primary.
Why was there this recklessness – moving so quickly toward the direct
primary – in the face of evidence that at best it was a flawed solution to
the problems of party nominations, and at worst might be counterproduc-
tive? This is an issue to be explored more fully in the next three chapters,
but there is one key point that should be made now. Debate about the direct
primary began and continued during a period of continuing change in laws
governing party nominations. From one perspective, the recklessness that
was to be displayed over the direct primary was little different from the
frantic attempt to write and rewrite laws on party nominations in the 1890s.

[60] *Nation*, July 31, 1902, 85–7.   [61] *Nation*, October 13, 1904, p. 290.
[62] "Direct Primary Nominations," *Citizens Union*, 1910.

Yet, the explosion of legislation on direct primaries, especially between 1903 and 1910, was to have a much greater impact on America's parties in the long term; it was to make possible the domination of the candidate and, thereby, the atomization of American parties.

7. The States Convert to Direct Primaries, 1903–15

The period of what might be dubbed "experimentation" with the direct primary lasted only a few years. During these years, some states were making direct primaries optional, others were mandating its use for particular counties, while two states were requiring its use for virtually all public offices. This period lasted until about 1906. By that year, Wisconsin (1903) and Oregon (1904) had enacted laws requiring the direct nomination of most public officials; Minnesota (1899) and Nebraska (1905) had mandated the direct primary for their most populous cities; Pennsylvania (1906) required its use for all but statewide offices; Delaware (1903) had made its use optional; and several other states had passed laws that in some way facilitated the direct primary – Missouri (1901), Massachusetts (1902), New Jersey (1903), Michigan (1901 and 1905), and South Dakota (1905). In other words, by the beginning of 1907 nearly one-third of the non-southern states had started to legislate for the practice of direct nominations, and there were yet other states, such as Ohio, where parties in particular counties had converted to the voluntary use of direct nominations in the 19th century. However, these years may properly be regarded as ones of "experimentation," in that only two states had embraced the direct primary for all offices, and Wisconsin was the only one to have moved directly from a caucus-convention system deployed throughout the state to the comprehensive use of direct nominations.

After 1906, change was much more rapid, and between 1907 and 1915 nomination practices in the states changed enormously. The transformation was evident in three respects. First, many states that had not experimented with direct nominations earlier now passed legislation mandating it. Second, states that had made direct nominations optional, or that had mandated them for only some counties or some offices, started to require their use for all offices. Third, a number of other states followed Wisconsin in moving from a system based wholly on caucuses and conventions to one based entirely on the direct primary within one year.

The states (or territory, in the case of Arizona) legislating on direct nominations for the first time are shown in Table 4.1.

Only three states – Connecticut, Rhode Island, and New Mexico (a territory until 1912) – had not adopted the direct primary in some form by 1915.

As for the adoption of direct primary laws that covered virtually all public offices, here, too, the notable feature is just how rapidly the

TABLE 4.1. *Date of First Legislation on Direct Primaries for States without Such Legislation before 1907, 1907–1915*

1907:	Iowa, North Dakota, Washington
1908:	Kansas, Oklahoma, Ohio
1909:	Arizona, California, Idaho, Illinois*a*, Nevada, New Hampshire
1910:	Colorado, Maryland
1911:	Maine, New York, Utah, Wyoming
1912:	Montana
1915:	Indiana, Vermont, West Virginia

a Illinois had first passed legislation mandating the use of direct primaries in 1908 but this had been struck down by the courts (see Chapter 5).

TABLE 4.2. *Year of Adoption of Primary Laws Covering Most Offices within a State, to 1915*

1903:	Wisconsin
1904:	Oregon
1907:	Iowa, Missouri, Nebraska, North Dakota, South Dakota, Washington
1908:	Kansas, Oklahoma
1909:	Arizona, California, Idaho, Illinois, Nevada, New Hampshire
1910:	Colorado
1911:	Maine, Massachusetts, New Jersey, Wyoming
1912:	Minnesota, Montana
1913:	New York, Ohio, Pennsylvania
1915:	Vermont, West Virginia

transformation of the nomination system proceeded. The states adopting such legislation between 1903 and 1915 are shown in Table 4.2. By 1915, twenty-eight of the thirty-seven nonsouthern states had moved over to direct nominations for virtually all public offices in the state. To this list might be added two further states whose primary laws were close to providing for universal nomination by direct primary. The Indiana law of 1915 provided for nomination by convention for the state governor and U.S. senators, but only in some circumstances: A "preference primary" was held for these two offices and the result of that was binding on a state convention should one candidate receive an absolute majority of the votes cast. In effect, Indiana was close to having a comprehensive direct primary law. The situation in Maryland was broadly similar. Michigan was more removed from having a comprehensive law; its law of 1909 kept various statewide offices, although not the governorship and US Senate seats, in the control of party conventions.

TABLE 4.3. *States Enacting Direct Primary Laws for the First Time, and Passing "Complete" Laws in Doing So, 1907–1915*

1909:	Arizona, California, Idaho, Nevada, New Hampshire
1910:	Colorado
1911:	Maine, Wyoming
1912:	Montana
1915:	Vermont, West Virginia

Of the remaining six states, two (Delaware and Kentucky) were still further away from having universal direct primaries: Each party in these states remained free to decide whether to use direct nominations or not. That leaves four states, of which one, Utah, used direct primaries for elections in larger cities but for no other offices. The last three states were Connecticut, New Mexico, and Rhode Island, and they were to hold out against the direct primary for decades.

The third feature of the years between 1907 and 1915 was that nearly half of the states that had not previously enacted any legislation relating to the direct primary made it mandatory for all offices now, and did so with a single piece of legislation. Before 1907, only Wisconsin had made this kind of leap in the dark; after 1907, eleven of the twenty-three states enacting direct primary legislation for the first time took this route (see Table 4.3). The more cautious approach to nomination reform employed by many states in earlier years was replaced by one that was altogether bolder and, arguably, riskier.

The new approach was that of Progressives in many western states who were faced by very different kinds of political opponents than were to be found in the East. As Shefter argues, "opponents of the patronage system . . . were able to overwhelm the regimes that governed the cities and states" in the West, while in the East "where party organizations were stronger and more broadly based, the Progressives were unable to destroy these organizations and reconstitute the electorate."[63] Differences in party organizational strength were crucial:

In contrast to their counterparts in the Northeast, politicians in the territories and states of the West did not build highly structured and broadly based party organizations during the late nineteenth century. Strong party organizations failed to emerge during these decades partly because the West had only recently been settled, but also because politicians did not find it necessary to construct them in order to gain or retain power.[64]

---

[63] Martin Shefter, "Regional Receptivity to Reform: The Legacy of the Progressive Era," in Shefter (ed.), *Political Parties and the State*, Princeton, N.J., Princeton University Press, 1994, p. 169.

[64] Shefter, "Regional Receptivity to Reform," p. 177.

They did not need to do so, because their parties could draw on the resources of the interests that dominated the economies and political institutions of the region, namely the railroads.

In the East, party organizations developed before the rise of the railroads, companies whose size and ability to influence politics was greater than any previous economic institutions in the country. Politicians in the east often ended up by championing railroad interests, but they had their own power base in the party organizations created during the Jacksonian era, and these continued to expand and develop. By contrast, in the West, parties were becoming established at the same time, or after, the railroads were a major presence in these states and politicians there tended to draw on their resources rather than establishing the kind of party organizations found in the East. More recent settlement and weaker party structures had important consequences for political behavior in the West. As Shefter's data demonstrates, voter turnout was much lower in that region in the late nineteenth century, and in gubernatorial elections, for example, the Republican vote was much more volatile from one election to another.[65] In short, parties had much less grip over their potential voters than they did in the East.

The significance of this for reform in the early twentieth century is twofold. First, the close links between politicians and major economic interests meant that assaults on economic power would more likely take the form of political reform designed to constrain politicians who were promoting that power. Because the inhabitants of eastern states were less dependent on particular companies for their livelihoods, and because the connections between economic and political leaders were more complex, economics and politics were not quite so intertwined. Second, the western parties were less able to withstand assaults on their practices from reform-minded politicians – the weaker links between parties and voters meant that popular uprisings against the parties could be less easily contained.

Consequently, it would be expected that there would be significant variations in how the direct primary came to be adopted in the two regions. However, before turning to this, it is necessary to discuss briefly how the two regions are to be defined. Shefter himself used the Mississippi River as the dividing line – states to the east of it were part of what he called the "north east," while to the west of the river were the western states. It is proposed here to use a slightly different way of separating the regions, which involves reclassifying two states, Missouri and Wisconsin. The problem with Shefter's classification is that Missouri, which attained statehood by 1820, is part of the West, while Wisconsin, which was settled rather later, and which did not attain statehood until the mid-1840s, is classified as part of the northeast. The classification proposed here is the one

[65] Shefter, "Regional Receptivity to Reform," p. 170.

employed in Chapter 2, and involves using the achievement of statehood as the main variable: The longer a place had been a state, the more structured its parties would likely be at the end of the century; thus, Missouri should count as part of the East and Wisconsin should be classified as western.[66] Unfortunately, this way of proceeding provides an anomaly in the form of West Virginia, which did not become a separate state until 1863, although as part of Virginia it had a long history of party politics. To overcome this, the East is defined here as those places that had congressional representation before 1840.

Clearly, when looking at regional differences in relation to the direct primary, its early introduction is of less interest. As was shown in Section 1 of this chapter, the direct primary originated in an eastern state, Pennsylvania, as the "Crawford County System," and it is not surprising that some of the places to which it was transplanted early on, without legislation, were in neighboring eastern states, such as Ohio. Differences between east and west are more likely to be evident in relation to when states first introduced direct primary laws, how quickly they enacted laws that covered virtually all offices, and whether they introduced "complete" legislation at one time, without prior "experimentation" with it for particular offices or in particular counties.

In relation to the first legislation on direct nominations, it is clear that the older, eastern, states were more likely to be innovators than western states up to (and including) 1906 (Table 4.4). By the end of that year, 39 percent of eastern states (seven out of eighteen) had passed some form of legislation relating to direct nominations, while 26 percent of western states and territories (five out of nineteen) had done so. It is not surprising that early innovation was evident mainly in the East; these were the states with the more broadly based party organizations – organizations that had more to lose from unsatisfactory systems of nomination. In the next five years, though, this pattern of regional difference reversed. By the end of 1911, it was the western states that had been more active in enacting such legislation; nearly 90 percent of all western states (seventeen out of nineteen states) had some direct primary legislation compared with only 72 percent of eastern states (thirteen out of eighteen states). The East largely caught up again over the following four years, so that by the end of 1915 only 12 percent of eastern states (two in total) had no legislation relating to direct primaries compared with 5 percent of western states (just New Mexico).

---

[66] Naturally, these classifications are quite crude. Missouri's economy was much more like that in many western states, and the assault by early-twentieth-century politicians on organized interests there had much in common with the experience in western states. Yet, if party institutionalization did affect political outcomes, we would expect this to modify political behaviour in the state.

TABLE 4.4. *States Facilitating Direct Primaries through Legislation before 1907, by Region*

	States Enacting Legislation before 1907	States Not Enacting Legislation before 1907
Eastern States	Delaware (1903)	Connecticut (1955)
	Kentucky (1890)	Illinois (1909)
	Massachusetts (1902)	Indiana (1907)
	Michigan (1905)	Maine (1911)
	Missouri (1901)	Maryland (1910)
	New Jersey (1903)	New Hampshire (1909)
	Pennsylvania (1906)	New York (1911)
		Ohio (1908)
		Rhode Island (1947)
		Vermont (1915)
		West Virginia (1915)
Western States	Minnesota (1899)	Arizona (1909)
	Nebraska (1905)	California (1909)
	Oregon (1904)	Colorado (1910)
	South Dakota (1905)	Idaho (1909)
	Wisconsin (1903)	Iowa (1907)
		Kansas (1908)
		Montana (1912)
		New Mexico (1938)
		Nevada (1909)
		North Dakota (1907)
		Oklahoma (1908)
		Utah (1911)
		Washington (1907)
		Wyoming (1911)

Regional differences are also apparent in considering when states enacted direct primary legislation that covered virtually all offices. Such legislation was passed much earlier in the West (see Table 4.5), and that conclusion holds even if the slightly contentious cases of Indiana and Maryland are counted as having what Merriam called "complete" legislation. By the end of 1910, 74 percent of western states had this kind of legislation, compared with only 28 percent of eastern states. Even by the end of 1915, the East lagged behind – 78 percent of states had these laws, compared with 95 percent of western states.

Not only did the West "overtake" the East in the enactment of direct primary laws, many of the states in the region that had not previously passed any such laws adopted them for nearly every office within one year

TABLE 4.5. *Year of Adoption of Primary Laws Covering Most Offices within a State, by Region*

	1903	1904	1905	1906	1907	1908	1909	1910	1911	1912	1913	1914	1915	After 1915
Eastern States					MO		IL NH MI	MD	ME MA NJ		NY OH PA		IN VT WV	CT DE KY RI
Western States	WI	OR			IA NE ND SD WA	KS OK	AZ CA ID NV	CO	WY	MN MT				NM UT

123

TABLE 4.6. *States Enacting Direct Primary Laws for the First Time, and Passing "Complete" Laws in Doing So, by Region*

Eastern States	Western States
Maine (1911)	Arizona (1909)
New Hampshire (1909)	California (1909)
Vermont (1915)	Colorado (1910)
West Virginia (1915)	Idaho (1909)
	Montana (1912)
	Nevada (1909)
	Oregon (1904)
	Wisconsin (1903)
	Wyoming (1911)

(Table 4.6). Forty-seven percent of western states (nine out of nineteen) did this, compared with only 22 percent of eastern states (four out of eighteen). Moreover, two of the eastern states that took this "fast track" to the direct primary did so very late in this period – both in 1915.

8. Insurgency and Party Reform in Wisconsin

The different political behavior of the older states compared with that of the new states was also reproduced within the first state to adopt "complete" primary laws, namely Wisconsin. Like much of the West, the parties in Wisconsin came strongly under the influence of the railroads, which, together with the lumber industry, were the dominant interests in that state. Especially after 1880, these two industries had enormous influence over both the state governor and the legislature with respect to prospective legislation that might affect them; one academic author even described the relationship in terms of the interests "virtually dictating" to the governor, legislature and state delegation in Congress.[67]

Now, one of the most interesting aspects of Robert La Follette's confrontation with the state legislature over the direct primary is that its resolution involved the issue being placed before the electorate in a referendum. This makes it possible for any possible territorial basis of support for the direct primary to be analyzed directly – something that is absent in most states. What emerges is a remarkable split in support for a measure that overall secured 61.9 percent of the vote in the referendum. In southern Wisconsin, most of which had been settled by 1850, only six of the

---

[67] Allen Fraser Lovejoy, *La Follette and the Establishment of the Direct Primary in Wisconsin, 1890–1914*, New Haven, Yale University Press, 1941, p. 18.

counties had a total vote in support of the direct primary that exceeded 60 percent of the county vote. The northern part of the state, which had been almost entirely unsettled before 1860, displayed far higher levels of support; in only four of these counties did support for the direct primary fall below 60 percent of the total vote.[68] As at the level of states themselves, the more recently settled parts of Wisconsin appeared more supportive of institutional restructuring than the older communities.

The political force that could exploit these sentiments in the more recently settled lands of America came to be known after 1908 as "insurgency."[69] Insurgency brought together groups that had often opposed each other in the nineteenth century, but after the depression of 1893–7, the "common threat of large scale enterprises drove them to submerge their differences."[70] Insurgency sought to remedy the consequences of economic maladjustments in the country, especially the increasing concentration of economic power, and "related in some of its phases to the problem of concentration of control in industry was a whole series of evils which arose from the rapid development of the railroads" in the post–Civil War years.[71] There were, of course, many Progressives in the northeast who were concerned about the impact of monopoly, but it was in the "new" midwest and the far West that discontent with the actions of various economic actors was most intense. This was the heartland of insurgency, and it operated there primarily through the Republican party simply because the democracy was not really competitive in these states.[72] Arguably, this concentration of insurgents on the dominant party contributed to their success; in other states, the complexity of the interaction of intraparty and interparty competition made for less clear cut outcomes. However, the real point about the concentration of insurgency in the "new" midwest and the far West was that these were the states where politicians were most in collusion with a few economic interests. In the "old" midwest and in the Atlantic seaboard states, relations between party politicians and economic interests were rather more complicated. As Hechler noted, "Outside of the middle west it was extremely difficult to stir much enthusiasm for progressivism."[73]

Because of the domination of the parties by economic interests in the "new" states, there was much more obviously a dual track approach by their opponents to break the power of the interests directly and to

---

[68] Lovejoy, *La Follette*, pp. 84–91.

[69] Hechler notes that the term "insurgency" was used little before President Taft's inauguration in March 1909; Kenneth William Hechler, "Insurgency," Columbia University, PhD. dissertation, 1940.

[70] David P. Thelen, *Robert M. La Follette and the Insurgent Spirit*, Boston and Toronto, Little, Brown, 1976, pp. 21–2.

[71] Hechler, *Insurgency*, p. 18.   [72] Hechler, *Insurgency*, pp. 17–18.

[73] Hechler, *Insurgency*, p. 26.

transform the parties in ways that would put them beyond the reach of these interests in the future. Reform in the socioeconomic sphere was to go hand-in-hand with the breaking of the interests' grip on the parties. La Follette's real significance in relation to nomination reform is that he was not only the first major insurgent, he also was the first to maintain that the direct primary was the device that would transform the parties. Unlike most of the earlier antiparty reformers in the northeast in the 1890s, La Follette was not someone who had been excluded from party politics, and who therefore saw the erosion of party power *per se* as the path to greater influence. To the contrary, he was a "regular" party politician who had been a district attorney before spending six years in Congress. In this regard, La Follette was rather like the insurgent politicians in Congress in 1909–10, of whom Sanders has noted:

Comfortable, conservative lawyers, the insurgent Republicans were preeminently good politicians. When the people of their states and districts began to show dissatisfaction with national Republican policies and local corruption, they seized on the discontent and turned failed or failing political careers into near invincibility.[74]

La Follette's support for the direct primary followed his being out-organized at the 1896 state convention for the Republican nomination for the governorship. He then alighted on the direct primary as the means by which he and others could avoid being out-organized in the future, and he linked his campaign for the direct primary with an attack on economic power in Wisconsin. After winning the governorship in 1900, his strategy was to focus on just two issues – the direct primary and a railroad tax – thereby annoying local insurgents who had a broader political agenda. In fact, "fewer insurgent bills passed in 1901 than had passed in 1897 or 1899 when governors had left the initiative to others."[75] Together with his refusal to compromise with the state legislature on direct primary legislation in 1901, this tended to limit La Follette's popularity in the state, and by 1904 he was being characterized as a troublemaker in the state press.[76] Although the referendum approved the direct primary, his electoral performance in his subsequent reelection (in 1906) was rather weak.

However, the passage of the direct primary legislation in 1904 did provide an important symbol for other insurgents – especially in the western states. As Mowry observed of California, "Throughout the early progressive campaigns in California, Folk's St. Louis and La Follette's Wisconsin were cited repeatedly as a city and a state that had freed themselves from the old iniquitous politics."[77] Wisconsin showed what could be done,

---

[74] Elizabeth Sanders, *Roots of Reform: Farmers, Workers and the American State, 1877–1917*, Chicago and London, University of Chicago Press, 1999, p. 166.

[75] Thelen, *Robert M. La Follette*, p. 35.   [76] Lovejoy, *La Follette*, p. 84.

[77] George E. Mowry, *The California Progressives*, Berkeley, University of California Press, 1951, p. 90.

thereby prompting imitation elsewhere in the region. In essence what happened in many of the western states was a copying of the La Follette agenda, in making the direct primary the centerpiece for the attack on the economic interests' grip on the parties. Imitation did not always extend to the details of the Wisconsin legislation and there were important differences in the operation of the direct primary within the West – for example, with respect to tests of party membership. However, there is a real sense in which La Follette's successful efforts did prompt those in other states. In doing so, La Follette thereby ensured that, even more than in the east, attention in the western states was to be focused exclusively on the supposed "solution" rather than on what the nomination problems actually were and how they might be resolved. This issue of the "solution" taking over from "the problems" is one to which we return in Chapter 7.

9. Concluding Remarks

It has been seen that, after 1906, the enactment of direct primary legislation was occurring more rapidly in the West, and by 1915 more states in that region had "complete" primary laws than in the east. But how significant is this in understanding the rise of the direct primary? Three points can be made that must qualify any emphasis placed on insurgency in explaining regional differences in the approach to nomination reform. First, even if there had been no regional variations with respect to insurgency, it would have been expected that, in many cases, eastern states would have adopted the direct primary more slowly than western states. This is because of the effects of the practice of office rotation in rural and small town communities. As will be seen in Chapter 5, in Massachusetts one of the main sources of opposition to direct nominations came from politicians representing districts where, traditionally, offices were rotated between the various towns in a district; direct nominations would mean that there was no mechanism for ensuring rotation was practiced. In the older parts of the country, and, obviously, that meant in the eastern states rather those in the West, rotation was firmly established, and it would always have been more likely that this form of opposition would surface there.

Second, insurgency in the West did not lead to the dismantling of parties there in all respects. It is true that some devices, such as the introduction of nonpartisan elections for local government, were much more common in the West, and were intended to weaken party control. But, in relation to nominations, parties were not always opened up in the West in ways that they might have been. For example, California's notorious cross-filing provision – under which a candidate could enter (and possibly win) the primary of more than one party – was not imitated elsewhere. Moreover, with regard to who could vote in primaries, western states generally remained as protective of party interests as eastern states. By 1915, only three western states

(Colorado, Montana, and Wisconsin) had open primaries – in which voters could choose, without hindrance, on election day, which party's primaries they wished to vote in; this was the same number of states as used this system in the East (Massachusetts, Michigan, and Vermont). Most states – in both East and West – used a closed primary, in which primary voters did not have that form of choice.

Third, in many ways the most remarkable aspect of the rise of the direct primary is not that its introduction happened more quickly in the West but that it became used so commonly in the East as well. By 1915, 88 percent of eastern states had some laws relating to direct nominations, and just over three-quarters of them had laws requiring direct primaries for nearly all offices. In spite of the much greater relative autonomy of party organizations in the East – a point on which Shefter is surely correct – most of those organizations accepted the direct primary. But why? It is easy to see why they should have experimented with the direct primary for some kinds of offices: It might provide a solution to some of the problems they were facing in nominating candidates. But why would they adopt so widely a reform that was advocated by many reformers who were antiparty in orientation, and that, in hindsight, seemed to run counter to the interests of parties?

These are the questions addressed in the next three chapters. Chapter 5 considers the argument that features in many popular accounts of the Progressive era – that the direct primary was one of the areas in which urban-based, and often antiparty, reformers took on urban party bosses and defeated them, requiring them to accept a form of nomination that they could manipulate less easily. Chapter 6 examines an argument that has found more favor with political scientists than with historians – that direct primaries resulted from a decline in party competition in much of the United States in the years after the 1890s. Chapter 7 provides an alternative explanation, derived from the evidence presented elsewhere in this book, that party elites turned to the direct primary as the only possible "solution" to a problem they believed both demanded a solution and for which, they thought, a solution must exist.

WHY THE DIRECT PRIMARY WAS INTRODUCED

5

Reformers versus Urban Machines?

One common interpretation of the rapid rise of the direct primary is that it emanated from a conflict between reformers, usually based in cities and often antiparty in orientation, and urban political machines. On this view, as exemplified, for example, in the account presented by Steven J. Diner, Progressive legislation on institutional reform at the state level was an extension of these reformers' assaults on the power of urban bosses.[1] Consequently, the introduction of the direct primary is usually portrayed as highly conflictual, with the major protagonists being antiparty reformers, on the one side, and the urban machines on the other. This view would seem to make sense. After all, it has already been seen that, at the end of the 1880s and in the 1890s, both in relation to the Australian Ballot and the legal regulation of party nominations, anxieties about the practices in the large urban areas were crucial in prompting legislation. But is this actually what happened?

If the account were accurate, it would be expected that such conflict would be most evident in the states containing the largest cities. It was there that the stakes would be highest for the party organizations, because of the benefits they could extract from control of local government; it was there also that the highest concentrations of the middle classes would be found, and it was these classes, on whom, relatively, the highest tax burdens tended to fall in the nineteenth century, that formed the main base of reform movements. To see whether that account is accurate, this chapter examines how direct primary legislation was enacted in the states containing the five largest cities in America in 1900 – Massachusetts (Boston), Pennsylvania (Philadelphia), Missouri (St. Louis), Illinois (Chicago), and New York (New York). If there really was conflict between reformers and urban machines over the introduction of the direct primary, it would

---

[1] Steven J. Diner, *A Very Different Age: Americans of the Progressive Era*, New York, Hill and Wang, 1998, pp. 208–9.

surely be in these states. Each is examined in detail in the following sections of the chapter.

1. Massachusetts

The introduction of the direct primary in Massachusetts bears no resemblance to the conventional account about the interaction between reformers and political parties. As with the Australian Ballot, primarily one person was responsible for promoting the idea of direct nominations. However, the similarities between Richard Henry Dana, who was the principal initiator of ballot reform, and Robert Luce, who was the main moving force behind direct primaries, are not close. Dana had a purely instrumental attitude to parties – he would support a candidate irrespective of their party, thereby switching his loyalties from election to election, and he wished to weaken party influence over elections. As a result, he never held elective office himself, nor did he exercise influence within a political party during his career; rather, his influence derived in part from his connections to individual politicians and in part because the idea he was promoting – the official ballot – offered a clear solution to a problem that was widely recognized within the parties as being serious.

Luce was a party loyalist. Having been a Democrat until 1894, he became a Republican winning election as a representative to the Massachusetts legislature, and, later in his career, he served as a member of Congress. Unlike Dana, his influence derived from his role as an elected politician. Many of the bills on direct primaries introduced into the state legislature between 1900 and 1911 were sponsored by him, and by the time all state offices were covered by the direct primary (in 1911) the issue was one that was very much identified with him. Luce was not a maverick politician, however; in Abrams's words, he was:

> . . . not only . . . a good Republican, but a Republican with leadership potentialities. Although the party leadership distrusted him because of his unorthodox political views, he was not an "outsider". . . . In addition, for all his unorthodoxy, Luce never broke party regularity at election time. Insisting on "party government," he liked to emphasize that his primaries system would help eliminate the independents and Democrats from Republican nomination contests.[2]

Moreover, Luce was operating in a context in which overt opposition to the direct primary was muted, and where many politicians were willing to consider whether a proposed solution was a practical one.

The reform journal *Outlook* claimed in 1898 that the direct primary had been given "its indorsement by both the Republicans and the Democrats of

---

[2] Richard M. Abrams, *Conservatism in a Progressive Era: Massachusetts Politics, 1900–1912,* Cambridge, Mass., Harvard University Press, 1964, p. 181.

Massachusetts in 1893."[3] By 1896, legislation was introduced to make the Board of Aldermen in Boston subject to direct nomination. That legislation failed, as did a similar bill in 1897, although it was passed subsequently. By 1899, the Secretary of the Commonwealth of Massachusetts appears to have taken up the matter of direct nominations. In an official report to the legislature, he wrote:

I commend to the serious consideration of the Legislature the subject of nominating candidates by direct vote as far as practicable, without the intermediate process of delegate conventions. I am convinced that there is a strong sentiment in favor of bringing the nomination of candidates as close to the people as possible.[4]

However, the next legislation on direct nominations was not until 1901, when an act was passed requiring direct nominations in Suffolk County (Boston) for state senators and for members of the state committee in each of the senatorial districts in that county.[5] This meant that nine of the forty senate districts came to be subject to direct nominations. One of the significant aspects of this piece of legislation is that it exposes a key point – that pressure to control nominations in problematic areas could well arise from within the party most affected. The main areas of Boston in which the problems of the caucus system were most pronounced were Democratic, yet it was the Democrats themselves who petitioned originally for direct nominations, although it was enacted by a legislature controlled by the Republicans and signed into law by a Republican governor. The apparent success of the measure led the Democrats, at their State Convention in October that year, to support the extension of the direct primary – to include all offices selected below the level of a state convention, and even to candidates on the state ticket when 5 percent of voters supported such a proposal.[6]

The following year further legislation was enacted. A number of bills were introduced into the state legislature in 1902, but the most comprehensive was Robert Luce's. Luce had spent the summer of 1901 visiting both Minnesota and Wisconsin investigating how the nomination systems worked there.[7] By early 1902, though, the state's Republican establishment was becoming concerned about the legislative developments in the state. U.S. Senator Henry Cabot Lodge wrote to Governor Murray Crane on February 27 about the matter (in a letter marked "personal"), and wrote again to Crane on April 12 (in a letter marked "personal and confidential").

[3] *Outlook*, September 17, 1898.
[4] Joseph Walker Papers 1907–1933, Box 2, Massachusetts Historical Society; the date and the content of this communication to the legislature is contained on a separate sheet attached to the written version of a speech given by Joseph Walker on May 17, 1910.
[5] Robert H. Whitton, "Political and Municipal Legislation in 1901," *Annals of the American Academy of Political and Social Science*, 20(1902), p. 382.
[6] *Outlook*, October 26, 1901. [7] *Outlook*, November 1, 1902.

In both letters, the concern expressed was not about the *principle* of direct nominations, but rather the pace at which legislation might be enacted. On February 27 Lodge noted:

... my general opinion was that it would be wise to wait until the subject had been thoroughly treated in Boston. I can say to you, however, that I feel very strongly that it would be unwise to pass this bill at present. Let us see how the new system works in Boston before we try to revolutionise the politics of the State.[8]

The letter on April 12 followed the reporting of the bill to the state House, and Lodge reiterated his point about trying the system in Boston first, adding, "Cannot something be done to prevent what seems to me very hasty action at this time [sic]."[9]

Something was done. Pressure was brought to bear on Republicans in the state legislature, and the scope of the bill was restricted. In particular, Lodge's desire that the experiment be confined to Boston was successful. The compromise involved some nominations for seats in the lower chamber of the state House becoming subject to direct nomination, as well as those elective city offices in Boston in which voting was conducted in two or more wards of the city, but with the exception of members of the School Committee.[10]

The following year (1903) Luce enjoyed further legislative success, this time sponsoring the Joint Caucus Bill. This required parties to hold their nominating caucuses at the same time, and also subjected that stage of the nominating process to the kind of regulation that turned them into elections. For example, *Outlook* commented:

The vote at the primary will be in all, or almost all, respects exactly like that at the election. It will be in charge of the paid election officers who have charge of elections, the two leading parties being equally represented. The voter must audibly state with which party he wishes to vote.[11]

Primary voters were prevented from taking part in the nominating process of the other main party within the year following their participation in a primary. However, they were allowed to participate in a party's primary for *municipal* nominations, even if they had voted in the other party's primary for state elections;[12] this separation of municipal from state nominations was not the result of any antipartism but, rather, an attempt by Republicans to weaken Democratic influence in city elections.

[8] Henry Cabot Lodge to Murray Crane, February 27, 1902, Lodge Papers Box 18, No. 448, Massachusetts Historical Society.
[9] Henry Cabot Lodge to Murray Crane, April 12, 1902, Lodge papers, Box 18, No. 251, Massachusetts Historical Society.
[10] *Outlook*, November 1, 1902.   11. *Outlook*, July 4, 1903.
[12] *World's Work*, August 6, 1903, p. 3716.

Nevertheless, Luce and his fellow legislator, John N. Cole of Andover, failed to obtain the passage of a bill they introduced that would have provided for direct primaries for virtually all offices, and it was not until 1911 that such legislation was enacted.[13] The impact of the "softly, softly" approach advocated by senior Republicans, notably Henry Cabot Lodge and Murray Crane, meant that radical reforms were not going to be enacted without a period of experimentation. However, this did not stop Luce from trying to increase the use of direct primaries. For the next few years, he was always attempting to expand the scope of the direct primary legislation beyond the offices covered by the 1901 and 1902 acts. Nevertheless, Luce himself was far from being a radical reformer in a hurry; he took pride in the incremental Massachusetts style of policy reform. In 1907, he told the annual conference of the National Municipal League in Providence:

In Massachusetts, with annual elections, we have a persistent habit of doing things piecemeal, a little at a time year after year. . . . We do not proceed with the leaps and bounds that seem to be the normal habits of Oregon and Washington and other Western States, but we crawl, and so we have crawled in this matter of primary reform.[14]

Furthermore, he was certainly not moving in the direction of opposition to parties *per se*. He also told the same Providence conference:

. . . it has been suggested this afternoon that if national party lines were wholly taken out of municipal elections the probabilities would favor better results. I can tell you of a Massachusetts city where for years in municipal elections there has been no such thing as a Democrat or a Republican; where for something like ten or twelve years a mayor has been in office who has been the subject of constant criticism, and the allegation has been frequent that it is one of the worst governed cities in Massachusetts.[15]

Luce's attempts to convert the state to the wholesale use of the direct primary remained largely unsuccessful until 1911. Nevertheless, by 1910, 150 of the 240 representatives in the state House, and thirteen of the forty state senators, were subject to direct nomination.[16] The main problem was not opposition from the Democratic party organizations in Boston. Indeed, by 1907, the Democratic party leaders from the city wanted to extend the principle of direct nominations to other offices in their county. (Martin Lomasney, one of the two or three most powerful Democrats in the city, for example, tabled an amendment to the Luce Bill of that year to provide

---

[13] *Boston Post*, March 5, 1911.
[14] Robert Luce, "Massachusetts Primary Law," *Proceedings of the Providence Conference for Good Government and the 13th Annual Conference of the National Municipal League*, 1907, p. 38.
[15] *Ibid.*, pp. 42–3.
[16] Data cited in a speech by Joseph Walker, January 18, 1910; Joseph Walker papers 1907–1933, Box 1, Massachusetts Historical Society.

for direct nominations for the office of district attorney in Suffolk County.[17])
For Republicans, institutional reform in Boston was largely a means of
keeping the Irish and the Democratic party under control. For example, this
was the purpose of the provision in the new city charter of 1909 that made
Boston city elections nonpartisan.[18]

It was the rural areas and the smaller cities – many of them Republican
strongholds – that resisted the direct primary. One prominent argument
made by opponents was that it would interfere with traditional principles
of office rotation – from one town to another – that had been long practiced in rural areas and in small towns. It was advanced, for example, in
opposition to the unsuccessful 1907 Luce bill, by a representative from West
Springfield, Mr. Cook, and by Mr. Brigham from Marlboro; Cook's argument was "where the district included several towns the smaller places
would be outvoted by the larger, whereas by the agreed rotation system all
were treated fairly."[19] This was the backbone of opposition in the state and
it provided good reasons for the Republican leadership to continue to resist
Luce's more ambitious proposals for nomination reform.

It was an unstable equilibrium, however. Direct nominations could be
made an electorally attractive proposal, and the Republican leadership's
position would be susceptible to defections from its own ranks and from
the threat of a strengthened Democratic party. Both conditions were to
be present by 1910. The cause was taken up by the Speaker of the State
Assembly, the ambitious but previously conservative Joseph Walker. Walker
had opposed the direct primary, just as he opposed direct legislation and
any other manifestations of what he regarded as nonrepresentative democracy. By the beginning of 1910, though, he was moving to support a modest
extension of direct nominations. In a public speech on January 18, he stated:

I do not intend to discuss the question of direct nominations tonight. I realize that
there are two sides to the question. I believe Massachusetts can afford to go slowly
in this matter and watch the experiments already being tried in other states. I think
it wise at this time to confine direct nominations to senatorial and representative
districts and to allow each district to decide the question for itself.[20]

He had introduced a bill to this effect, but was already facing opposition
from those concerned to protect the practice of office rotation. His new
position was revealed further in an interview on January 24, when he stated
unequivocally: "Rotation in office by which the office of representative is

[17] *Boston Herald*, May 10, 1907.
[18] Thomas H. O'Connor, *The Boston Irish: A Political History*, Boston, Back Bay Books,
   1995, pp. 177–8.
[19] *Boston Herald*, May 10, 1907.
[20] Joseph Walker Papers 1907–1933 (MS N–202), Box 2, Massachusetts Historical Society,
   speech of January 18, 1910.

passed from town to town is not for the best interests either of the district or of the Commonwealth."[21]

The bill failed, but 1910 saw an electoral resurgence of the Democrats in the state. The Republican party had little to lose now from the extension of the direct primary system, and they made it a plank in the party platform. However, the Democrats captured the governorship, while the Republicans retained a majority in the legislature, with Walker then being reelected as Assembly Speaker in January 1911. This shift in the balance of power in the state made it certain that some form of direct primary legislation was going to be passed that year; as the *Boston Post* noted on February 12: "It is already conceded that the direct nominations bill will be passed in the Legislature and there is a rush to get on the bandwagon."[22] The real division was among the Republicans. Luce and his allies were pushing ahead with the kind of all-encompassing bill that he had always backed. Walker, however, "was very ambitious to have his name attached to any direct primaries law that might be passed," a move that would bolster his impending bid for the Republican gubernatorial nomination.[23]

In the changed political circumstances Walker was now willing to contemplate a far more complete reform than he had supported a year earlier, particularly as he believed that his own chances of securing the gubernatorial nomination were much greater under a direct primary.[24] However, the experience of his own bill in 1910 appeared to suggest to him that a comprehensive reform would be susceptible to defeat by a coalition composed of two elements that could be detached from each other. One was those politicians (including some senior Republicans) who opposed direct nomination for statewide office, and the other were the rural politicos seeking to protect the practice of rotation for lesser offices. Walker's strategy was to submit two bills, because in "his opinion it would be easier to get through the two bills separately than to secure the adoption of an omnibus bill."[25] This strategy was akin to the stereotype of a general foolishly using the experience of the previous war to fight the present one. The Democrat resurgence meant that the coalition opposing direct nominations was much weaker than Walker seemed to believe. Furthermore, Walker's gubernatorial ambitions were now drawing opposition from senior Republicans, and they had no desire to have Walker get the credit for a measure that was going to pass anyway. The bill that emerged from the Assembly committee bore "the tag of the committee," even though it largely resembled the original Luce proposals.[26]

[21] Joseph Walker Papers 1907–1933 (MS N–202), Box 2, Massachusetts Historical Society, transcript of interview on January 24, 1910.
[22] *Boston Post*, February 12, 1911.   [23] *Boston Herald*, March 26, 1911.
[24] *Boston Herald*, March 26, 1911.   [25] *Boston Herald*, March 26, 1911.
[26] *Boston Post*, March 26, 1911.

By 1911, the use of direct nominations had become widespread in Massachusetts, but that state's experience bears little resemblance to the conventional wisdom about the introduction of direct nominations. Antiparty reformers were not the moving force behind the legislation nor were they decisive in its final enactment. Moreover, urban machines were not a major source of opposition to direct nominations, and regular politicians in Boston often supported their extension. In addition, as far as institutional reform of the parties was concerned, Boston's Democrats would have been largely at the mercy of their opponents before 1910, should conflict have arisen. Opposition came from rural areas, worried about the principle of rotation, and from senior Republicans anxious to avoid radical reforms that might destabilize the party. In the end, intraparty and interparty competition helped to complete a transfer to direct nominations, a process that had actually begun much earlier than in most other states.

2. Pennsylvania

While the Massachusetts legislature debated the introduction of direct primaries for various offices for well over a decade, in Pennsylvania most offices came to be covered by state legislation providing for direct nominations within a matter of a few months, in early 1906. (Only statewide offices were not covered by that legislation, and they were added in 1913.) The Pennsylvania experience contrasts with that of Massachusetts in a number of important respects, not least in that, while the latter had passed considerable legislation regulating parties before the introduction of direct primaries for most offices, in Pennsylvania county parties had been able to regulate their own nominations right up until the introduction of the 1906 Act. The contrast is well illustrated in the following way. In 1911 the Massachusetts legislator John Cole, one of the long-time advocates of the direct primary, justified his position by blaming earlier legislation for constraining the parties; he said:

I believe in the old fashioned caucus where public questions are fought out and men get shoulder to shoulder to shoulder, but we have gone far afield from it today. We began wrong a long time ago in putting our election laws into a mass of complicated machinery.[27]

In Pennsylvania, though, just a year before the introduction of state-mandated direct primary elections in 1906, a report to the *National Municipal League* noted that parties in that state were still covered by legislation of 1881, and

... the essential principles of the original Acts of 1881 have been undisturbed, and the primary legislation of Pennsylvania may be briefly summarized as a formal and

[27] *Boston Post*, March 2, 1911.

authoritative vesting of political organizations with complete power to make any rules they please for determining who may participate in a primary; how, when and where a primary shall be conducted; who shall determine the result of a primary; and how the result shall be authenticated.[28]

Until 1906, Pennsylvania was one of the minority of states that had not enacted legislation on party nominations in the period since 1890.

Not only had the Pennsylvania parties been free to run their nominations as they wished but, as noted in Chapter 3, a remarkable variety of different nomination procedures had been adopted in the various counties. Most famously, the state had given birth to the direct primary – the Crawford County System – but many other forms of nomination had been devised, especially in rural counties. Given this diversity, it is not surprising that nomination reform had not been a major item on the political agenda; grassroots revolts were always likely to get in the way of any move towards direct nominations. That this did not occur in 1906 was the result of a serious crisis facing the Republican party that had emerged the year before.

Pennsylvania was one of the more heavily Republican states in the union. It had last voted for a Democratic presidential candidate in 1856, and it would not be captured by the Democrats again until Roosevelt's landslide of 1936. Unlike New York State, where the major cities leaned Democratic, in Pennsylvania the largest city (Philadelphia) was a bastion of Republicanism. Even during the Democratic surge under Cleveland in 1892, when in congressional elections the Democrats ran ahead of the Republicans by 5 percent of the total vote, in Pennsylvania they had trailed the GOP by 6 percent of the total. The aftermath of the economic depression and the Bryan candidacy was simply to cement the Republicans' advantage. By the early twentieth century, Republicans were capturing at least 60 percent of the vote in congressional elections in the state. In part, Republican dominance had been consolidated from the mid-1880s onward by Matthew Quay, who created one of the most effective statewide party organizations in the nation. Quay controlled:

... the flow of legislation and appropriations through the state legislature, and this in turn was contingent on his ability to subject party subordinates who staffed the state government to his discipline.[29]

However, a sequence of scandals, involving the deposition of state funds in favored banks culminated in 1905 when the State Treasurer deposited

[28] Scott Nearing and Lawrence W. Trowbridge, "Political Organization and Primary Legislation in Pennsylvania, 1881–1904," *Proceedings of the New York Conference for Good Government and the 11th Annual Meeting of the National Municipal League*, Philadelphia, 1905, p. 293.

[29] Peter McCaffery, *When Bosses Ruled Philadelphia: The Emergence of the Republican Machine, 1867–1933*, University Park, Pennsylvania State University Press, 1993, p. 79.

funds in "a dubious New Mexico railroad scheme."[30] The Democrats ran a reform mayor as their candidate for treasurer that year, and backed by several minor parties as well, William H. Berry won in a highly publicized campaign. He was the first Democrat to win statewide office in twelve years.

The Republican establishment was shaken.[31] This was a party that controlled the state assembly by 179–15 and the senate by 39–10. To seize the initiative back for his party the governor, Samuel W. Pennypacker, announced, just five days after the election, a special session of the legislature for early 1906, a move that seemed to have taken political leaders in Philadelphia by surprise.[32] Pennypacker had been in office since 1903, and was a good example of the kind of "blue chip" candidate that party organizations often selected to head the state ticket in order to broaden their electoral coalition. He had been a judge, with few political resources of his own, but he was both a cousin of Matthew Quay and a staunch Republican. Before 1905 his record in office was based on providing an efficient administration; like Quay himself, he had embraced various reforms, although in other matters, including the state's libel laws, Pennypacker had proved to be a conservative.[33] Quay died in 1904, and because of both this and his own position as the senior Republican officeholder in the state, Pennypacker was able to take the initiative in countering the threat of a resurgent democracy.

Nevertheless, Pennypacker's agenda was not a radical one. He made seven recommendations – including reapportionment of state House and Senate districts – as ones that were to be addressed by the special session of the legislature at the beginning of 1906. Significantly, reform of the party nominating system was not among them. Within two days, efforts were being made to persuade Pennypacker to expand the scope of activity for the legislature in 1906; the mayor of Philadelphia, who had temporarily broken with the Republican party, regretted publicly the absence of ballot reform from Pennypacker's proposals, while the *Philadelphia Inquirer* observed that pressure was being brought to bear on Pennypacker to enlarge the scope of his proposals, and, in particular, to bring about the "adoption of a uniform system of primaries."[34] The wording of this statement is highly

---

[30] Philip S. Klein and Ari Hoogenboon, *A History of Pennsylvania*, Second Edition, College Park and London, Pennsylvania State University Press, 1980, p. 421.

[31] Even the highly partisan *Philadelphia Inquirer*, a paper that two days before the election had the words "The Only Republican Newspaper in Philadelphia" emblazoned across its front page, could admit "[T]he plurality for Berry is not an overwhelming one, as majorities have gone in Pennsylvania of late years, but it is sufficient to show that in a great Republican commonwealth there was an unrest that took shape in voting for the Democratic candidate for State Treasurer," November 24, 1906.

[32] *Philadelphia Inquirer*, November 12, 1905.

[33] On Quay, see McCaffery, *When Bosses Ruled Philadelphia*, p. 81.

[34] *Philadelphia Inquirer*, November 14, 1905.

significant, for, unlike any other state, the adoption of the direct primary in Pennsylvania came about with hardly any public debate about the issue of direct-versus-indirect nominations. Throughout the entire period of the legislation, the issues being addressed publicly were largely those of bringing party nominations under state law and requiring the parties throughout the state to adopt the same procedures. As Pennypacker was to note later in the process (January 22, 1906):

The purpose of a uniform primary law is to provide a plan for the holding of primaries of all parties at the same time and in a way which will throw the greatest safeguard about the election.[35]

That the procedures that were to be used were direct nominations – a form of nomination that was far from widespread – elicited virtually no comment.

Despite receiving requests that the scope of the legislative session be expanded, Pennypacker's initial reaction was to reject such advice. On November 15, the day after the first public calls for expansion, he decided not to do so, with the *Philadelphia Inquirer* claiming:

Many prominent citizens and good Republicans have informed the Governor that they favor the adoption of a uniform primary election law, but while the Governor is not out of sympathy with the idea, he feels that the subject is altogether too important to make hasty action advisable.

His proposal was that any action should be delayed until after the 1906 elections.[36] This approach got the backing of U.S. Senator Penrose, the man who had replaced Quay as the most powerful organizational leader in the party; on November 17, when asked about ballot reform and uniform primary elections, he replied simply, "These matters have been gone over thoroughly."[37] Nevertheless, the following week, Pennypacker appeared to be changing his mind about the desirability of taking early action on primary elections.[38] Yet, having appeared then to endorse early action, he changed tack once again. On December 3, he argued, on the one hand, that to modify his original call for a legislative session would be to "lead to endless confusion in the extra session," while, on the other hand, he claimed that he was not satisfied that he had "a legal right to amend his original call."[39]

The member of Congress for the 11th District, Henry W. Palmer, who had written to Pennypacker originally on November 14, wrote to him again on December 24. He urged Pennypacker to include a Uniform Primary Law in the package of legislation, citing personal experience of campaigns "in

[35] *Pittsburgh Gazette*, January 22, 1906.   [36] *Philadelphia Inquirer*, November 15, 1905.
[37] *Philadelphia Inquirer*, November 18, 1905.
[38] *Philadelphia Inquirer*, November 23, 1905.
[39] *Philadelphia Inquirer*, December 3, 1905.

which money has been used to secure nominations." He went on to describe "the delegate system" as "rotten to the core," a phrase he had used also in his November letter.[40] Pennypacker appears to have received rather limited correspondence on the subject, but all of it urged him to take action. However, none of his correspondents either raised the matter of the principle of direct nominations, or provided detailed justifications for requiring its use; as was to be the case throughout the period from November 1905 to February 1906, the case for, and against, direct nominations was largely notable by its absence from public discussion.

By January, the cautious Pennypacker had changed his mind for the final time. On January 9, and seemingly to "the great surprise of his official advisers," he issued a call for several other issues to be considered by the legislature, and this included an act providing for a uniform primary law.[41] The timing of Pennypacker's shift is significant, because it came on the day that the City Party – a breakaway party of dissident Republicans formed in Philadelphia in 1905 – won a large victory in a special election for a state senate seat. It was clear that just calling the special session might well not prove sufficient to stabilize the Republican party. With gubernatorial acceptance that primary election reform fell within the brief of the special session, five bills on the subject were introduced between January 15 and 19, at least one of which – that of Senator White – would have abolished nominating conventions: "there is to be direct voting for candidates, so that all nominating conventions will be avoided."[42]

Not surprisingly, given that this was an issue that had been rushed onto the legislative agenda, it was clear that there were considerable differences of opinion about the scope of the legislation to be enacted. Pennypacker was of the belief that the question of uniformity was entirely separate from that of direct elections. In an interview with the *Pittsburgh Gazette* published on January 22, he expressed the "opinion that the method of nominating candidates is a matter of party regulation and is a question which does not need to be dealt with in the uniform primary election law." It was on this occasion that he made the observation (quoted earlier) that a uniform primary law was about fixing the timing of primaries and about providing legal safeguards for their conduct. It was also clear that he thought that the thorny matter of rotation – the issue that was proving so problematic in Massachusetts and elsewhere – had to be considered, for he claimed that "no law will prevent the counties of a congressional district

---

[40] H. W. Palmer to Samuel W. Pennypacker, December 24, 1905, Pennypacker Papers, Pennsylvania State Archive, Harrisburg, Level 1258, Folder on Primary Election Law, 1905–6. In his letter of November 14, Palmer had argued "the business of running for delegate is well understood and the business of buying them after they are Elected has become well Established."

[41] *Philadelphia Inquirer*, January 10, 1906.   [42] *Philadelphia Inquirer*, January 16, 1906.

from making an agreement to allow rotation in office or fix the number of terms each county is to have the representative."[43]

However, Pennypacker was in no position to restrict the legislation in the way he preferred. Had he taken a firm position on a uniform primary bill much earlier – and insisted that the legislature could consider only the matters of the timing and legal supervision of primaries – it is possible that the result might have been different. As it was, he was boxed in. Not only had he claimed (on December 9) that he was not "endeavoring to influence the attitudes of House or Senate members," but his whole strategy for party revival was based also on passing legislation.[44] He could not now hold out for more limited legislation, if that increased the likelihood of an impasse, with no legislation on the subject being enacted. It was an issue on which all kinds of considerations would affect the votes of legislators, and thus the outcome was always going to be one of political bargaining.

This was bargaining that was being undertaken in a very brief period – the special session was a short one, and in the event the legislation was completed by February 14. Among the difficult matters to be addressed was the cost of state-supervised primary elections (with counties objecting to having to bear the costs themselves), and later the question of when the bill was to take effect (with Penrose's supporters demanding that it not be put into effect immediately, since Penrose had already secured, under the existing arrangements, many of the Philadelphia delegates to the 1906 State Convention).[45] Reports of conflicts in the committee handling the legislation emerged frequently, and as the *Pittsburgh Gazette* noted on February 10, "there are a number of members who do not desire any bill and the others are divided on the kind they want."[46] Perhaps the most important point to note, though, is that what emerged was not the minimalist bill favored by Pennypacker. The bill that passed was Senator White's, although it did not include statewide offices under the direct nomination; it passed the lower house with ease (157–22) in spite of all the difficulties that chamber had experienced in obtaining agreement.

That it was not a minimalist bill might be taken as evidence of the power of antiparty reformers. Nothing could be further from the truth: The legislation was enacted by partisan legislators elected in the prescandal year of 1904 and who had been called back into session by a governor who wanted to protect the interests of his and (for the overwhelming majority) their party. Had direct nominations really been a matter that was of key importance to them, those concerned to protect party interests could have followed the governor's lead and passed a much more restricted law, perhaps on the lines that New York had enacted in the 1890s. Like the governor,

[43] *Pittsburgh Gazette*, January 22, 1906.   [44] *Philadelphia Inquirer*, December 10, 1905.
[45] *Philadelphia Inquirer*, January 26, and February 14, 1906.
[46] *Pittsburgh Gazette*, February 10, 1906.

the Republican-dominated legislature needed to pass legislation to restore public confidence in the party. Party nominations were an area in which there was public disquiet, and some form of public control of elections would have to be enacted. However, they were not under pressure to concede vital party interests in doing so, and had direct nominations been seen as contrary to the interests of the party it is inconceivable that they would have been traded away. Other legislation had been passed by the special session to restore electoral popularity, some legislation on primaries could be passed anyway, and legislators could always have hidden "behind the Governor's skirts," if they had wanted minimal change to the nomination process. The fact is that moving from a predominantly caucus-convention system for offices other than statewide offices to a system of direct nomination was not a matter that party politicians in Pennsylvania saw as a means by which the parties would be destroyed. There was scarcely any public debate on that matter.

If antiparty reformers did not form one side of a confrontation over direct nominations, as the conventional wisdom about primary reform claimed they did, then what of the supposed other side of the conflict – the urban party machines? As the state Republican party leader, in a state in which party power was more concentrated on the state level than it was in many states, Boies Penrose was in a position to exert leverage over the outcome. Given that much of his political power base was in Philadelphia, he would have been expected to be in a position to swing opposition against the direct primary. However, his main concern was to prevent any threat to his own nomination for the U.S. Senate that year, and his supporters in the state legislature fought successfully to prevent the Act coming into effect until November 1906.[47] There is no evidence that a move toward direct primaries was seen as a serious threat to their overall operations by the major urban party organizations in Pennsylvania.

Pennsylvania appears to be a curious case, therefore. Antiparty reformers seem to have got the result they would have wanted, but the role they played in securing it was small – beyond helping to convince Governor Pennypacker that uniform primary legislation should be considered by the legislature. (It is an example of Brian Barry's point that, "[W]ith enough luck you can get everything you want without any power."[48]) Since there were individuals in the party – like U.S. Representative Palmer – who were trying to do the same thing, the origins of the Pennsylvania legislation cannot be said to lie in antipartisanship. The moves that led to direct primary legislation were started by a party politician trying to protect his party, and who thought he was promoting much more limited legislation

[47] *Philadelphia Inquirer*, February 12, 1906; the vote in the Assembly was 121–54 to defer the introduction of the Act until November.
[48] Brian Barry, "Is it Better to Be Powerful or Lucky?," *Political Studies*, 28(1980), p. 184.

than was enacted. The legislature that enacted it had not been elected on a wave of reform but had come into office over a year earlier when major reform was not on the political agenda. The resulting legislation was a compromise between various kinds of party interests and the interests of individual politicians.

Furthermore, Pennypacker's overall strategy of moderate reform as a way of restoring trust in the Republicans worked. After Berry, no Democrat was elected to statewide office until 1931, and the City Party had collapsed by 1907. Republican dominance was restored. The party organization was little affected by the Uniform Primary Act; as McCaffery notes of its effect in Philadelphia, the Act "which in theory made selection of party candidates for public office fairer and more competitive, did not in practice affect the ability of the city boss to control Republican party nominations."[49] Furthermore, in the suburban counties surrounding Philadelphia, arguably the effect of the introduction of the direct primary was to have "increased the advantages of countywide organization and the incentives for maintaining it."[50] In other words, the direct primary may have facilitated the development of formal party organizations and systems of party funding in these counties, and hence increased party power. After the direct primary, the Republicans were to continue their domination of Pennsylvania politics until the New Deal.

3. Missouri

The conventional account of the direct primary in Missouri makes it appear as though it conforms to the standard Progressive version of the origins of direct nominations; in Missouri's case it was the reform Democrat Joseph Folk who supposedly directed the attack on "machines." Thus, Thelen writes:

The central mechanism to give "ordinary citizens" power over "professional politicians," Folk believed, was the direct primary for nominating candidates. Removing the nominating caucuses and conventions at which power broker brokers had used patronage and money to deflect voters, the 1907 gave a popular majority the direct power to nominate candidates for state office.[51]

---

[49] McCaffery, *When Bosses Ruled Philadelphia*, p. 182.

[50] Charles E. Gilbert, *Governing the Suburbs*, Bloomington and London, Indiana University Press, 1967, p. 67. Gilbert's detailed study of politics in three suburban Philadelphia counties is interesting and worth considering, but it is clear that his argument is based on long-term developments, rather than on a detailed knowledge of the decade immediately following the introduction of the direct primary. This is evident from his belief that Pennsylvania did not introduce the direct primary at the county level until 1913, and he seems to have been unaware of the 1906 legislation.

[51] David Thelen, *Paths of Resistance: Tradition and Dignity in Industrializing Missouri*, New York, Oxford University Press, 1986, p. 248.

On closer inspection, though, Missouri comes no nearer to the accepted wisdom that primaries were a new device imposed by reformers on urban bosses, and in the face of entrenched opposition by the latter, than either Massachusetts or Pennsylvania.

The first point to note about Missouri is that direct nominations had long been used for some offices in some counties; for example, the Republican party in St. Louis county had made direct nominations for the St. Louis House of Delegates since the late 1870s.[52] As in Pennsylvania, the direct primary was not a wholly alien institution that made politicians wary about its implementation; in this respect, therefore, Missouri was very different from Massachusetts where caution pervaded discussion of direct nominations at nearly every stage. Nevertheless, Missouri was unlike Pennsylvania, in that there had not been a wide variety of nominating mechanisms in use in different counties, so that public discussion was not couched, as it was in Pennsylvania, in terms of the legislation providing simply for uniformity of nominating procedures. While press coverage of the 1906 Pennsylvania legislation emphasized the matter of uniformity, in Missouri at the same time the press coverage that there was did focus on the fact that it was direct nominations that would now be used throughout the state.

Second, Missouri had already made direct primaries optional for cities with populations greater than three hundred thousand.[53] This is highly significant. The 1901 legislation predated the "reform" administration of Joseph Folk by nearly four years, and, indeed, it was enacted the year before Folk began his much publicized prosecution of St. Louis Democratic boss, Edward Butler; that is, it occurred at a time when, supposedly, Missouri was still run by representatives from "regular" party organizations. Given this, the principle of a direct primary would appear to have been remarkably unthreatening for such politicians. It suggests that, as in many other states, the direct primary was not a "stick" used by reformers to beat party organizations. (Presently we see that this could not have been the case in Missouri because of the peculiar strength of partisanship there.) In fact, the attitude of "regular" politicians to direct nominations reflected how their particular interests were affected – and those interests could vary. Thus, in 1900 the leaders of the two main Democratic organizations in Kansas City – Jim Pendergast and Joseph Shannon – differed as to whether the mayoral candidate should be nominated in a "ballot primary" or at the city convention. Pendergast favored the former because he could count on getting out the vote in the wards in which he was powerful; he prevailed, and duly got his candidate nominated at the primary election.[54]

---

[52] *St. Louis Post-Dispatch*, January 11, 1907.

[53] Charles E. Merriam and Louise Overacker, *Primary Elections*, Chicago, University of Chicago Press, 1928, p. 63.

[54] Lyle W. Dorsett, *The Pendergast Machine*, New York, Oxford University Press, 1968, p. 28.

Third, there was little public debate about the 1907 legislation, and that legislation generated little controversy. From the introduction of bills by Senators Fields and Avery in early January until the passage of the bill in mid-March, there was limited newspaper coverage of the legislation, and the coverage that there was tended to emphasize its relatively uncontroversial nature.[55] Some major daily papers, including the *St Louis Post-Dispatch* gave the topic hardly any coverage at all during the two and a half months between Governor Folk's biennial message and mid-March. Typical of the press coverage was an editorial in the *Kansas City Star*, when the Fields bill was first passed by the Senate:

With very little "fuss and feathers" the State Senate of Missouri has passed an admirable election law applicable to all elective offices of the state and its various subdivisions. Only school and municipal elections not held at the same time with a general election are exempted from its provisions.[56]

This is not to say, though, that the measure was without opponents. However, it was not an especially high priority issue for those opponents, and the opposition that there was tended to follow party lines. In the House the bill "was passed by a strict party vote, with the exception of the five Republicans who voted for the bill."[57] The significance of this partisan dimension to the legislation is discussed shortly.

Fourth, the experience of the direct primary in getting an "easy ride" through the legislature was not replicated by other legislative proposals that year, so that there was no question of primary reform having a fast passage through the state assembly on the crest of a "reform wave." On a number of matters, the legislature was not enacting Folk's reform agenda; at the conclusion of the legislative session on March 16, he called a special session of the General Assembly, for April 2, to consider legislation that had not been enacted. Among the more controversial measures that had not been adopted in the regular session of the Assembly was a bill to provide for direct primary elections for U.S. Senators, the Simmons bill. This bill's failure was the result of its likely impact on the career ambitions of particular politicians. Thus, as in Pennsylvania, it was the effect of particular provisions of a reform bill on senior politicians that tended to generate disagreement, rather than matters of general principle.

Fifth, like any U.S. governor, Folk was not in a position to dictate to the legislature that specific legislation be enacted. Indeed, by the time the direct primary legislation was introduced in 1907, more than two years had elapsed since his election, so that there could be no question of a legislature complying with his wishes because of his recently displayed electoral popularity. The *Globe-Democrat* made this clear at the very beginning of the legislative session:

[55] *St. Louis Globe-Democrat*, January 9, 1907. [56] *Kansas City Star*, February 28, 1907.
[57] *Kansas City Star*, March 7, 1907.

The senate will organize itself independently of administration influences, and, though this does not necessarily mean that the senate will be unfriendly to the governor, it does mean that it will resent anything that presents the appearance of dictation on his part.[58]

As the session proceeded, Folk was to lose a number of important disputes with the House, which originally had been the chamber more inclined to follow his lead. In particular, on the Simmons bill all the House Democrats voted against the timing for the primary favored by Folk, one that would have advanced his own cause against incumbent Senator Stone in 1908. In other words, both House and Senate Democrats were willing to oppose Folk, and they did so. It is in this context that the easy passage through the legislature of the Fields bill must be understood. It was not a measure that split the Democratic party, nor one for which Folk had to mobilize against a significant element in his party, even though there were other bills on which he did face such opposition.

These five points seem to suggest that, while Folk's governorship might have been the catalyst for Missouri's adoption of the direct primary throughout the state, it was no more than a catalyst. So why did the state move toward direct nominations with such apparently limited opposition to it? That question has to be addressed because Missouri was a state in which organized parties were especially powerful; for example, it had been the only state to adopt the "shoestring" ballot (in 1897) after having adopted a "blanket" ballot – the "shoestring" ballot being the ballot form most favorable to party control of the electorate. Given party strength in Missouri, the conventional account of the origins of the direct primary seems inadequate in explaining why it should have been so uncontroversial. Why did "regular" Democrats from St Louis and Kansas City, in particular, not revolt successfully against Folk on this issue?

One important consideration is that Missouri combined highly partisan politics with the dominance of rural areas. Of the states containing the five largest cities in 1900, Missouri was easily the most rural; only 36 percent of its population lived in urban areas, the corresponding figures for the other states being 54 percent (Illinois), 86 percent (Massachusetts), 73 percent (New York), and 55 percent (Pennsylvania). If the conventional wisdom were correct in assuming that it was primarily urban politicians who would oppose the direct primary, then Missouri would be a state in which they might be expected to have least influence because they were so outnumbered in the state legislature by rural representatives.

Another factor, but one that requires rather more explanation involves issues considered in Chapter 4 – the difference between reform in the eastern and western halves of the country. Missouri can be considered as both an eastern and a western state – a curious hybrid in which reform movements

[58] *St Louis Globe-Democrat*, January 2, 1907.

more characteristic of the West went hand-in-glove with the deep partisanship characteristic of the east. Like Wisconsin and other western states, Missouri's economy was open to exploitation by economic monopolies, many based outside the state, and by the early twentieth century there was a major popular reaction against that. As in Wisconsin, political reform followed on from an attack on economic interests and on their ability to exert influence through the parties. Both Joseph Folk and his Republican successor Herbert Hadley made their political careers by using legal measures to tackle the economic-political nexus in the state – Folk as circuit attorney in St. Louis and Hadley as, first, a prosecutor in Kansas City and, later, as state attorney general. Thelen is correct in arguing that there was popular support for their assaults on the "interests," and the scope of their action against them was much more akin to La Follette's actions in Wisconsin than reform in the eastern seaboard states.[59]

Nevertheless, there was a particular intensity to party loyalties in Missouri that was rather different from that usually found in the west. Missouri was not only older than the western states, attaining its statehood by 1820, its location as a border state meant that conflicting Civil War loyalties sharpened political divisions. In Thelen's words, "Missourians voted for the political arm of the army in which their fathers had fought."[60] The consequences of this for the parties were enormous; party really mattered in Missouri because of the long and bitter conflict between opposed subcultures within the state. In the Progressive era, therefore, the parties could not be dismantled as they were in California, or much weakened, as they were in Wisconsin. Reform took place within the context of strong parties, and most politicians, with the possible exception of Folk himself, would not seek to weaken party as an intermediary between people and politics. (It is significant, perhaps, in this context, that Folk, for all his legislative achievements did not serve in major elected public office again.) As Hadley observed in 1912, "The only government that we know in this country is party government."[61]

That parties were so important in Missouri meant that political reform aimed at removing the power of economic interests could not possibly have succeeded if political elites believed that parties themselves were threatened. However, many Democrats were at one with Folk on the principle of using direct primaries because they saw no particular threat to party interests from the use of this mechanism. As noted earlier, some, like Pendergast, could see advantages to their own factions from having direct primaries. While a few state legislators from "regular" party organizations in St. Louis and Kansas City might have taken a different view, it was not an issue on

[59] Thelen, *Paths of Resistance.*   [60] Thelen, *Paths of Resistance*, p. 23.
[61] Thelen, *Paths of Resistance*, p. 24.

which they could win and they followed the party line in the final vote in the House.

There is a final significant aspect to the role of party in Missouri. Given that it was the Democrats who had the larger, and more problematic, urban organizations in the state – Butler's in St. Louis and the Pendergast and Shannon factions in Kansas City – it might be imagined that it would have been the Republicans who would have taken the lead in passing direct primary legislation. That is, the direct primary might have been seen by Republicans as a weapon that they could use for partisan ends. However, this was not the case. Direct primary legislation was not enacted in 1905, when the Republicans gained control of the House, despite the fact that Folk had included support for such legislation in his inaugural address.[62] Both the 1901 and the 1907 laws were enacted by Democratic majorities in the two legislative chambers. This was not an instance of a party being able to use an issue to divide its opponents.

4. Illinois

In none of the states examined so far – Massachusetts, Pennsylvania, and Missouri – was the introduction of the direct primary characterized by a fight between antiparty reformers on the one side and leaders of urban party machines on the other. The same point is also a striking feature of the experience in Illinois. There was conflict in Illinois, and that conflict prolonged the successful introduction of direct primary legislation, but the conflict was one between the courts and the politicians. Three successive acts of the state legislature were declared unconstitutional, mainly on technical grounds, so that the permanent introduction of the direct primary was delayed until 1909. While superficially, therefore, Illinois appears to more closely resemble Massachusetts, with respect to the time it took to enact statewide direct primaries, than it does Pennsylvania and Missouri, where relatively quick passage of extensive legislation was evident, the resemblance is illusory. In Massachusetts, a political style of enlightened conservatism meant that reform tended to proceed on a piecemeal basis; in Illinois politics had little to do with the delayed introduction of the direct primary.

A more interesting comparison concerns the pattern of legislation on party nominations before the introduction of the direct primary. Here it is Pennsylvania that is the outlier, with its direct primary being introduced without any prior legislation regulating party nominations – or, rather, none since the largely unrestrictive legislation of the early 1880s. Illinois fits the more common pattern. Early legislation in the late 1880s was followed by legislation in 1898 and 1899. The more important bill of 1898 placed the expense of conducting primary elections, at least for parties that gained 10

---

[62] *St. Louis Daily Globe-Democrat*, January 10, 1905.

percent of the vote at the previous general election, onto the public purse and applied general election laws to the primaries. First used in the Democratic primaries of March that year, they were pronounced a success by the reform journal *Outlook* which proclaimed them to be "eminently satisfactory."[63] As in many other states, Illinois did not leap straight into the adoption of the direct primary. Indeed, the 1905 and 1906 legislation found unconstitutional by the courts did not actually provide for direct nominations. It was not until 1908, following an Act that later was also held to be unconstitutional, that the direct primary was first used in the state.

However, by far the most revealing point of comparison to be made in relation to Illinois is the role played by individual politicians. In two of the states discussed so far one or two particular politicians appeared to play a crucial role. In Massachusetts, legislator Robert Luce kept the issue of direct primaries alive for many years, while Joseph Walker's self-interested maneuverings were important to the ultimate passage of a comprehensive bill on direct primaries. In Pennsylvania, Governor Samuel Pennypacker eventually became converted to the belief that the direct primary was a necessary component of a legislative package that could restore the credibility of his party following the electoral revolt against it in 1905. Only in Missouri was there no such key champion. In Illinois, the support of one politician, the Republican Governor Charles S. Deneen, was crucial to the adoption of the direct primary. Of the individuals discussed so far, Deneen was far more like Walker than he was the others, in that not only was he a politician at the heart of his party's traditional organization but his support for direct nominations was linked directly to his own political self-interest.

Charles Deneen was not just a loyalist to the Republican party organization, as was, say, Robert Luce, he was a staunch defender of party power in many of its traditional forms. During his 1904 campaign for the governorship he declared, "I am not a civil service reformer or civil service agitator. Not at all. I believe that positions ought to be held out as inducements for political work."[64] Moreover, he personally used power in the time-honored way, and was seen by political reformers in that light. For example, in 1910 the reform journal *World To-day* provided a long account of Deneen's role in the introduction of the direct primary, and noted in its conclusion, "Even before the passage of the present primary law, Governor Deneen was planning to thwart the will of the people and deprive them of the right to rule."[65] One of the instances it cited of Deneen's earlier behavior was his role in 1906 in depriving a leading candidate, Andrew Russell, of the Republican nomination:

[63] *Outlook*, March 26, 1898, p. 753.
[64] Cited in Thomas R. Pegram, *Partisans and Progressives: Private Interest and Public Policy in Illinois, 1870–1922*, Urbana and Chicago, University of Illinois Press, 1992, p. 169.
[65] *World To-day*, September 1910, p. 944.

It is a matter of well-known political history in Illinois that Governor Deneen, forseeing that Mr. Russell could not be nominated on the first ballot, called in his officeholders from all parts of the state on the day and evening before the convention, and through them forced into line a sufficient number of delegates to assure the nomination of his friend Smulski, who was practically without support in the convention on the first ballot outside of the Cook county delegation.

It is clear, therefore, that Deneen was in no sense antiparty, and that any understanding of why he became such a vehement supporter of the direct primary must confront that fact.

Three factors are important in explaining Deneen's behavior – the opportunity provided by the changed role of the governorship, the particular electoral coalition he had constructed before his first election in 1904, and the opportunities for securing his own reelection. Each of these factors will be examined briefly in turn.

Intense internal conflict within the Republican party enabled a governor in the early years of the twentieth century to build up a personal power base in the party. This point was been well demonstrated by Pegram, whom it is worth quoting at length:

The governor was a key figure in party organization and governmental authority in progressive-era Illinois. . . . Within the GOP, a bitter struggle between rival patronage networks . . . reflected the contest between the senior United States senator from Illinois and the governor for control of the state party. The turbulence of this conflict fragmented the Illinois Republican party into several competing factions divided by organizational jealousies and ambitions and by ideology. Within a shattered consensus, the office of governor became the most secure base of party power. The new politics of executive authority, expressed through a legislative program and a firm direction of policy toward the state institutions, allowed the governor to build a stronghold of personal supporters in the General Assembly and the state service that could withstand the assaults of factional party rivals.[66]

Deneen was the first governor to make use of the resources that his office could now command, and that helps to explain why he was able to drive through the General Assembly four successive bills on nomination reform. However, it cannot explain why he, a politician steeped in party organization, should have adopted primary reform as an issue in the first place. To explain this we must turn to the second factor.

Within Chicago Charles Deneen's power base was in the Scandinavian wards in the southwest of the city.[67] Having secured the support of William Lorimer, the most powerful Republican politician in Chicago in the 1890s, Deneen then broke with Lorimer in 1903 and launched a bid for the party's nomination for the governorship. Certain kinds of political reform were

---

[66] Pegram, *Partisans and Progressives*, p. 166.
[67] Joel Arthur Tarr, *A Study in Boss Politics: William Lorimer of Chicago*, Urbana, University of Illinois Press, 1971, p. 126.

advocated vigorously by Deneen, and the reason for that lay in the cultural values of the particular groups he was in a prime position to mobilize against Lorimer. In the words of Joel Arthur Tarr, Lorimer's biographer, Deneen's Scandinavian political base drew him toward a rather different policy agenda than Lorimer's:

The pietistic religious orientation of Swedes made them prohibitionists and supporters of reform-oriented government. Lorimer, on the other hand, represented an area inhabited largely by Catholic and Russian Jewish immigrants. These groups regarded government with an occupational and entrepreneurial attitude, and their ritualistic religious orientation caused them to reject an activist reform government. The differences that existed between Lorimer and Deneen stemmed not only from a conflict of power but also from different cultural values in their constituents, a formula that explains many of the political conflicts of the progressive era.[68]

Reforming the nominating system was good politics for someone in Deneen's situation – that is, for a Cook County (Chicago) state's attorney who was ambitious for higher office.

However, by itself, that cannot explain why it was the *direct* primary to which Deneen turned. In fact, Deneen had been an opponent of the direct primary. In 1898, Roy O. West, who was Deneen's main adviser for many years, gave an address to the National Conference on Practical Reform of Primary Elections in which he defended the caucus-convention system.[69] Moreover, as noted earlier, the first two bills (1905 and 1906) passed by the Illinois legislature, and then invalidated by the state's Supreme Court, did not provide for the direct primary. However, by 1907 Deneen had two powerful reasons for changing tack. One reason was that he had committed himself to nomination reform, and had been unable to deliver on that; the compromises he had to make with regular Republicans had helped to make the laws unconstitutional, and he was in danger of losing credibility among his supporters. Moreover, Deneen now had a personal stake in the direct primary; he "believed that without a direct primary his opponents would block his renomination in the convention."[70] Almost certainly, he was right in this belief that the direct primary strengthened the position of incumbents in high profile offices. As one of Deneen's rivals observed in 1912, "Under this primary law it is practically impossible to defeat the Governor in office for nomination if he uses his office to renominate himself," and Deneen was to become the first two-term governor in a generation.[71] Once governor, therefore, the pursuit of his own political career provided a strong incentive to push for direct nominations. There was some danger in doing this, however. In abandoning a policy of compromise with some

[68] Tarr, *A Study in Boss Politics*, p. 127.
[69] *National Conference on Practical Reform of Primary Elections*, pp. 96–8.
[70] Tarr, *A Study in Boss Politics*, p. 186.
[71] Cited in Pegram, *Partisans and Progressives*, p. 170; see also p. 167.

of his fellow Republicans he ran the risk of failing in the pursuit of a more extensive reform. Building legislative coalitions across party lines in support of the so-called Oglesby bill of 1907 resolved that problem.

Deneen's problems with the state Supreme Court were not yet over, of course; the 1907 bill also would be found unconstitutional. But the bill had served Deneen's purpose: the direct primary was used for his renomination in 1908, and after it was invalidated he pressed for a further (direct primary) bill in 1909 that, finally, did not find disfavor in the courts. Nevertheless, there is a further point to consider about the courts: were they, as political appointees, upholding the interests of those elements of the party organization that opposed Deneen? The answer to this question is – no. The arguments used by the Court were precisely those that would appeal to antiparty reformers, rather than party regulars. For example, in striking down the 1906 law, the Court held that a primary was an "election" within the meaning of the state constitution. Moreover, the Court denied that parties could have the right to restrict the number of candidates nominated to contest seats under the cumulative voting system used for the state legislature. One of the features of that electoral system is that it is very much in the interests of a party to calculate the optimum number of candidates to nominate in each district. For the Court to deny that power to the parties was a most radical stance contrary to the interests of parties. In taking it, the Court was adopting a position that no defenders of parties would have supported, so that there can be no suspicion that the Court was acting in the interests of Lorimer and other opponents of Deneen.[72]

The argument outlined in this section has been that in Illinois conflict over the direct primary did not pitch reformers outside the parties against urban political bosses; to the contrary, the conflict was mainly within the Republican party, and centered on politicians whose electoral bases lay in different ethnic groups within Chicago. To use the pejorative language of antiparty reformers, the main protagonists were very much urban-based "bosses" whose interests were affected in very different ways by the possible introduction of direct nominations.

5. New York

It is only when the discussion turns to New York that it is possible to find the kind of conflict over the adoption of the direct primary that bears any resemblance to the account that is often presented. However, even in New York, the conflict does not quite conform to the standard version. More significantly, perhaps, it can be shown why New York is atypical rather

---

[72] Leon E. Aylsworth, "Notes on Current Legislation: Primary Elections – Illinois," *American Political Science Review*, 6(1912), 569–71.

than being an example from which to generalize about nomination reform in the eastern industrial states, let alone the country as a whole.

There were three main stages to nomination reform in New York, the first two of which were highly conflictual while the third was not. The first stage occurred in the governorship of Charles Evans Hughes. There were clear parallels between the Republicans' selection of Hughes in 1906 as their gubernatorial candidate and the legislative response to the election results of 1906 made by Governor Pennypacker in Pennsylvania. Both were reactions to scandal: as McCormick says of New York, "In the aftermath of scandal came 'reform'."[73] In the Empire State the scandal had been one involving life insurance, and Hughes had been the person chosen in 1905 to head an official investigation into it. By later selecting him as the gubernatorial candidate, the New York Republicans were deploying the established strategy of choosing a "blue chip" candidate to lend the party credibility. However, it was not until 1908 that Hughes took up the matter of direct nominations in earnest, and from then on it was to be one of the most high profile causes with which he was associated.[74]

In 1909, he backed the unsuccessful Green-Hinman bill, which required the use of direct primaries in the state. This measure failed again in 1910, though by smaller majorities in the state legislature. Hughes even called a special session of the state assembly later that year to get a compromise proposal considered, but that too failed. Much of the "standard account" of primary reform is apparent in New York in the Hughes era. Hughes was a "good government" reformer and his legislative proposals were backed by the various reform journals based in New York City. Crucially, opposition in the state assembly to the bills came from "regulars" in his own party; without their backing he could not hope to prevail, and he did not.

Whereas Hughes had been associated with institutional reform before he came to office, this was not true of the governor under whom the matter next arose, the Democrat William Sulzer. It was known early in 1913 that he favored direct primaries, but the radical nature of the measures he supported was not known until later that spring.[75] Whereas Hughes's commitment to reform was genuine, in Sulzer's case it was more political ambition that seemed to drive his conversion to reform. In this regard, Sulzer bears some resemblance to Charles Deneen in Illinois – another politician who tried to use the direct primary as a means of consolidating his position in his own party. As Wesser observes:

---

[73] Richard L. McCormick, *From Realignment to Reform: Political Change in New York State, 1893–1910*, Ithaca and London, Cornell University Press, 1981, p. 256.

[74] McCormick, *From Realignment to Reform*, pp. 243–7.

[75] Robert F. Wesser, *A Response to Progressivism: The Democratic Party and New York Politics, 1902–1918*, New York and London, New York University Press, 1986, p. 113.

Not all reform Democrats supported the statewide primary, and they ably rehearsed the arguments against the Sulzer bill. But of greater significance than the debate itself were what many concluded to be the realities behind it. Few doubted that the governor harbored clear-cut political objectives. "He hopes that by using [the primary] he will be able to gain control of the Democratic Party in the State of New York," claimed one reformer unabashedly.[76]

Sulzer's bid for power was unsuccessful, though. Like Hughes, he failed to enact his primary bill because he could not carry his own party with him. But Sulzer's failure to convince Tammany Hall and other regular Democratic organizations to back the bill was part of a far more general estrangement from his party. His attitude toward his political opponents produced bitterness within his own party, and led to investigations of his use of political money, investigations that culminated in his impeachment later that year. Consequently, while this second stage of nomination reform in New York was highly conflictual, it was not straightforwardly a fight between reformers and bosses, as at least, to some extent, it had been under Hughes.

The third stage of the process followed Sulzer's removal from office by impeachment. His Democratic successor, Martin Glynn, called a special session of the state assembly in late 1913, requesting a number of reforms to be enacted. One was the direct primary. This time Tammany Hall did not oppose their own governor, and the direct primary bill passed with little opposition from either party. Tammany's position had been undermined by the election of "Fusion" reformer John Purroy Mitchel, to the mayoralty of New York City in November.[77] Like all political bosses, Tammany's Charles Murphy could read the election returns, and he knew when he was in a weak position to sustain opposition to a measure he would otherwise oppose. Consequently, in the end, the direct primary came to New York more with a whimper than a bang.

Overall, the standard account of the rise of the direct primary fits the experience under Hughes fairly well. The fit with the Sulzer experience is less clear-cut. Not all reformers backed his measure, and within his party opposition to him and his proposal extended well beyond regular Democrats. Nevertheless, even in relation to Hughes there are two further points to be made that suggest that the New York experience does not quite accord with the standard account of primary reform. First, the bill supported by Hughes was intended to be a compromise that regular organizations would find acceptable. It incorporated a device that came to be known as the "Hughes Plan," a modified version of which would later be used by a few states, including Colorado.[78] Under the plan, the official party

---

[76] Wesser, *A Response to Progressivism*, p. 114.

[77] Wesser, *A Response to Progressivism*, p. 140.

[78] R. John Eyre and Curtis Martin, *The Colorado Preprimary System*, Boulder, Bureau of Governmental Research and Service, 1967, pp. 5–7.

committees could designate a candidate as the official candidate, and that candidate would then be given first place on the primary ballot. Hughes's support for this measure, which would have retained considerable party power in the nomination process, was designed not just for strategic purposes. Indeed, as strategy, it was singularly unsuccessful, since it failed to bring the support of party regulars while at the same time diluting the enthusiasm of some reformers. Rather, as McCormick suggests, there is evidence that Hughes himself favored strong parties, and that he saw the "Hughes Plan" as strengthening them.[79] Consequently, the standard depiction of the direct primary as a fight between antiparty elements on one side and party regulars on the other does not quite capture even the Hughes years.

The second point is that the standard view sees the reformers triumphing over the party regulars. However, in the case of Hughes it was the regulars who prevailed. In New York, it was not a head-on clash between reformers and bosses that brought about the direct primary but a rather complicated set of political circumstances following the unusual event of the impeachment of a state governor. Nevertheless, despite these qualifications, the high-profile nature of the conflict under Hughes was clearly different from that evident in the four other states; that raises an obvious question – why was New York different? Why was there more of a battle between reformers and bosses there than elsewhere? Before answering the question, it is useful to remember two aspects of earlier political reform in the state – features that seem to point in opposing directions.

One feature concerns New York's introduction of the Australian Ballot. As was seen in Chapter 2, under Governor David Hill this issue provoked a high profile political dispute of a kind that was unusual in other states. For example, early on the equally competitive state of Indiana had devised a form of official ballot that protected party interests and that came to be copied elsewhere. That is, conflict appears to be more central to institutional reform in New York than in many other states. That conflict was exacerbated by the fact that New York's reformers were much less integrated into major political parties than they were, say, in Massachusetts. However, counteracting this impression, that reform might be difficult to achieve in the Empire State, is the fact that the state regularly passed detailed legislation relating to the nomination of party candidates. In fact, between the late 1880s and 1912, it was far more active than most other states in this regard. Using the data about state legislation on nominations collected by Merriam and Overacker, it is evident that the only years in which there was no such legislation in New York were 1891 and 1894.[80] Only Massachusetts had a (slightly) more productive record, and most

---

[79] McCormick, *From Realignment to Reform*, pp. 244–5.
[80] Merriam and Overacker, *Primary Elections*, Appendix D.

states did not come close to matching theirs. Initially, this suggests a paradox – despite the fact that political reform could generate long and divisive political battles in New York, much legislation on the subject could still be enacted. This apparent paradox is useful when approaching the issue of why New York appears to be atypical in its introduction of the direct primary.

The crucial difference between New York City and other major American cities was that New York State's largest city contained a much greater proportion of its state's population than did any other large American cities (except Baltimore). This meant that the city-based machines in New York State could exercise considerably greater leverage in state politics. The relatively small size of cities then – in relation to overall state populations – is well illustrated by looking at the seven largest cities in the United States in 1900. In descending order they were New York, Chicago, Philadelphia, St. Louis, Boston, Baltimore, and Cleveland. With two exceptions, the cities on this list ranged from Cleveland, which contained less than one-eighth of the population of Ohio, to Chicago, which contained about 35 percent of the population of Illinois. One exception was Baltimore, which had grown rapidly, and which by 1900 contained 43 percent of the population of Maryland. However, Baltimore lacked the influence in Maryland that this should have brought it: The state was notoriously malapportioned in the early twentieth century – Baltimore had only four of the twenty-seven members of the state senate and twenty-four of the 101 member of the lower chamber.[81] Consequently, like relatively smaller cities (in relation to overall state population), Baltimore could only be a "light puncher" in the state legislature. New York, though, was very different – there the urban bosses could play a much more important role in the state legislature.[82] By 1900, 47 percent of New Yorkers were living in New York City, and with a powerful regular Republican organization in the city, as well as Tammany Hall and the Brooklyn Democratic organization, the "urban machines" could play a very different role from the ones their counterparts in other states could play.

[81] Leon E. Aylsworth, "Notes on Current Legislation," *American Political Science Review*, 2(1908), p. 582.

[82] Interestingly, in 1894 Republicans in the state legislature did succeed in introducing rules for future legislative reapportionment into the state constitution that would reduce the power of New York City once it contained a majority of the state's population. Each of the sixty-two counties in the state was guaranteed at least one member of the lower chamber, and membership of that chamber was fixed at 150. In the case of the Senate, no two counties that were divided by a river could have between them more than one half of that chamber's membership; this rule was designed specifically to limit the joint representation of Manhattan and Brooklyn. Although New York City was to become underrepresented in the legislature, it was still a much more significant force in the state than were other major cities in their states. See Warren Moscow, *Politics in the Empire State*, New York, Alfred A. Knopf, 1948, pp. 166–7.

Size gave urban party organizations a power at the state level to block reforms of which they were suspicious. That was why David Hill faced major difficulties over the introduction of the Australian Ballot. However, this power was not an absolute veto for party bosses, nor anything like that. It was a power that depended on the context in which a legislative proposal was introduced, as well as on how threatened the organizations' interests appeared to be, and, to some extent, on how intraparty rivalries among regular organizations could be overcome. These factors are relevant in explaining why so much party reform legislation was passed in New York; that legislation included, for example, the Ferris-Blauvelt bill of 1911 – a compromise measure supported by the Democratic majority that provided for the direct primary for "all nominations except for members of the state ticket."[83] Moderate reform was always possible in New York, providing the matter did not become a high profile one. When that happened the reform might produce a division on partisan lines – as happened over the Australian Ballot. Alternately, it might lead to factional fissures within a party that those who opposed the reform might exploit for their own ends.

Hughes misjudged the situation between 1908 and 1910 in two respects. By pushing for a major reform "in one leap," he turned the issue into one that Tammany Hall could deem to be of major significance, thereby making it likely that they would utilize their blocking power, but this was in circumstances in which Tammany had no particular reason for believing they would incur major costs for such opposition. Tammany-nominated candidates had won every mayoral election in New York City since 1903, and electorally they had outmaneuvered the main threat to their control of the city, William Randolph Hearst. The pressure to desist from opposition, that the Mitchel victory was to bring in late 1913, was absent in these earlier years. Moreover, Hughes also miscalculated in believing that the "Hughes Plan" would bring in the regular party organizations as supporters of reform. The plan was precisely the kind of compromise that might have worked had it been proposed during a stalemate over a much more radical primary reform. In that respect, it might be thought of as analogous to the "shoestring" ballot, which resulted from the conflict over the official ballot two decades earlier. However, by introducing it earlier, Hughes made it possible for the regular organizations to find official reasons for opposing it, and Hughes lost a bargaining device as well as the enthusiasm of the more antiparty elements among the reformers.

Sulzer's frontal assault on the nomination process also failed because it was conducted in circumstances in which there were no particular reasons why Tammany should not exercise its muscle. Indeed, that Sulzer's move toward direct nominations was widely interpreted as a bid for control of the Democratic party statewide gave it every reason for opposing him.

---

[83] Wesser, *A Response to Progressivism*, p. 113.

There is no doubt that, generally, the regular party organizations in New York did not want direct nominations for those elected offices that mattered to them. That part of the standard account of nomination reform is correct. It was far from being their main priority, though; Tammany could, and did, survive the advent of the direct primary, so that it was never going to make "a last stand" on the issue. It would oppose direct nominations when the cost of doing so was not that high. However, opposition to reform was not always feasible. For example, Tammany Hall wanted to avoid creating, or perpetuating, conditions in which all its potential enemies were allied against it. Hence its capitulation at the end of 1913. Furthermore, as in any area of politics, priorities mattered. To the extent that nomination reform was lower down the organizations' priority ordering among the current issues before the state legislature, the more likely it would be an issue on which they would compromise. Consequently, even in New York, where the city organizations were more powerful at the state level than elsewhere, nomination reform was far from being an impossibility.

Consequently, the standard account of nomination reform is not just wrong, it propounds a view that is utterly implausible. Even if all the major cities had been of a (relative) size in their states so that they would have had the bargaining power that the regular organizations had in New York, the overall result would not likely have been different from what actually happened. It was *high-profile conflict* between antiparty reformers, on the one side, and party regulars, on the other, that could doom nomination reform to failure. It was the one circumstance in which reform was difficult to achieve because it made it more likely that party organizations would utilize their blocking power. Hughes failed and Sulzer failed, and others would surely have failed in those sorts of conditions.

6. Concluding Remarks

There are three important points to be made about the links between antiparty reformers, regular party organizations, and the adoption of the direct primary. These are: (1) most reformers who wished to weaken parties did see the direct primary as an important weapon in the fight for their objectives; (2) many regular urban organization leaders, though not all, would have opposed the introduction of the direct primary had the choice been theirs; and (3) it was long-term problems associated with candidate selection in the cities that had produced a mass of legislation on the subject since the late 1880s. However, these points cannot substantiate the conclusion that the introduction of the direct primary was the result of a conflict between such reformers and urban bosses, any more than saying that the fact that Australia and Italy were on opposite sides in World War II means that the war is to be explained as a conflict between these two protagonists. Of course, any account of the war is inadequate without a discussion of their role, but to place them at the center of an analysis would be misleading. So it is with the antiparty reformers and the urban bosses. Certainly, they existed and they did take part in the processes that led to the adoption of the direct primary, but their role was often not the central one it is sometimes supposed to be.

One of the reasons they could not play the role usually attributed to them is that, with the exception of New York, they were operating in political arenas in which they were outnumbered. The largest cities formed between only about one-quarter to one-third of the populations of a state. The machines' power base was in the cities themselves but it was not the cities that could legislate on the nomination process. Similarly, it was in the largest cities that the main concentrations of antiparty reformers were to be found. The majority of the legislators who voted on direct primary bills were not from these cities; they had grown up in a political world that was party-dominated, but not boss-dominated, and yet in most states these legislators chose to introduce the direct primary. The important question is "why," and aspects of that question are examined further in the next two chapters.

6

The Impact of Party Competition

It is widely acknowledged that political competition in a regime can affect which issues come to the forefront of the political agenda and how those issues are then resolved. For example, as was seen in Chapter 5, the threat of an increased Democratic challenge in Pennsylvania at the end of 1905 prompted the Republican governor to sponsor a number of legislative proposals at a special session of the state legislature, including, eventually, the direct primary. It would not be surprising, then, if political scientists had sought to link the rise of direct nominations to some aspects of electoral competition. However, what is remarkable is that far from arguing that competition (or the threat of it) facilitated the introduction of the direct primary – as in Massachusetts or Pennsylvania – some of them have sought to argue the opposite. That is, they argue that it was the absence of political competition that had this effect. Thus, V. O. Key claimed:

The spread of the direct primary is commonly attributed to its appeal as an instrument of popular rule, yet the probability is that the nature of the party structure in the areas of its origin stimulated its growth. In many states in the 1890s the party system had broken down in the sense that a single party dominated many states and localities.[1]

It is clear from the context that Key is referring not just to the South but also to Wisconsin and its surrounding states. Another expert on America's political parties to make a similar point was Frank J. Sorauf, and he made the argument an even more general one. He claimed:

The quick success of the direct primary movement happened during the years of the greatest one-partyism in American history. In the early years of the twentieth century sectionalism was rampant, and one party or another dominated the politics of many states. One-partyism made the nomination of the major party crucial. Although the

[1] V. O. Key, Jr. *Politics, Parties and Pressure Groups*, Fourth Edition, New York, Thomas Y. Crowell, 1958, p. 412.

failings of the conventions might be tolerated when a real choice remained in the general election, they could not be borne when the nomination of the dominant party was equivalent to election ... so the Progressives who fought economic monopoly with antitrust legislation, fought political monopoly with the direct primary.[2]

Superficially these sorts of arguments might seem quite plausible, but was there really this connection between alleged one-partyism and the switch to direct nominations? To answer the question requires an extended discussion on a subject that is frequently misrepresented in the political science literature, the nature of party competition both before and after the 1890s.

1. Competition in the United States before the Mid-1890s

In most accounts that emphasize the uncompetitiveness of party politics in the early twentieth century, a contrast is drawn with the period that ended in the early-mid-1890s. In Burnham's words those years saw the "destruction of party competition": a system in which "vigorous party competition extended from individual localities to the nation itself" was replaced by a polity that Schattschneider had earlier named "the system of 1896."[3] One important question is just how "vigorous" this competition was, and what form it took. If the level of competition was somewhat lower before the mid-1890s than is usually suggested, it would indicate that the transition from the late-nineteenth-century party system to the early-twentieth-century system was less stark than it is often portrayed, and, in turn, that would weaken the claim that the alleged transformation to "political monopoly" had triggered the rise of the direct primary.

Certainly, competition was intense at the national level between the late 1830s and the early 1890s, with most presidential elections being decided by narrow margins of victory. In the last three presidential elections before 1896, the pluralities in the popular vote were 0.25 percent (1884), 0.8 percent (1888), and 3.09 percent (1892). This seemingly narrow margin of victory in 1892 actually provided the largest plurality for the Democrats since 1856; it indicates just how competitive the national political system was, and how relatively small pluralities, by the standards of later decades, marked major shifts in party support. However, that did not mean that all of the states were highly competitive, and, from one

[2] Frank J. Sorauf, *Party Politics in America*, Second Edition, Boston, Little Brown, 1972, p. 210.

[3] Walter Dean Burnham, "The Changing Shape of the American Political Universe," in Burnham (ed.), *The Current Crisis in American Politics*, New York and Oxford, Oxford University Press, 1982, p. 46 and pp. 46–7. E. E. Schattschneider, *The Semisovereign People*, New York, Holt, Rinehart and Winston, 1960, p. 81.

TABLE 6.1. *Competitiveness of States in 1884, 1888, and 1892 Presidential Elections*

DEMOCRATIC DOMINANT STATES [Democrat plurality over Republicans at least 10% in each election]	Alabama Arkansas Georgia Louisiana	Mississippi South Carolina Texas
DEMOCRATIC SAFE STATES [Democrat plurality over Republicans at least 4%, but in at least one election it fell below 10%]	Florida Kentucky Missouri North Carolina	Tennessee Virginia
DEMOCRATIC LEANING STATES [States won by Democrats in all three elections, but in at least one their plurality fell below 4%]	Connecticut Delaware Maryland New Jersey West Virginia	
MARGINAL STATES [States won by Democrats in at least one election, but not in all 3 elections]	California Illinois Indiana New York Wisconsin	
NON-DEMOCRATIC LEANING STATES [States not won by Democrats in any election, but in at least one election their share of the vote was less than 4% below Republican share]	New Hampshire Ohio	
NON-DEMOCRATIC SAFE STATES [States lost by Democrats in all three elections, but in at least one election their vote share was less than 10% below Republican share]	Iowa Massachusetts Michigan Minnesota	Nebraska Oregon Pennsylvania Rhode Island
NON-DEMOCRATIC DOMINANT STATES [States lost by Democrats in all three elections, and in which their vote share was always at least 10% less than the Republican share]	Colorado Kansas Maine Nevada Vermont	

perspective, at least, many were not. To illustrate this, Table 6.1 classifies each of the thirty-eight states according to how well the Democrats did in the presidential elections of 1884, 1888, and 1892. There were seven types of state.

1. Democratic Dominant (DD) states are ones in which the Democrats' plurality over the Republicans was at least 10 percent in each of the elections. There were seven such states – all in the South (Alabama, Arkansas, Georgia, Louisiana, Mississippi, South Carolina, and Texas). In the 1880s, they accounted for 17 percent of Electoral College votes in the 1880s.

2. Democratic Safe (DS) states gave the Democrats at least a 4 percent plurality in each election, but in one or more of the elections the party failed to exceed a 10 percent plurality. There are six states in this category – two border states (Kentucky and Missouri) and four on the outer rim of the South (Florida, North Carolina, Tennessee, and Virginia). In the 1880s, they, too, accounted for 17 percent of Electoral College votes.

3. Democratic Leaning (DL) states were won by the Democrats in all three presidential elections, but in at least one of them the plurality was less than 4 percent. There are five states in this category, three being border states (Delaware, Maryland, West Virginia) and two in the northeast (Connecticut and New Jersey). In the 1880s, they accounted for 7 percent of Electoral College votes.

4. Marginal states were won by the Democrats on at least one occasion but not on all three. The five states in this category included three in the midwest (Illinois, Indiana, and Wisconsin), one in the northeast (New York), and one in the west (California). Some of the most populous states were marginal, and they accounted for 23 percent of Electoral College votes.

5. Non-Democratic Leaning (NDL) states were not won by the Democrats at any of the three elections, but in at least one of the elections they were less than 4 percent of the vote behind the Republicans. There are only two states (New Hampshire and Ohio) in this group, and they accounted for 7 percent of Electoral College votes.

6. Non-Democratic Safe (NDS) seats were lost by the Democrats in all three elections; they were always at least 4 percent behind the Republicans, although in at least one election they were less than 10 percent behind. There were eight states in this category – four in the midwest (Iowa, Michigan, Minnesota, Nebraska), three in the northeast (Massachusetts, Pennsylvania, and Rhode Island), and one in the west (Oregon). They accounted for 22 percent of Electoral College votes.

7. Non-Democratic Dominant (NDD) states were always lost by the Democrats and in all elections they were at least 10 percent of the vote behind the Republicans. Of these five states, two were in the west (Colorado and Nevada), two in the northeast (Maine and Vermont), and one in the midwest (Kansas). They accounted for 7 percent of Electoral College votes.

Several points should become apparent from analyzing party competition in this way. The first is that few states were microcosms of the national polity: only 32 percent of states were in the Marginal, DL, or NDL categories. They included some of the largest states, so that they accounted for 37 percent of Electoral College votes, but the fact remains that less than a third of states could be said to be truly competitive in national elections. A plurality of 4 percent of the vote was a large margin nationally in the late nineteenth century – no party achieved it between 1872 and 1896 – and yet two-thirds of the states could produce that kind of margin regularly for one of the two major parties over its rival. A second point is that there was a quite distinct regional pattern to party competition. The DD and DS states were all in the south or the border region, and, apart from three border states that were DL, no states in these regions fell into any other category. Although some states in the northeast, midwest, and west were in the DL, Marginal, or NDL categories, most of the states in these other regions were in the NDS or NDD categories. While the regional patterns of party support were not quite as clear cut as they were to become after 1896, they were most certainly evident in the earlier period.

Two states, Indiana and New York, were both highly competitive and large, and for both major parties usually they formed the focal point of any presidential election campaign. Typically, the party that won these states won the election, though, in the "stolen election" of 1876, the Democrats had won both but lost the presidency. The other states fell in behind these two in descending order of competitiveness. The result was that, from a presidential perspective, nineteenth-century America resembles most other competitive political systems using territorially based units of election, in that much of the country was safe territory for one party or another. (For example, in every British general election from 1950 to 1979 no party's plurality was more than 6 percent of the vote but only about one-fifth of seats were, in any sense, marginal and there was a strong regional pattern of electoral support for the Conservative and Labour parties.)

However, in arguing that, perhaps, only about 13 percent of states were highly competitive, a further 19 percent competitive, and 68 percent were safe for one party in presidential elections, there is a serious danger of appearing to understate the extent of competition in the United States at that time. It was a polity characterized by a particular kind of party mobilization. Most voters were partisans and the key to electoral victory was for a party to mobilize its own supporters as effectively as possible; unlike the contemporary era, much less effort was put into persuading "undecided" or "independent" voters to vote because there were relatively few of them. When both parties could get their core supporters to the polls the election would be won by whichever party had the numerical advantage among adherents in that state. That is why there are so few states in the

Marginal category in Table 6.1, and why even in the large victory achieved by the Democrats in 1892, they carried only two states (California and Wisconsin) that they had not won in either of the two preceding elections. Nevertheless, especially in the period between presidential elections, party coalitions could break down, and when that happened congressional delegations and state governments could be controlled by the party that was really the "minority" party in national contests.

Party coalitions would break up temporarily for two main reasons. The party winning the presidency and state governorships in presidential election years rarely had enough patronage to satisfy all those party loyalists who felt they had some claim on the party. The resulting disillusionment invigorated the factionalism that was always at the center of state politics, and in turn that could affect adversely voter turnout in off-year and midterm elections. However, parties could also come under stress from particular issues that threatened to split their electoral base. On the Republican side, one of these main issues up to the 1890s was Prohibition. For example, Summers has provided a good account of how the Republican party in Ohio was split by proposed Prohibition legislation between the 1880 and 1884 elections; these splits made it possible for the Democrats to win the governorship and the state legislature in a state where the Republicans held a relatively narrow, but decisive, advantage when both parties were at full voting strength.[4] Even states that were normally safe for the Republicans occasionally came under threat; for example, the Democrats won the governorship of Pennsylvania in 1890. It was this pattern of the parties fragmenting and then cohering again every few years that was so distinctive of politics in America during that era, and that contributed to the impression of a polity that was highly competitive. In this process, "fusion" with smaller parties – a process discussed in Chapter 2, Section 8 – was an important weapon for parties; it was especially important for the Democrats in overcoming the electoral disadvantage they faced in most of the nonborder states outside of the South.

The competitiveness of the nineteenth-century party system did not emanate, therefore, from the major parties being of equal size in most states. In all save a handful of states they did not have the same underlying potential electoral support, and the advantage to the majority party was decisive providing it was not split; competition was then made possible largely by factors that encouraged such splits in the larger of the two parties. This view of competition in those decades contrasts markedly with the view normally presented by scholars who argue that the rise of the direct primary was linked to the demise of party competition after the mid-1890s.

---

[4] Mark Wahlgren Summers, *Rum, Romanism and Rebellion: The Making of a President 1884,* Chapel Hill, University of North Carolina, 2000, pp. 84–90.

Schattschneider, for example, had claimed that "[B]efore 1896 the major parties contested elections on remarkably equal terms throughout the country."[5]

2. Party Competition after the Mid-1890s

Misunderstanding the nature of nineteenth-century party competition, and thereby overemphasizing how competitive the system was constitutes part of the reason why changes in competition can be invoked to account for the rise of the direct primary. The other reason is that the nature of the change in competition after the mid-1890s also has been misinterpreted. According to Key, Schattschneider, Burnham, and a whole host of others, the United States entered a political "dark age" in which party competition was largely absent until the New Deal electoral realignment. To make this account plausible, the entire period from the 1890s to the early 1930s is treated by them as a single entity – in Schattschneider's phrase, "the system of 1896." However, this interpretation ignores two obvious problems. First, for the most part, outside the South, party competition had been restored by 1910, and it survived until the Democratic party coalition started to fall apart from 1916 onwards. Second, that later period of Republican dominance was much greater than it was in the period 1893–1910, and it is only by combining data for the two eras that the earlier years can be made to appear part of some longer term trend to regionally based one-party dominance. So what did happen to party competition after the mid-1890s?

In the South, longer-term political trends reached a critical point in the early-to-mid-1890s. As noted earlier, there is a strong case for treating the South as an entirely separate political system, one that was connected to the non-South through federalism but that operated in a very different way. Electoral turnout in the South was starting to decline by the early 1890s, before turnout decline was evident in the non-South; that decline was then accelerated enormously by the systematic disenfranchisement of black southerners, and also some poor whites, from the early 1890s onward.[6] Whereas there was a sharp rise in turnout (to record levels) outside the South in the elections of 1894 and 1896, in the South turnout in both 1894 and 1896 was significantly lower than it had been twelve years earlier. The South was a different country, one in which party competition after the Civil War depended on an artificial factor – the role of federal military forces in controlling southern whites; although Republicans remained

---

[5] Schattschneider, *The Semisovereign People*, p. 80.

[6] On southern disenfranchisement, or "disfranchisement" as it was called at the time, see Michael Perman, *Struggle for Mastery: Disfranchisement in the South 1888–1908*, Chapel Hill, N. C., and London, University of North Carolina Press, 2001.

fairly strong in a number of southern counties after 1876, and until the 1890s, at the state level Republican competitiveness ended shortly after Reconstruction.

In the 1890s southern politics changed in ways that made certain that there would no longer be any possibility of an electoral coalition between blacks and poor whites. Quite how this happened has become a matter of scholarly debate. The orthodox view, following Woodward, Key, and Kousser, sees the key actors as primarily richer whites, who were entrenched in the Democratic party and who wished to preserve their own power by making any challenge to the Democratic monopoly impossible. More recent scholarship suggests that, at least in some states – notably Alabama, Georgia, and Louisiana – the elimination of black political participation was a goal of white "outsiders" who had earlier tried to mobilize black political support. Finding that Bourbon power over the black population prevented this, they then changed their political strategy, and sought to defeat their opponents from within the Democratic party and by eliminating black people as actors in the political process.[7]

Whichever interpretation is correct, the result was the same. In the southern states, all of which had been either in the DD or SD categories, the remaining elements of the post-1876 Republican party disappeared as political institutions were reformed in ways that bolstered a Democratic monopoly. The direct primary was useful in this regard. To the extent that the primary was a device of a private organization, the Democratic party, it could be used to exclude those whose participation was not wanted from the political process. To some extent – as Key, Sorauf, and others have suggested – its introduction helped to legitimize politics in states where, for most offices, the general election was noncompetitive. In the South, therefore, the argument that the direct primary was the result of changes in political competition is, in some sense, quite plausible.

What of the non-South? A major part of the case for there being a "system of 1896" was the claim that there was a massive electoral realignment that year. However, more recent scholarship on electoral realignment indicates that there was not; in Nardulli's words, citing Chubb and Peterson, there were really "rather modest electoral shifts in 1896," or, as Bartels puts it, "the electoral pattern established in 1896 was much less

---

[7] On the orthodox view, see C. Vann Woodward, *The Strange Career of Jim Crow*, Third Edition, New York, Oxford University Press, 1974, V. O. Key Jr, *Southern Politics*, New York, Alfred A. Knopf, 1949, and J. Morgan Kousser, *The Shaping of Southern Politics: Suffrage Restrictions and the Establishment of the One-Party South, 1880–1910*, New Haven, Conn., Yale University Press, 1974. For alternative arguments, see Gerald H. Gaither, *Blacks and the Populist Revolt: Ballots and Bigotry in the "New South,"* University, Alabama, University of Alabama Press, 1977, especially pp. 109 and 115, and Russell Korobkin, "The Politics of Disenfranchisement in Georgia," *Georgia Historical Quarterly*, 74(1990), pp. 20–58.

durable than previous scholarship has suggested."[8] In many ways, the Democratic party recovered remarkably quickly from a defeat in which they lost a presidential election by the massive margin (for the late nineteenth century) of over 4 percent of the total vote. For example, in the midterm House elections of 1898, the Democrats' share of the total vote was 1 percent higher than that of the Republicans; the distribution of the votes meant that the latter still controlled the House, but, even so, it was scarcely the performance of a party reeling from a massive defeat. Indeed, the 1898 election was viewed by at least some journalists at the time as a "censure of the [McKinley] administration."[9]

However, it was not until 1910 that the old order was restored completely. The really significant point about 1910 is that the pattern of Democratic strength that year bears a strong resemblance to that evident in 1888. The states in which the Democrats were at least competitive in 1910 were generally those states where they had been similarly placed in 1888. In Tables 6.2 and 6.3, these two years are compared with respect to the relative performance of Democratic and Republican congressional candidates in the median district in each state;[10] in states where the performance of the Democratic candidate in the median district was such that he ran no more than 6 percent of the total vote behind the Republican, the state is regarded (for these purposes) as being competitive (Table 6.3). In 1888, there were fourteen competitive states (using this definition), eleven of which were still competitive in 1910. Leaving aside Delaware, which was undergoing a long-term shift of support toward the Republican party, these states could be said to form the key to Democratic success. In 1888, when the Democrats fell ten seats short of a congressional majority, these ten states provided 42.9 percent of all Democratic seats (with the South providing 45.6 percent of the seats).[11] In 1910, they provided 44.4 percent of Democratic seats (with the South's contribution amounting to 41.6 percent).

[8] Peter F. Nardulli, "The Concept of a Critical Realignment, Electoral Behavior, and Political Change," *American Political Science Review*, 89(1995), p. 18; John E. Chubb and Paul E. Peterson, *The New Direction in American Politics*, Washington, D.C., Brookings Institute, 1985; Larry M. Bartels, "Electoral Continuity and Change 1868–1996," *Electoral Studies*, 17(1998), p. 316. See also David R. Mayhew, "Electoral Realignments," *Annual Review of Political Science*, 3(2000), pp. 449–74.

[9] Andrew E. Busch, *Horses in Midstream: U.S. Midterm Elections and their Consequences, 1894–1998*, Pittsburgh, University of Pittsburgh Press, 1999, pp. 155–6.

[10] Districts in which a candidate ran as both the Democratic and Republican nominee are disregarded in calculating the median district. In districts when one of the two major parties did not have a candidate, the notional "plurality" is taken to be the share of the vote obtained by the candidate of the other party. (Obviously, this has a negative value in the case of a Republican being the only major party candidate.)

[11] The states are Connecticut, Illinois, Indiana, Kentucky, Maryland, Missouri, New Jersey, New York, Ohio, and West Virginia.

TABLE 6.2. *Median Plurality in Each Nonsouthern State of Democratic Congressional Candidates in 1888 and 1910 Elections*

	1888	1910
California	−1.5	−11.3
Colorado	−14	+2.5
Connecticut	−1.2	−3.1
Delaware	+11.7	−4.8
Illinois	−5.3	−0.7
Indiana	−0.7	+4.6
Iowa	−9.6	−14.2
Kansas	−22.5	−8.7
Kentucky	+10	+12
Maine	−13.1	+1.4
Maryland	+1.1	+3.6
Massachusetts	−8.9	−1.9
Michigan	−4.5	−16.5
Minnesota	−12.1	−21.2
Missouri	+6.1	+6.0
Nebraska	−14.2	−1.1
Nevada	−9.8	−11.8
New Hampshire	−1.5	−7
New Jersey	−1.5	+7.5
New York	−3.5	+2.1
Ohio	−2.9	+5
Oregon	−12.3	−16.9
Pennsylvania	−11	−9.8
Rhode Island	−12.4	−10.6
Vermont	−42	−43.6
West Virginia	+0.9	+6.5
Wisconsin	−7.7	−18

The contribution of the seventeen other nonsouthern states was much less in both elections – they provided 11.5 percent of all Democratic seats in 1888, and 12 percent in 1910.[12] This was not so much because they had few seats (106 in 1910, as against 156 in the "key" states), but because most of these states were safe Republican territory. In 1888, Democratic candidates won a mere 17.0 percent of all districts in those seventeen states, while in the ten "key" states they won 50.8 percent of districts. In 1910, the difference in the relative success rate was even greater – 25.4 percent and 64.1 percent being the respective rates of success.

[12] The contribution of new states to the Democratic House majority was similarly slight; these eight states provided a mere 1.3 percent of Democratic seats in 1910.

TABLE 6.3. *Competitive and Noncompetitive States in 1888 and 1910 Congressional Elections, Measured by Democratic Candidate's Plurality over Republican Candidate in Median District in Each State*

1910

	+10%	+6%	0%	−6%	−10%	1888
Kentucky			Delaware			
	Missouri					+10%
		Maryland				+6%
	New Jersey West Virginia	Indiana New York Ohio	Connecticut Illinois	New Hampshire	California Michigan	0% 1888
			Massachusetts		Iowa Nevada Wisconsin	−6%
		Colorado Maine	Nebraska	Kansas Pennsylvania	Minnesota Oregon Rhode Island Vermont	−10%

The central point is that, in broad outline, the electoral geography of 1910 was very much the same as 1888. Nevertheless, there had been some important changes, and, in part, they support the claim that, in some sense, there was less competition in 1910 than twenty years earlier; however, the data presented in Tables 6.2 and 6.3 do not really capture the transformation. In 1910, it had become even more difficult for the Democrats to win elections in a number of states that had been Republican in orientation earlier but that were now much more heavily inclined to the GOP. These states included Iowa, Michigan, and Pennsylvania. For example, in Pennsylvania not only was the surge to the Democrats in 1910 much weaker than it was nationally, but they actually won a smaller share of House seats than they had in 1888 – a year when the Democrats had lost control of the House (28 percent of the total compared with 22 percent in 1888). Moreover, the weakness of the Democrats in the state was to be revealed in 1912, when Wilson won a mere 32.5 percent of the vote.

The conventional account of the Democratic recovery of 1910 is not to see it as a belated reestablishment of a political order but to treat it as the product of a split in the Republican party between its progressive and conservative wings. Those who do so emphasize Taft's attempts to defeat insurgents in the Republican primaries.[13] However, there are two obvious objections to this approach. First, there was no formal split in the party that year; that did not occur until 1912. While the formation of a separate Progressive party undoubtedly benefitted the Democrats in 1912, at least in the short term, it cannot account for their success in 1910. At 94 percent, the two-party share of the vote was high in 1910 – only 1 percent lower than in 1906 and 3 percent lower than in 1908, while turnout was the same as in 1906.

Second, if it is argued that the Democrats recovered in 1910 only because there were tensions in the Republican party, then there is a clear retort to that: It was precisely because of intraparty divisions that the nineteenth-century party system appeared to be so competitive. What happened in 1910 was just what had been happening regularly until the mid-1890s. The important questions, therefore, are why that pattern of regular fission and fusion within parties no longer provided the dynamic of party politics after the mid-1890s, and what were the consequences of its absence, if any, on the adoption of the direct primary?

On the former question, it is possible here to provide only an outline sketch to the answer – a complete answer would require a separate chapter or, more likely, a book to develop the argument fully. Three factors can be identified, which are discussed in ascending order of importance. The first is that the decisive Republican victories in 1894 and 1896 gave that party the opportunity to change the rules of the game in many states – and they took it. For example, antifusion laws were passed as were revisions to the Australian Ballot in the direction of mechanisms that favored straight-ticket voting (see Chapter 2, Section 8). Both measures hurt the Democrats, who tended to be more dependent on fusion for their victories.

The second factor was that a number of urban parties became rather more stable and more centralized in the decades after the mid 1890s. Since the early part of that period coincided with large Republican victories in presidential elections, the position of the Republican party there was more consolidated than it would otherwise have been. The Democrats' relative weakness in urban areas between the 1890s and the 1930s was not just the product of the evident rural bias of some of its presidential candidates; it stemmed also from Republican entrenchment in some cities. That entrenchment was made possible because of reforms whose effect was to provide for greater centralization of powers in city government. The more centralized was local government, the more centralized could the local party organization become. Ironically, therefore, machine politicians would often pursue the same policies as municipal reformers because they could see the advantages to their party. Thus, in Philadelphia, Simon Cameron and Matthew Quay had favored "centralizing power and responsibility under a strong mayor; it would strike a decisive blow against

---

[13] Busch, *Horses in Midstream*, p. 84.

councilmen and ward 'bosses' because the practice of having executive departments controlled and administered by committees of the Councils would be eliminated."[14]

Consequently, by the end of the nineteenth century, patronage was much more centrally controlled in Philadelphia than it had been twenty years earlier, and this stabilized the party's electoral grip on the city. It was now much more difficult for a minority party, the Democrats in the case of Philadelphia, to mobilize against a more centralized dominant party. The partial coincidence of a period of municipal reform, in which, generally, local government powers were consolidated rather than dispersed, with that of the twelve-year period of Republican advantage in presidential elections was significant. It meant that it was the Republicans who, on balance, benefitted from the consequences of changes in urban government. (In cities like Cincinnati, for example, where there was a so-called new charter in 1891, both administrative reform and the greater stability in political alliances after the early-to-mid-1890s helped to consolidate the Republicans' position.[15]) Of course, there were some cases, such as New York City, where they did not, but usually it was a factor working to the GOP's advantage. It proved to be a long-term problem for the Democrats that was not resolved by them until the New Deal realignment.

The key factor disadvantaging the Democrats, though, was that how voters connected with parties was starting to change slowly. Nineteenth-century politics had been dominated by loyalty to a party; the personality of the candidate at the head of the ticket was important only in so far as it acted as a catalyst to make certain that loyalists did turn out to support their party. Although military heroes, especially, might be used for this purpose in presidential elections, who was at the head of the ticket mattered a lot less in the nineteenth century than it did later. The very approach of a presidential election would tend to bring most of the loyalists back to the party. However, as was seen in Chapter 2 (Section 7), Reynolds and McCormick's evidence from New Jersey and New York shows a marked change in voting behavior around the turn of the century. The introduction of the Australian Ballot reduced ticket splitting low down the ballot, and in the 1890s ticket splitting was actually lower in these states than it had been earlier. But from 1904 ticket splitting increased, and it did so at the top of the ticket as voters responded positively or negatively to charismatic politicians.[16]

---

[14] Peter McCaffery, *When Bosses Ruled Philadelphia: The Emergence of the Republican Machine, 1867–1933*, University Park, PA, Pennsylvania State University Press, 1993, p. 73.

[15] Zane L. Miller, *Boss Cox's Cincinnati*, New York, Oxford University Press, 1968, Chapter 6.

[16] John F. Reynolds and Richard L. McCormick, "Outlawing 'Treachery': Split Tickets and Ballot Laws in New York and New Jersey, 1880–1910," *Journal of American History*, 72(1986), p. 856.

The main problem facing the Democratic party after 1896 was the need to present voters with presidential candidates to whom they would respond positively. However, as is argued shortly, the party was in a worse position to do this than the Republicans. Consequently, local parties had to devise strategies for overcoming their disadvantage, and what is interesting about the effects of the 1896 election is just how quickly the Democratic party could rebound in state and local elections. In New Jersey, there emerged a bifurcated electoral system in which "the generally low correlations between presidential and off-year elections for the whole of the post-1896 era . . . portray voting decisions in non-presidential elections as more heavily influenced by short term or nonpartisan considerations."[17] State Democrats sought to decouple presidential and off-year elections, and through this strategy they succeeded in keeping the party competitive locally even while it was doing badly in presidential years. The 1896 election did not mark a serious break with the past in New Jersey, for "as late as World War I the party's vote was as much a function of its 1888 vote as any other presidential election."[18]

That 1896 did not mark a major discontinuity in patterns of electoral support was evident also in Indiana:

The election of 1896 in Indiana was less a sudden shift than a temporary deviation. After reaching its peak in 1884, Democratic strength slowly eroded until the election of 1904, when it fell rather sharply. Only the increased Democratic vote for president in 1896 departs from this trend. Nor was there any appreciable shift in the areas from which the parties obtained their support.[19]

However, it should not be concluded, from the evidence of states like New Jersey and Indiana, that the experience of the early 1890s changed nothing. The Democratic party was less able to sustain a serious challenge in some states where it might have "had a shot" in a good year earlier. New Hampshire and Wisconsin are good examples of how the party's ability to mount a fierce challenge to its opponent was significantly reduced by 1910.[20] However, disentangling long-term shifts in voter support in particular states from the effects of the 1893-6 upheaval is difficult. But perhaps the most significant point is just how much electoral support in 1910 resembled that of 1888. The states that had been competitive before

---

[17] John F. Reynolds, *Testing Democracy: Electoral Behaviour and Progressive Reform in New Jersey, 1880–1920*, Chapel Hill and London, University of North Carolina Press, 1988, p. 86.

[18] Reynolds, *Testing Democracy*, p. 86.

[19] Philip R. VanderMeer, *The Hoosier Politician: Officeholding and Political Culture in Indiana, 1896–1920*, Urbana and Chicago, University of Illinois Press, 1984, p. 13.

[20] There were a few states, though, where the Democratic disadvantage had largely been eroded by 1910; Colorado and Nebraska provide clear-cut examples of this, and it was partly true of Maine and Massachusetts as well.

1893 tended to be competitive between 1910 and 1916. The states where there was a Republican advantage before 1893 still tended to have an advantage in 1910, and in some cases that advantage had been consolidated. The central problem for the Democrats was not that an electoral realignment had marginalized them nationally, but that they failed to find presidential candidates who could win.

3. Why the Democrats were Disadvantaged

Why, then, after the mid-1890s were the Democrats less able than the Republicans to bring forward presidential aspirants who could command broad-based support? Three factors are relevant in explaining the role played by presidential elections in stymieing the Democratic advance.

First, to have a reasonably sized pool of attractive potential candidates from whom to choose a nominee, the party actually had to put together a run of good results in state elections so that there were sufficient alternatives available – especially among state governors – to be a major threat to William Jennings Bryan. The main legacy of 1896 for the Democrats was not, as popularly believed, that they lost their electoral base in much of the country, but that they were left with Bryan thereafter. He was both the major asset and the main liability for the Democratic party. He brought to the party a radical programme, based in rural America, that was essential for any Democratic victory in the early decades of the twentieth century. But Bryan himself was unelectable; his antiurbanism, first evident to most American voters in 1896, meant that he continued to be treated with suspicion by potential Democratic elites and voters in urban areas. Bryan dominated the party for most of the decade and a half after 1896 because there were few who could challenge him, and the reason for that was that the Democrats could not string together enough successive victories outside the South for such challengers to emerge. Failure begot failure – at the national level – and that in turn hindered recovery at the state level. It was not until 1910 that they did well enough in a single election to produce a number of attractive candidates for the following presidential contest. Until then the Democrats were in a vicious circle, with Bryan usually being in a position to claim the presidential nomination if he wanted it.

Second, the Democrats' long-standing nominating rules meant that the nominee was someone who was likely to be merely acceptable to the party, rather than a vote-winner among a broader public. From the 1830s until the 1930s, the Democrats required that the nominee receive the votes of two-thirds of the delegates to the National Convention. This had been designed to produce a southern veto on the choice of candidate, but in doing so it tended to restrict the party's choice of nominee. Even more than in the Republican party, the process tended to throw up a nominee who was "acceptable" in one of two ways. The one sort of candidate had the sole merit of having fewer enemies in the party than other potential nominees; it was into this tradition that the nominee of 1904, Alton Parker, fell. But there was another sort of nominee, one who was the "lowest common denominator" in a rather different way. He might be acceptable enough to sufficient elements in the party to win the nomination, but in the absence of a simple-majority decision-making system, the party would end up with someone who had little chance of broadening his support beyond that base. William Jennings Bryan was the classic instance of such a candidate.

It is arguably the case that in 1896 Bryan did better in the presidential election than any other Democratic candidate could have done. But Bryan did not win then, and he could not win later either. His lack of appeal to urban Americans, especially those in the northeast, consigned the Democratic party to defeat in presidential elections time after time. However, Bryan was always a strong contender for the nomination because others were not. Had the Democratic party used majority voting procedures, Bryan's advantage would have been less because it would have been easier for other candidates to have detached support from him in the earlier stages of the nomination process. Rather paradoxically, perhaps, and given the party's nomination rules, the scale of the defeat in 1896 actually helped Bryan to dominate a party that he had led to defeat.

Third, as McGerr has shown, political campaigning was undergoing a slow transformation in the sixty years after 1865.[21] By the end of the nineteenth century, the presidential nominee was no longer someone who retired to his home and left the party organizations to undertake the campaigning. James Blaine had been criticized in 1884 for breaking with the traditional style of campaigning, but by the end of the nineteenth century the candidates were leading from the front and that practice developed further in the twentieth century. Consequently, it now mattered a lot more who the presidential nominee was; it had to be a person who could attract votes for the party as an active political campaigner. Someone like Alton Parker might have been elected in 1880 or 1884, but twenty years later he was a liability for a party that needed a challenger to oppose actively Teddy Roosevelt.

Together these three factors made it much more difficult for the Democrats to build on recoveries that they were making at the state level in the years between presidential elections. Rather than being the elections that tended to heal party divisions and rebuild their electoral coalition, as they had been before 1896, presidential elections now tended to impede the Democrats' recovery. Their nominating procedures meant that they were in a worse situation than the Republicans would have been, were they facing similar adversity, and they were less well fitted than the Republicans for

---

[21] Michael E. McGerr, *The Decline of Popular Politics: The American North, 1865–1928*, New York and Oxford, Oxford University Press, 1986.

competing in the new era of presidential politics. Nevertheless, despite this, and despite the fact that after 1896 the Democrats were never again able to equal the Republicans in political finance, the party did recover electorally within fourteen years.

4. Changes in Party Competition and the Rise of the Direct Primary

The argument being made here is that under changed conditions, the party system no longer "self corrected" between elections as it had done in the nineteenth century. The major defeat of 1896 made it difficult for the Democrats to defeat the Republicans in presidential elections, and that, in turn, restricted the recovery state parties could make. However, the party system was not turned upside down, as is frequently alleged. Nor is there any evidence that, outside the South, participants at the time believed that they had entered a "dark age" of political monopoly. To the contrary, there was considerable evidence that mass electorates might yet punish those whose behavior in office fell short of expectations. As was seen in Chapter 5, it was precisely this fear of voter revolt that led the Pennsylvania Republicans under Governor Pennypacker to introduce reforms, including the direct primary for many offices. This example is interesting because it happened in a state that was safe Republican territory before the mid-1890s (and thereafter) – but the fear of possible voter revolt was still evident in 1905.

Consequently, it would be expected that, in the absence of a transformation in the 1890s to a world of political monopoly, it would be unlikely that any general linkage between the absence of political competition and the introduction of the direct primary would be found. The states experimenting with the direct primary before 1904 included those where the Democrats remained competitive, such as Maryland, those where they remained competitive at the local level (for example, New Jersey) and those such as Minnesota and Oregon, where there was Republican dominance.

However, when examining the timing of the introduction of primary laws that covered virtually all state offices, it appears as if there may be a link between their early introduction and Republican party strength (see Table 6.4). Those states that were safely Republican in 1910 – where the Democratic candidate in the median congressional district received at least 6 percent of the total vote less than the Republican candidate – were much more likely to have given an early passage to such legislation. Does this indicate that Key, Sorauf, Burnham, and others might have been correct in seeing a direct link between party monopoly and the introduction of the direct primary? The answer to that is no. Underlying the apparent relationship between the two variables is a different factor – region. As was seen in Chapter 4, regional differences are important in explaining the

TABLE 6.4. *Relationship between the Level of Party Competition in the States in 1910 and the Timing of the Adoption of Direct Primary Laws Covering Most Offices*

	1903	1904	1905	1906	1907	1908	1909	1910	1911	1912	1913	1914	1915	No Laws Before 1916
Republican plurality over Democrat in median Congressional district in 1910 less than 6% of total vote					MO NE	OK	IL	CO	ME MA NJ		NY OH		WV	CT DE *IN* KY MD
Republican plurality over Democrat in median Congressional district greater than 6% of total vote	WI	OR			IA *ND* *SD* *WA*		CA *ID* *NV* NH		WY	MN MT	PA		VT	RI *UT* MI

Western states are shown in italics.

179

timing of the introduction of the direct primary, and, once region is taken into account, much of the apparent connection between the direct primary and political monopoly dissolves.

Nevertheless, electoral competition was not without significance. Within the particular contexts of a given state, the presence of party competition could be a factor that affected the introduction of direct primary legislation, even though there is not a simple, direct relationship between the two. It is to this consideration that the discussion now turns.

5. Competition as a Stimulant to Nomination Reform

The five states discussed in Chapter 5 have already provided some evidence that the related forces of competition and political ambition could provide a decisive push in the direction of nomination reform. In Pennsylvania, it was the threat of a Democratic resurgence following political scandals that led a Republican governor to call a special session of the state legislature that passed, among other measures, a direct primary bill. In Illinois, it was intraparty rivalries that led Republican governor, Charles Deneen, to champion the direct primary – it was popular among the sort of Republican voters that he had encompassed in his own electoral coalition. In Massachusetts, Democratic revival and the political ambitions of the State Assembly Speaker, Joseph Walker, were important in his change of mind over the direct primary. In some states, though, it was not just the fear of party competition, or intraparty competition among rival politicians, that contributed to the introduction of direct primary legislation, but direct competition between parties in the electoral market. Two states that illustrate well the circumstances in which this could occur are Indiana and Maine.

Indiana had been one of the most competitive states before the political upheavals of the early 1890s and it was one state that remained highly competitive afterwards, even before the 1910 recovery. It was a state of party "regulars" in which virtually all the practices associated with mid-nineteenth-century American parties were well known. So close were elections there that some voters were paid to vote, although the myth of the role of money in Indiana politics was somewhat at variance with reality. (A famous instance of this was the claim by the Secretary of the Republican National Committee, Stephen W. Dorsey, that $400,000 had been spent by the party in 1880 to win the state. In fact, nothing like this amount was either needed or spent in the state that year.[22])

Nevertheless, if Indiana is a good example of what euphemistically might be described as the robust side of nineteenth-century democracy, this aspect of its politics did not prevent it from being innovative in institutional

---

[22] R. D. Marcus, *Grand Old Party: Political Structure in the Gilded Age 1880–1896*, New York, Oxford University Press, 1971, pp. 48, 53, and 56–7.

reform. As shown in Chapter 2, following the lead of Kentucky and Massachusetts in adopting the Australian Ballot, Indiana produced a version of it – the party column ballot – that retained advantages to the parties, in preserving voter-party links, while making it possible to eliminate ticket-splitting at lower levels of the ballot. Later, when public debate about direct nominations became prominent, Indiana was like a number of states, in that many of its politicians recognized the advantages in having local offices subject to direct nominations. Thus, as early as 1907 legislation was passed in Indiana requiring counties containing large cities to have direct primaries for city, township and county offices.[23] A significant proportion of elites in both parties, however, remained unconvinced that a further extension of direct primaries was either necessary or desirable.

Nevertheless, as VanderMeer shows, the Democrats moved toward supporting such an extension after 1914.[24] The decline in the Progressive Party's vote that year would likely result in the complete demise of the party by 1916, and its remaining voters would be open to being won over by one of the two major parties before then. Winning a majority of those voters, therefore, was the key to the Democrats retaining office in 1916, and adopting an issue that was highly salient to Progressive Party voters was an obvious strategy for the party. It was opposed by a number of leading Democrats, including the state governor, largely on the grounds that the quality of public officials would decline because the people were "fallible." (Of course, this was an effect of direct nominations that Thomas L. Johnson had observed in Cleveland two decades earlier.) Divisions between Democrats resulted in the legislation being held up in the state's General Assembly, but eventually, because other legislation was also stalled, a compromise version of the bill was passed so that the party would have legislative accomplishments to show for their term as a majority party. VanderMeer's verdict on this was that:

... legislative action in 1915 was due less to a generally weakened state of parties than to a particular set of political circumstances . . . it was ultimately not a general decline of party loyalty but unique electoral circumstances – a brief period when party critics represented the swing vote – which led to legislative action. Even with this change in the rules, however, party organizations remained active and influential.

In other words, this is a classic instance of how the incentive to "claim credit" for adopting a particular policy from a group of voters led to the adoption of a policy that would not otherwise have been enacted. Party competition produced results that would not have come about in its absence.

---

[23] VanderMeer, *The Hoosier Politician*, p. 34.
[24] The account in this paragraph is largely drawn from VanderMeer, *The Hoosier Politician*, pp. 36–7.

There is a further point about Indiana that should be noted in passing: In one or two states, including Indiana, the presidential campaign of Theodore Roosevelt in 1912 did have an indirect effect on the progress of the direct primary. That campaign had focused attention on aspects of direct democracy – including the direct election of U.S. Senators – but its effect on direct primaries was relatively limited, simply because so many states had already adopted them by then. However, in a highly competitive state that had not extended their use, like Indiana, Roosevelt's erstwhile supporters were important for electoral coalition building, and as already noted, the pursuit of their votes by the parties helps to explain why direct nominations were adopted in the state.

Another example of the impact of political competition is Maine. Maine was unusual in that it moved from being dominated by the Republicans in the early 1890s to being far more competitive by 1910. In 1890, the year of a crushing midterm landslide for the Democrats, Republican candidates in the state were outpolling their Democratic counterparts by more than 16 percent of the total vote; in 1892, they led the Democrats by 9 percent. Even as late as 1902, the Republicans were winning more than 60 percent of the vote. By 1908, part of the Democratic party's strategy in making itself competitive in state elections was a commitment to a direct primary law – a classic case of a strategy designed to broaden an electoral coalition. So successful was their overall effort to make themselves competitive that by 1910 not only had the Republicans followed suit in committing themselves to direct primary legislation, but, more significantly, the Democrats actually won control of the state legislature.[25]

Both parties wanted to claim credit for enacting direct primary legislation, or, in Hormell's words in 1923, "The Republican members of the legislature were not willing . . . to leave to their Democratic colleagues the task and honour of providing the state with a direct primary law."[26] The result was the introduction of rival bills. There was only one critic in the legislature of the principle of direct nominations in the legislatures (a Democratic senator), and the controversy centred entirely on which version would pass. Eventually, one of the bills was put before voters in a special election in September 1911 where it secured the support of about three quarters of those voting, although, interestingly, Hormell noted that the measure seemed to have attracted very little public interest by then.[27] Unlike Indiana, Maine was not noted for its tightly organized parties, but in both states the effect that competition could have in particular circumstances is observable.

---

[25] They controlled the state House by 87–64 and the Senate by 22–9.
[26] Orren Chalmer Hormell, "The Direct Primary Law in Maine and How it Has Worked," *Annals of the American Academy of Political and Social Science*, 106(1923), p. 128.
[27] Hormell, "The Direct Primary Law," p. 129.

However, it is important to note that, just as the rise of the direct primary cannot be explained by the absence of interparty competition, so, too, was its presence not necessarily the key factor in explaining the introduction of direct nominations. Illinois, Massachusetts, Missouri, and New York are all instances of competition not playing the role that it did in Indiana, or the slightly different role it played in Maine. It was only in particular circumstances that it emerged as a decisive factor pushing one party, or both, to treat the issue as one from which direct electoral benefit might be derived.

6. Party Competition and Political Exclusion: Southern New England

While party competition could be a stimulus to the adoption of the direct primary there were also circumstances in which the fear of competition drove party leaders to retain the caucus-convention system of nomination. In other words, unlike the South, where Key's argument about political monopoly are applicable, in the North the desire to preserve or create political dominance could have the opposite effects. This was what happened in Connecticut and Rhode Island. Although there are important similarities between the two states, there were also some differences. In particular, in the nineteenth century, Rhode Island had always been tightly controlled by a political elite, and the Democrats rarely got in sight of victory at any level of office above that of counties. Connecticut had the appearance of being much more competitive; in Section 2 of this chapter, Rhode Island was classified as an NDS state, while Connecticut was classified as Marginal. However, classifications using either presidential or congressional voting patterns can give a misleading impression of politics in a state. For institutional reasons, to be discussed shortly, Connecticut's Republicans could exercise far more power at the state level than they could have in a truly competitive state. There was an opportunity, unavailable in states where there was genuine competition at the state level, for Republican leaders to consolidate their position – and they did so.

In examining the issue of the direct primary, Connecticut may be compared with its superficially similar neighbor, Massachusetts, where the direct primary had been on the legislative agenda since the 1890s – its adoption occurring in three stages between 1903 and 1911. Two states with rather similar social and economic profiles were to produce radically different responses to the direct primary.

Not surprisingly, perhaps, given their physical proximity, Connecticut and Massachusetts had similar social and economic histories. Both states urbanized rapidly, and by 1890 both had a majority of their populations living in urban areas; Massachusetts was the most urban state in the Union with 82 percent of its population living in cities with more than five thousand people and Connecticut (with 51 percent) was the fifth most urban state. (The only other states that had more than half their populations living in urban areas in 1890 were New Jersey, New York, and Rhode Island.) Industrialization created a demand for labor that could not be satisfied by the existing populations, and from the 1840s onward there was a massive influx into the region of Irish immigrants. Later in the century, other immigrant groups, including Italians, moved into the rapidly growing cities, with the result that the populations of both states nearly doubled between 1880 and 1910. By 1910, foreign-born persons formed 30 percent of Connecticut's population.[28]

In spite of these obvious similarities there were some crucial differences between the two states. One dissimilarity was that, although in the national context Connecticut was an advanced industrial and urban state, its rural population was relatively that much greater than Massachusetts'. This had consequences for the building of political coalitions in the state. Another difference between the two states affecting the potential for coalition building relates to the kind of urban populations that there were. In Connecticut, the cities generally were on a much smaller scale. Its total population was only one-third of that of Massachusetts, and none of its cities even approached the size of Boston. It was urban, but small scale, a feature that was still evident in 1929 when Lancaster noted:

The state is essentially one of small towns and medium-sized cities, there being no cities of metropolitan rank in it and few or no towns in which agriculture is self-sustaining. . . . At the census of 1890 the state for the first time became definitely urban, but for several generations before that the small towns had been slowly drained of their population and had lost their rural character.[29]

Politically, the two states had rather similar histories. Both had been centers of support for Federalism in the 1790s, for the Whigs in the 1840s, and, later, for the Republican party in 1856 and 1860. However, during and after the Civil War, Connecticut leaned much less consistently to the Republicans than did its neighbor. Lincoln won the state only narrowly in 1864 and, thereafter, even when they won the presidential election, the Republicans' margin of victory was always narrow – until the 1890s. By contrast, Massachusetts was a bastion of support for the Republicans. In both states, though, the advance of the Democracy's vote had been stimulated by Irish immigration, with the Republican party remaining staunchly Yankee. In 1901, for example, 98 percent of all Republicans in the Connecticut House of Representatives were Yankees.[30]

Given the discussion in Section 5, it might have been expected that it would be in Connecticut, rather than Massachusetts, that the impact of party competition might become a factor prompting outbidding by the

[28] Joseph I. Lieberman, *The Power Broker*, Boston, Houghton, Miflin, 1966, p. 23.
[29] Lane W. Lancaster, "The Background of a State 'Boss' System," *American Journal of Sociology*, 35(1929–30), p. 785.
[30] Duane Lockard, *New England State Politics*, Chicago, Henry Regnery, 1959, p. 241.

parties on the issue of the direct primary. However, there was one crucial institutional difference between the two states, and it prompted radically dissimilar responses to the direct primary. Connecticut's constitution, which had been drawn up in 1818, gave political supremacy to the legislative branch and gave sole power for initiating constitutional change to that branch. However, the state's legislative branch was heavily dominated by the old, small towns. This was not the result of malapportionment but of constitutional design. The 1818 constitution granted to each existing town, regardless of size, two representatives to the lower chamber of the state legislature; new towns could only have one representative, and, although this was later increased to two for towns with a population of more than five thousand, the result was that small towns were heavily over-represented in the lower chamber. As an example, it may be noted that Union, with a population of 322, had the same representation as New Haven with over 130,000; one estimate was that a majority of members of the state House were from districts that contained only 12 percent of the population.[31]

The partisan consequences of this constitutional requirement were devastating for the Democrats. Even in years when the party was doing well electorally in the state it still could not control the General Assembly.[32] For example, in both 1892 and 1912, the Democrats won the state governorship and a clear majority of congressional seats, yet they trailed the Republicans 114–137 (in 1892) and 120–130 (in 1912) in the Connecticut General Assembly. In most years the Democrats did not even come this close to control of the House; between 1892 and 1914 Republicans there usually outnumbered Democrats by two-to-one, and sometimes by as much as five-to-one.[33]

The state senate had a more proportional system of representation, though even there the largest districts could contain more than three times as many people as the smallest ones.[34] The weakness of the governorship – a marked contrast with, for example, the situation in Illinois – combined with the constitutional entrenchment of small-town power in the legislature meant that, for purposes of governing the state, it did not matter with whom the immigrants combined. The Democrats might win the governorship with the help of the immigrant vote, they might win a majority of the

[31] John D. Buenker, "The Politics of Resistance: The Rural-Based Yankee Republican Machines of Connecticut and Rhode Island," *New England Quarterly*, (47)1974, p. 215.

[32] On the malapportionment of the Connecticut legislature, see Peter H. Argersinger, "The Value of the Vote: Political Representation in the Gilded Age," in Argersinger (ed.), *Structure, Process and Party: Essays in American Political History*, Armonk, N.Y., M. E. Sharpe, 1992, pp. 76–86.

[33] Frederick Morrison Heath, "Politics and Steady Habits: Issues and Elections in Connecticut 1894–1914," Ph.D. dissertation, Columbia University, 1965, p. 43.

[34] Lancaster, "The Background of a State 'Boss' System," p. 790.

vote in U.S. House elections, but under the constitution small-town Yankees would always control the state House, and that meant they could control the state. While these Yankees were nearly always Republicans, in the years between 1894 and 1912 not all Republicans were committed to the preservation of small-town power. Indeed, at the very beginning of the twentieth century, some Republicans supported the so-called Fyler plan, a measure that would have given cities greater representation for every additional twenty thousand inhabitants. However, the bill was defeated decisively in the House, 145–61.[35]

Between 1894 and 1912 the Connecticut Republican party was heavily factionalized, but this form of intraparty competition generated no opportunities for excluded groups – and most especially immigrants – to benefit from the splits. There were three reasons for this. One was that, whatever the stakes, rural and small-town politicians would never do anything to endanger their constitutionally entrenched position – that was something that they were not going to trade away. Second, the factions were highly fluid.[36] This meant that there was no permanently excluded group among the Republicans, and hence no incentive for anyone to break ranks and consider alliances with the Italians and other immigrant groups who were swelling the populations of the larger cities. After 1912 factionalism declined in the Republican party, with J. Henry Roraback constructing a much more hierarchical party that united business interests with the small town Republican base. Third, the weak position of the governorship meant that, unlike Illinois, it was not an office around which intraparty competition for votes could develop. There could be no equivalent in Connecticut to Illinois' Charles Deneen – someone who could use the resources of a governorship to create personal support for himself, possibly outside traditional party voters.

The opportunity, available in Connecticut, for simply excluding immigrants from political influence in governing the state did not exist in Massachusetts. Yankee antagonism to immigrants could be, and was, played out in many ways in the Bay State, but immigrants could not just be shut out of politics. The possibility of political coalitions that included immigrants had already been evident in the aftermath of the Mugwump revolt of 1884. Of the states in the East, the Mugwump revolt against the Republican nominee James Blaine had been strongest in those states where there were preexisting groups of political Independents and where there was newspaper support for a "bolt."[37] Thus, it was strong in Massachusetts and

[35] Edwin McNeil Dahill, "Connecticut's J. Henry Roraback," Ph.D. dissertation, Columbia University, 1971, pp. 37–8. Again, in 1902, a state constitutional convention advocated some reform, but high voting turnout in the subsequent referendum by rural and small-town voters led to its defeat.

[36] Dahill, "Connecticut's J. Henry Roraback," p. 14.

[37] Gerald W. McFarland, *Mugwumps, Morals and Politics, 1884–1920*, Amherst, University of Massachusetts Press, 1975, p. 19.

New York, but relatively weak elsewhere; in Connecticut, it was strong only in New Haven. In Massachusetts, and unlike New York, a number of Mugwumps allied themselves with the Democratic Party, through an organization known as the Young Men's Democratic Club of Massachusetts (YMDC), which was formed in 1888. Part of the significance of the YMDC is that Irish as well as Yankee Democrats were willing to encourage "their people" to participate in this organization.[38] By 1891, the Democrat Governor William E. Russell could describe the YMDC as the "strongest political organization in New England," which, if it was an exaggeration, at least gives some indication of the potential for coalition building across ethnic divisions in the state.[39]

This working through of cooperation between ex-Mugwumps and immigrant politicians was well illustrated by the Mayor of Boston in the mid-1890s, Josiah Quincy. An ex-Mugwump who had served in the Cleveland administration, Quincy had become a Democrat whose "complete commitment to the Democratic party reflected a belief that the political party was not merely an unfortunate expedient but a crucial instrument of social progress."[40] Quincy's whole strategy as mayor was to ground his program in cooperation with the Boston "machine."[41] Of course, the impact of the national electoral upheavals of 1893–6 was felt in Massachusetts, as elsewhere. Unlike New Jersey, for example, the state party system was not able to insulate itself from the national system, and the Democrats did not become competitive again in the state until 1910. The first two of the three laws introducing the direct primary were passed before this – that is, during the period of Republican ascendancy. However, the key point is that it was an ascendancy in which the possible future revival of the Democratic party as a major influence in state government could not be ruled out. That kind of development could be ignored in Connecticut, though.

Political competition, thus, had less impact on the political agenda in Connecticut than it did in Massachusetts. In 1910, not only did the Connecticut Republicans retain, as always, control of the state House, but the Democrats won the governorship only by putting forward as their candidate an ex-Mugwump, Simeon Baldwin, whose political agenda was completely acceptable to a great many conservative Republicans. As a former Republican governor said at the time, "There was not one thing which Baldwin suggested that the state ought not to adopt."[42] This boosted Baldwin's vote; the Republican candidate's share of the vote was about 4 percent less (of the total vote for the office) than that obtained by

---

[38] McFarland, *Mugwumps, Morals and Politics*, p. 60.
[39] Russell is cited in Geoffrey Blodgett, *The Gentle Reformers: Massachusetts Democrats in the Cleveland Era*, Cambridge, Mass., Harvard University Press, 1966, p. 84.
[40] Blodgett, *The Gentle Reformers*, p. 246.   41. Blodgett, *The Gentle Reformers*, p. 260.
[42] Rollin S. Woodruff cited in Frederick H. Jackson, *Simeon Eben Baldwin*, New York, King's Crown Press, Columbia University, 1955, p. 174.

Republicans running for other major offices.[43] Even in 1912 the split in the Republican party had a relatively limited effect on the political agenda. It did allow the Connecticut Democrats to make major advances, including gaining control of the state senate, but once the breach in the Republican party had closed, at least partly, the Republicans resumed their position of ascendancy. After 1914 they controlled the senate once more by 30 to 5. Unlike Massachusetts, the rise in party competition in the years 1910–14 was much more apparent than real. Moreover, beginning in 1912, Connecticut party politics was to follow a very different path from Massachusetts', in that the "open" nature of the polity came to be undermined by the centralization of power within the Republican party. On a 19–16 vote, the Connecticut Republican party installed as Chairman and treasurer of the Republican State Central Committee J. Henry Roraback – a man, who in many ways, was to become the most powerful political boss in the United States in the twentieth century. From 1912 until his suicide in 1937, he would exercise tight control over all Republicans in the state in a machine that linked business interests, particularly his public utilities interests, to small city Republicanism.

Rather similar political conditions to those in Connecticut were also present in Rhode Island, and it is significant that, apart from New Mexico, it was the only other state that had not switched to the direct primary before 1916. Like Connecticut, Rhode Island persisted with caucus-convention forms of party nomination until after World War II.[44] Rhode Island had long had a reputation of being a political fiefdom, and well into the twentieth century, for example, it still employed a property qualification for the franchise in local elections. It had been another Yankee state that underwent rapid urbanization from the mid-19th century onward, and by 1890 its level of urbanization was almost as high as that of Massachusetts. As in Connecticut, the state's constitution ensured that rural areas and small towns were massively overrepresented in the state

---

[43] Heath, "Politics and Steady Habits," p. 234.

[44] It is worth noting that the causes of resistance to direct nominations were very different in New Mexico than they were in Connecticut and Rhode Island. In the two New England states, the direct primary represented a potential threat to an established political order. In New Mexico, the crucial factor was opposition among the Hispanic American political elite. It was the only state in the union in which there was a large racial or ethnic minority that was not systematically disenfranchised. (Hispanics formed about 40 percent of the population in the 1930s.) Fear of losing influence in their parties, should the caucus-convention system be replaced, led that elite to oppose reform. While Hispanics remained divided between the two parties neither party could afford to alienate their leaders. However, in the 1930s, Hispanics shifted disproportionately to the Democratic party. Intense factional disputes in that state party, which no longer had to worry much about Republican appeals to Hispanic voters, led to the passage of direct primary legislation in 1938. Thomas C. Donnelly, *Rocky Mountain Politics*, Albuquerque, University of New Mexico Press, 1940, pp. 238 and 240.

legislature, although in Rhode Island it was the state senate that was the basis for Yankee power; it was estimated that 73 percent of the senate was elected in districts containing 18 percent of the population.[45] Consequently, providing the Republican party did not experience a serious split, Yankee control would be ensured, and, as in Connecticut, they acted to limit immigrant influence.

However, granted that in both Connecticut and Rhode Island, Yankees had a strong incentive to "hang together" and to seek to exclude immigrant groups from political power, it might be asked why the "politics of exclusion" should have led to opposition to the direct primary? After all, in the South part of the attraction of the direct primary was that it could be used to exclude black voters, while at the same time granting a veneer of democracy to the process of candidate selection. Why did the Connecticut Republicans not embrace the direct primary while at the same time continuing to use their small-town base in retaining a grip on the policy agenda? This is the issue to which we now turn.

7. Political Reform and the Direct Primary in Connecticut

Given the combination of Yankee political culture, on the one side, and strong political parties, on the other, it is not surprising that the history of political reform in Connecticut was one of legislative initiatives to protect overt abuses of the political process, combined with a high degree of autonomy being granted to the parties. In 1883, it was one of the first states to enact legislation to prevent overt fraud in the nomination process.[46] Then, in 1889, the year following the first Australian Ballot legislation in America (in Kentucky and Massachusetts), Connecticut legislated for the official ballot. However, it opted for the "shoestring" ballot, the mechanism that maximized party control. This legislation lasted until 1909, when that ballot was replaced by the "stronger" form of party-column ballot (PPC). This early legislation on the secret ballot, though, was not followed up in the 1890s with extensive legal regulation of party nominations. Unlike most of the nonsouthern states, there was not a spate of legislative activity that formalized the means by which parties selected candidates. They continued to be left to their own devices.

Yankee concern with political rectitude was evident in 1905, though, when the state legislature passed a bill that the *American Political Science Review* described in 1907 as a "stringent corrupt practices law."[47] The main features of that bill were: a prohibition on corporations and judges making

---

[45] Buenker, "The Politics of Resistance," p. 217.

[46] Charles E. Merriam and Louise Overacker, *Primary Elections*, Chicago, University of Chicago Press, 1928, pp. 15–16.

[47] "Notes on Current Legislation," *American Political Science Review*, 1(1907), p. 250.

contributions to political parties; a limit (of five) on the number of paid workers at the polls in each electoral district; sworn statements of expenses by all candidates and delegates to nominating conventions; a ban on expenditures for conveying voters to the polls – except for the sick and infirm; a limit on campaign expenditures; stiffer penalties in cases of bribery, and a four-year ban on holding public office for persons found guilty of corrupt practices. When passing this law the legislature also set up a five-person commission to investigate corrupt practices and primary laws. That commission, under the chairmanship of Judge John H. Perry, submitted its final report to the legislature in January 1907. In relation to direct primaries, it recommended that a direct primary be introduced for various offices: governor and lieutenant governor, representatives in the U.S. Congress, members of the state legislature, city and borough offices (including sheriffs), and probate judges. Thus, although it would not have covered all public offices in the state, many of them would have been included.

The report immediately prompted the introduction of a bill to the state legislature at the beginning of its session in 1907, but it drew criticism from the state governor whose remarks indicated that it was not a measure to his taste. In his message to the legislature on January 9, Governor Rollin S. Woodruff observed:

With regard to the recommendation for a direct primary I would add that the report will be found to be radical. Let me urge that no hasty judgement be given, but that the most careful consideration of the recommendations be taken, and that they be weighed calmly and judicially. The subject is a vital one to our electoral system and action one way or the other should be taken only after the matter has been given the considerations that it demands.[48]

However, before the legislature began its deliberations at the end of January, the *Hartford Courant*, arguably the most prestigious newspaper in the state, lent its support to the direct primary:

We know positively that in many states opposition has disappeared and cordial approval has taken its place, and this method of getting the opinion of the people has come to be considered essential. . . . You can often corral a town and not infrequently a convention, but you cannot corral and seldom can stampede an entire state. The abolition of the convention may worry some old stagers . . . but the public generally are sick of delivered delegates.[49]

---

[48] *Hartford Daily Courant*, January 10, 1907. It is interesting to note that on January 19 the reform journal, *Outlook*, chose to portray Woodruff's call for "careful consideration" of the Perry report as indicating support by him for the direct primary (p. 101). Following a much longer account of a recommendation by the New Jersey Governor to his state legislature for direct election of US Senators, *Outlook* stated: "This recommendation was followed in two days by the recommendation of Governor Woodruff, of Connecticut, that the Legislature of that State carefully consider the report of a legislative commission in favor of a direct primary."

[49] *Hartford Daily Courant*, January 29, 1907.

The legislature held hearings on the Perry report on January 30, but, while it proceeded to pass further legislation dealing with corrupt practices, it sat on the proposals for a direct primary.[50] By now, Governor Woodruff had become exasperated by what he saw as a general inertia in the legislature and in early April 1907 he issued a public statement critical of it. Notably absent from his criticisms was any reference to the failure of the direct primary legislation to make progress. This point was seized on by Representative Banks, when the legislature considered Woodruff's comments, and Banks went on to argue for the direct primary arguing that he "could name one man who more than all others in the past six years has had more to say about who should be the next governor than all the gentlemen present. The pending bill on direct primaries would remedy the present condition."[51] By the end of the legislative session in July the bill had still not been reported out of committee. Nevertheless, a further report from Judge Perry was commissioned – one that was to examine the progress of direct primary legislation in other states.

By the time the legislature next met in January 1909 the proposal for a direct primary was gaining rather more publicity. A major meeting at which the merits of the system were debated was held on January 8; among those speaking were Judge Perry, and also present at the speaker's table was the incoming Governor, George L. Lilley, who did not speak but said that he had "come to learn." The debate was given full coverage by the *Hartford Daily Courant*, with many column inches devoted to the argument presented by both sides.[52] The following month, Judge Perry reported to the state Senate and this, too, received full coverage in the *Courant*, with a direct primaries' bill again receiving the *Courant*'s endorsement.[53] It noted that the scheme proposed by Perry's commission would limit the expense involved, that participation would be restricted to party voters, and that it would prevent fraud. Judge Perry took to the road and addressed meetings on the subject, including, for example, one to the Business Men's Association in Rockville on March 3.[54] On March 10, he appeared before the legislature's Judiciary Committee and was questioned at length about his recommendations.

In a party-oriented state in which one party could always control the state political agenda, the bill had little chance of success – if the party leadership decided that it had a stake in opposing it. This was evident when the Chairman of the Republican State Central Committee also appeared before the Judiciary Committee, and, in referring to the direct primary,

[50] *Hartford Daily Courant*, January 31, 1907 and August 2, 1907.
[51] *Hartford Daily Courant*, April 19, 1907.
[52] *Hartford Daily Courant*, January 9, 1909.
[53] *Hartford Daily Courant*, February 10, 1909.
[54] *Hartford Daily Courant*, March 4, 1909.

noted that he "hoped the committee would give it careful consideration, for it is much easier to get a law on the statute books than to repeal it." He observed further that New York Governor Hughes "had recently changed his position on the matter."[55] While the Judiciary Committee did give a second hearing to the bill in May and concluded its work on the measure, it then just sat on it. In early June the *Courant* claimed that the Senate's own members:

showed little disposition to furnish it with work by making reports upon Senate bills. There are a considerable number of these upon which hearings have long been closed, but which are lying in tin boxes of the various committees for reasons which are not made public. The judiciary committee is especially wealthy in these matters as no reports have been made on the direct primary bill.[56]

There the bill remained until the end of the month when the judiciary committee recommended that it be referred to the next legislature, which would meet in January 1911.

The year 1909 represented the best opportunity for passing a direct primary bill; there was a "head of steam" nationally for direct nominations, and the energetic Judge Perry could generate considerable publicity for the cause. Yet, by simply doing nothing, the state legislature could provide the Republican party leadership with what it really wanted. Although there were some pressures for direct primaries in the party – and in Hartford the party had gone some way toward implementing it[57] – the state party organizations and the House leadership generally remained in the hands of those who opposed it.

By 1911, the governorship was held by Simeon Baldwin, who did give direct primaries a rather more positive endorsement than his two predecessors. However, this support was worth little simply because he was a Democrat. On a matter like the direct primary, whatever leverage the governor might have – and the constitutional position of the governor was not strong, of course – was much more likely to come through intraparty negotiations. A Republican governor committed to the direct primary cause would likely have had more influence, but, as noted earlier, it was unlikely that Connecticut would ever produce a Charles Deneen.

In any case, Baldwin was a feeble supporter of the direct primary. As an ex-Mugwump, he might favor institutional reform but, like many of his ilk, he also was worried about the increasing cost of politics. So that, although the *Courant*'s editorial observed that Baldwin's address to the legislature gave "a good word" to the direct primary bill, what Baldwin had actually done was to express support with the caveat that he was concerned about the possible expense involved. He said of the Perry report:

---

[55] *Hartford Daily Courant*, March 10, 1909.
[56] *Hartford Daily Courant*, June 8, 1909.   [57] *Hartford Daily Courant*, March 25, 1909.

The bill which it recommended had been made the subject of long investigation and study by competent men, and the measures so recommended merit your careful consideration. Their adoption would seriously increase the expenses of candidates for office, unless the state were to limit narrowly the kinds of outlay to be deemed legitimate and perhaps itself to assume the main burden.[58]

By linking the direct primary to campaign expense reform in this way, Baldwin was playing into the hands of its opponents who had their own reasons for opposing it.

In fact, the 1911 bill did make further progress than its predecessors, in that a version of it, permitting direct primaries in some circumstances, was passed by the state senate.[59] Inevitably, though, it made no progress in the House. Failure was inevitable for a reason that has been well summarized by Heath:

... greater and more direct participation by the people would mean more influence for the cities and less than the existing structure provided for smaller communities and their leaders.... Connecticut's neighbor Massachusetts enacted two primary bills. There the district system of selecting legislators, instituted in the 19th century, made non-city votes less important.[60]

After 1911, there was no possibility of the issue being revived, because the Connecticut Republicans became subjected to a much greater discipline than they had known hitherto. After 1912, the centralization of power in the party under Roraback removed any chance of legislation on the matter, for primaries would likely undercut the source of his power. Unlike many politicians who had been called bosses earlier, Roraback really did "call the shots" in his state:

He presided over the deliberations of the legislature from a suite in the Allwyn House where each evening a lieutenant brought him a box full of the day's bills. When he picked them up the next morning, Roraback's instructions were carefully noted on each bill. So complete was his mastery of the state that a critical newspaper editor once put down a protesting Republican governor by insisting, "I have as much right to my opinion as you have to J. Henry Roraback's."[61]

However, before 1912, why did the Republican party not take possible public support for the direct primary more seriously, and what did they have to fear from its introduction? Two main points should be made. First, as in other states, immediate and direct public pressure for reform was not strong; it was not an issue that, by itself, would generate voter revolt in the party's small-town heartland. Second, the party leadership would have understood all too well that its capacity for discipline would have been

[58] *Hartford Daily Courant,* January 5, 1911.
[59] *Connecticut Senate Journal 1911,* pp. 1573–5.
[60] Heath, "Parties and Steady Habits," p. 282–3.
[61] Buenker, "The Politics of Resistance," p. 213.

reduced were candidates nominated directly. On the first point, it is evident that Connecticut was not like Massachusetts – it was less possible for a "bright reformer" (like Richard Henry Dana or Robert Luce) to win over legislative support for their ideas. The possibility of preserving complete Yankee dominance in Connecticut meant that legislators were much less likely to risk unpopularity by acting as innovators on a party-sensitive issue than in Massachusetts. The impetus for reform came not from inside the party, but from an "outside" commission (Judge Perry's). This reduced any prospect of dividing Republicans such that a significant portion of them would end up supporting reform. By contrast, in the absence of a con-stitutional entrenchment of power for small-town Republicanism in Massachusetts, the possibility for party-oriented reformers there to be influential did exist. In other words, political conditions in Massachusetts provided opportunities for individual politicians to act as political entre-preneurs on policies, while those opportunities were generally lacking in Connecticut. That made it more difficult to mobilize public opinion around the issue in Connecticut. Connecticut, thus, provides further evidence for a central argument of this book. Nomination reform made progress when the parties took the issue on; when they did not, as in both Connecticut and Rhode Island, proponents of direct nominations lacked the resources to overcome opposition.

As to party discipline, it is obvious that senior Republicans in Con-necticut feared most the prospect of having to take account of the interests of immigrant voters. If they lost control over their own elected politicians, the possibility of some of those politicians entering into short-term alliances with the immigrant-dominated Democratic party could not be ruled out. The Democrats had the support of a significant minority of voters – on occasion they could even win statewide office. They were a political force whose potential for alliances might lead to the unravelling of Yankee dominance, if the Republican party did not hang together tightly and protect its small-town base. To the extent that the direct primary might undermine its ability to hang together, by throwing up "unreliable" state legislators, it had to be resisted. Of course, after 1912 even that small risk of loss of control was much reduced, as the party became highly central-ized – a centralization that provided the basis for the continued political exclusion of the immigrant voters for several more decades. The difference between this "politics of exclusion" and that in the South is that by the 1890s the minority party there had a small political base, except in a few places on the outer edges of the region. Consequently, the kind of centralized party control seen in Connecticut was neither necessary in the South, nor was it possible. Among other things, this facilitated a wholly different strategy toward the direct primary.

8. Concluding Remarks

By basing his analysis of the direct primary on the experience in the South, on which he was undoubtedly the greatest expert of his time, V. O. Key (and those who have followed his line) produced a highly misleading argument as to why the direct primary was enacted. Not only do those who take this line misunderstand the change in party competition after 1896, but there was absolutely no connection between the absence of competition and the likelihood of a state adopting the direct primary. To the contrary, both interparty competition and intraparty rivalries tended to produce the results that would be expected of them: In particular conditions, they facilitated the introduction of reforms that were broadly popular with voting publics. The views of these publics were not decisive, though. In some circumstances, as in Connecticut, they could be ignored when the interests of the party that was, in effect, dominant dictated.

However, if competition between parties and between party factions could be a factor making it more likely that direct primary laws would be adopted, it was not always effective in this way. For example, Missouri, which was discussed in Chapter 5, is one instance of a party system that had become more competitive, but where the direct primary was relatively uncontroversial and where the forces of competition played scarcely any role in driving the policy forward. Thus, while competition can be important in understanding the rise of the direct primary in particular states, it is not an explanatory variable that can account for developments in all states.

7

Explaining an "Irrational" Reform

With the benefit of that best of predictive instruments, hindsight, it has always seemed that the introduction of the direct primary was a reform that ran counter to party interests. Unquestionably, in the long term, it helped to weaken the parties. Consequently, explanations of why this reform was introduced have generally assumed that it was something parties would rather have not done, but that they could not prevent. Thus, one common explanation has been that it was the result of antiparty reformers triumphing over party regulars, while another explanation was that it followed from a supposed descent into one-party dominance in much of the North after the mid-1890s. However, the states studied in detail in the last two chapters demonstrate the limitations of these two accounts of the rise of the direct primary. In the West, the introduction of the direct primary was linked to the success of insurgency, but this occurred only after a number of states, many in the East, had started already to experiment with direct nominations. That is, in spite of the weakness of insurgency in the east, most states there did introduce the direct primary, and there is no evidence either that the legislation involved conflict between antiparty reformers and urban-based political machines. Furthermore, there is also no evidence that the absence of party competition was responsible for this legislation. To the contrary, in some circumstances restrictions on party competition were a factor hindering its introduction (Connecticut), while intense party competition could drive both parties into supporting the direct primary (Maine).

To begin constructing an explanation of why the direct primary should have introduced even in the eastern states, it is necessary to recapitulate some of the points that have emerged in previous chapters.

1. By the end of the 1880s and the beginning of the 1890s, party elites in many states had become concerned about how party nominations were being made. Nomination procedures did not appear to be

working as well as they had when electoral units were smaller and when electorates were more ethnically homogeneous. Because of the structure of the parties, effective reform could be enacted only through legislation, and from the last decade of the nineteenth century onward, there were a large number of state laws aimed at regulating candidate selection procedures. (Chapter 3)

2. The introduction of the Australian Ballot had helped push forward this legislation in two respects. An official ballot meant that disputes as to who really was the candidate of a particular party had become justiciable; challenges to a party's designation were now likely to be brought through legal action, whereas earlier they had been settled by the printing of rival ballots or through the use of "pasters." Furthermore, the apparent success of the Australian Ballot in protecting party interests helped to encourage a view that legislative reform could solve long-standing problems for the parties, while not weakening the parties or their role in the nomination process. (Chapters 2 and 3)

3. Although much of the legislation in the 1890s produced expectations that it would remove the practices that party elites wanted to eliminate from candidate selection, little of this legislation produced results that were regarded as wholly satisfactory. In many states, each session of the legislature produced new bills aimed at improving nominating procedures. (Chapter 3)

4. At the same time as party elites were turning their attention to the issue of candidate selection, there had been a steady increase in the use of direct nominations. Their use was still confined mainly to rural areas, but they had spread well beyond their region of origin – western Pennsylvania. Nevertheless, the caucus-convention system remained the main way of nominating candidates throughout the United States. One of the features of caucuses, though, was that in many places they had never been more than elections – elections of delegates to conventions. Even in those parts of the east in which, originally, caucuses had been more than mere elections, the element of discussion in caucuses had been weakened as electorates had increased in size. The result was that the difference between a caucus-convention system and a direct primary did not appear so great as it would have done had caucuses really contained an interactive element. (Chapter 4)

5. Until about 1906/7, experimentation with direct nominations had been more widespread in the East than in the West. The former contained the more urbanized states, the ones facing the greater problems from the older nominating system. Subsequently, insurgency in the West led to many states there adopting "complete" laws more quickly than did their eastern counterparts. However, by 1915, a large number of eastern states also had such laws. (Chapter 4)

6. As with any change in the rules of the game, a move to direct primaries would benefit one political actor but not another. In some cases the likely beneficiaries were those "regular" politicians who were more able to mobilize mass electorates than their rivals. Thus, for example, Charles Deneen's conversion to direct nominations can be explained in terms of his ability to use the governor's office to secure renomination in Illinois; given the base of his support in Chicago, renomination would have been more difficult for him had the caucus-convention system still been in use. Self-interest on the part of politicians would always influence their attitude to direct nominations, and, as with Deneen, some party regulars could come to believe that their own careers were better advanced by direct primaries. (Chapter 5)

All of the above considerations help to describe and account for the potential attraction of the direct primary. However, leaving aside the obvious point that self-interest would incline some party regulars to preserve the status quo, what would make politicians cautious about the direct primary?

7. Unlike the official ballot, it was unclear to most politicians how *party* interests would be affected by direct nominations. With the Australian Ballot, it became evident early on that parties could have the benefits of a system that eliminated practices such as "knifing" without loosening the ties to their own voters. All systems of the official ballot, except the POB, provided for this. With nomination reform, reconciling the many objectives of reform with preservation of party control over the nomination of a ticket proved so difficult that it was unclear where the interests of a party lay. Even for those members of a party elite who wanted to promote this interest, rather than their own career interests, identifying it proved difficult. (Chapters 2–6)

8. The experience of the direct primary in the first two large cities in which it was used – leaving aside the brief experiment in Philadelphia – was not auspicious. Most of the limitations with direct nominations – ones with which all party elites would become familiar later – were evident in Cleveland, where the Republican party deployed this nominating system after 1890. The problems exposed there were relatively well known elsewhere, and yet knowledge of them seems not to have deterred other urban localities from starting to use the system. Similarly, the scandal associated with the administration of "Doc" Ames in Minneapolis did not harm the progress of the direct primary in the early twentieth century. (Chapters 3 and 4)

If these eight factors had been the only ones influencing debates about nomination reform, then it is unlikely that the direct primary would have spread as quickly as it did – especially in the east. Probably there would have been a sustained period of experiments in some states, but not others, and at some levels of public office in those states, but not the kind of wide-ranging deployment of the direct primary within just a few years that was actually the case. Two further factors help to explain why the context in which party politicians were operating led them to behave far less cautiously than might have been expected. One factor was the role played by public opinion. The other was that the issue of nomination reform was transformed from one of a problem for which a solution was needed to one in which a supposed "solution" was placed at the very centre of political debate. Indeed, that was to be the really significant contribution of the antiparty reformers who, according to the conventional wisdom, supposedly introduced the direct primary into the United States. They would have lacked the power to overcome the opposition of party organizations, but the way in which they helped to shape the debate did affect the spread of the direct primary. In this chapter, we consider these two factors in turn. In doing so, we see how, although the direct primary emanated from a process of party institutionalization, the choices made by party elites were taken in a context in which some logically possible choices were precluded to them, or did not form the focus of their attention.

1. The Constraint Imposed by Public Opinion

Charles Merriam was in no doubt as to why the direct primary had been adopted. It was because public opinion demanded it. Thus, he noted of the period after 1899, "Despite the fact that in many cases the primary had been surrounded by practically all of the safeguards of an ordinary election, the public remained unsatisfied." It was a theme to which he kept returning in *Primary Elections*; thus, for example, he argued that "[S]tartling disclosures respecting the betrayal of public trust by party leaders aroused the people to a crusade for responsible party government," and also "[S]o rapid was the progress of public opinion and of legislation that in many instances a compromise measure of one session [of a state legislature] was followed by a thoroughgoing law in the next."[1]

The idea that reform of nominating procedures could have been driven simply by pressure of public opinion is arrant nonsense. On the one hand, often there is no direct connection between public opinion and legislation. Sometimes public outrage does produce a legislative response – as it did in the 1990s with the spate of state laws on child sex offenders ("Megan's laws"). However, in many cases organized interests can be effective in weakening legislative proposals even when public opinion appears to support

---

[1] Charles E. Merriam and Louise Overacker, *Primary Elections*, Chicago, University of Chicago Press, 1928, pp. 60, 61, and 63.

them; a classic contemporary example has been the role of the gun lobby in relation to the regulation of hand guns. In representative democracies, public opinion simply does not play the role Merriam imputed to it. On the other hand, evidence from many states in the early 1900s – of which Massachusetts, Missouri, and Pennsylvania are clear instances – indicates that the direct primary was not that high profile an issue in political debate. Had public agitation really been as intense as Merriam suggested, then both the reaction of politicians and also press coverage would have been very different.

Nevertheless, there is an important truth contained within Merriam's exaggerations. If they addressed it, nomination reform could become an issue from which politicians could derive credit – at least from some groups of voters. The impact of either interparty competition or of intraparty rivalries provided an incentive for particular politicians to take up the matter. (The case of Indiana, discussed briefly in Chapter 6, provides an example of the former, while that of Charles Deneen in Illinois is an example of the latter.) Like many issues, therefore, it was one to which a politician might turn as a way of bolstering support for his party or himself. Moreover, although the evidence is fragmentary, it does appear that public attitudes had changed between the middle and the end of the nineteenth century. There are obvious reasons why they did. Especially in urban areas, parties were facing increasing difficulties in running nominations on the traditional, informal, lines, and decades of exposure to newspaper criticisms about the "ways of the cities" had made mass publics more willing to support proposals to constrain politics in the cities. In the West, the penetration of parties by major corporations made mass publics there even more willing to support intervention. It is important to recognize, though, that while public opinion may have become more supportive of reform from the 1890s onward, the willingness of voters to support political reform was already evident by the mid-to-late 1880s in relation to the Australian Ballot. As was argued in Chapter 2 (Section 6), Governor David Hill's problems on the issue stemmed from the fact that it was generally a popular reform among many voters.

This last point is important because it would be misleading to see popular support for the direct primary as something that emanated just from the political turbulence, and changed political conditions, of the 1890s. There had been a longer term change in attitudes to parties – from largely uncritical pre-Civil War to being more open-minded about their practices. What remained, though, was a set of beliefs dating back to the Jacksonian era that, if parties were at the center of political life, they should be highly participatory, providing access to the political system for all those who wanted it. That these sorts of attitudes were widely shared meant that the options for those who wanted to change the nominating system were limited. The significance of this becomes more apparent both in Section 2 and also in Section 4, when we consider whether the parties could have done more than they did to protect their interests. For now the key point is that a more recent, skeptical, attitude to the current performance of parties combined with long-standing beliefs in their participatory role helped to limit how political elites could respond to the nomination problem. It was a major constraint on what they could do.

Nevertheless, there are those who have argued that a yet more central role was played by public opinion in stimulating reform in the early twentieth century. This argument parallels Merriam's in that it posits public opinion as triggering reform. Unlike the cruder Merriam version, in which a generally disgruntled public demanded a satisfactory reform, this version holds that it was political scandal that prompted reform; scandal either caused a public outcry, or led political elites to expect a public outcry, but in either case those elites responded by initiating reforms. One of the main proponents of this sort of argument is Richard McCormick. McCormick argues that between about 1903 and 1908 scandals and other factors acted as catalysts in both triggering legislation on political reform by party politicians and also in changing the rhetoric used by parties in competing with each other. His claim is that, in the second half of the nineteenth century, socioeconomic transformation, and most especially rapid urbanization, changed the opportunities open to business to use government in pursuit of its own interests. By the 1890s, this was prompting public debates both about the corruption of politics by business, and also about how best to control those areas of activity where corruption was most likely. One of the main areas of controversy was control of utilities, where the possible profits for the operating companies provided a strong incentive to "buy" influence. According to McCormick:

During 1905 and 1906 in particular, a remarkable number of cities and states experienced wrenching moments of discovery that led directly to significant political changes. Usually a scandal, an investigation, an intraparty battle, or a particularly divisive election campaign exposed an illicit alliance of politics and business and made corruption apparent to the community.[2]

According to McCormick, one result of this was that between 1906 and 1908 there was a massive increase in the amount of state legislation in a number of areas of political reform – regulation of lobbying, prohibitions on corporate campaign contributions, regulation of free railroad passes to public officials, mandatory direct primaries, and the regulation of railroad corporations by commissions. Another effect was on the Democratic and

---

[2] Richard L. McCormick, "The Discovery that Business Corrupts Politics: A Reappraisal of the Origins of Progressivism," *American Historical Review*, 2, no. 66(1981), p. 260.

Republican parties themselves; McCormick argues that in eight of the ten states for which he could obtain state party platforms for the years 1900–10 there was discussion by the parties of how business corrupted politics in the second half of this period. (These eight states were Iowa, Missouri, New Hampshire, New York, Indiana, Illinois, Pennsylvania, and South Dakota.) Only in New Jersey did the parties not address this issue in their manifestos, while in Wisconsin the issue was taken up much earlier – in 1900 and 1902.[3]

We are not concerned here with the application of McCormick's argument to other reforms, but only to the adoption of the direct primary. Was there really a link between the incidence of scandal and attempts at direct primary legislation? Certainly, relating the McCormick argument to the direct primary is revealing for some states. The experience in both Pennsylvania, where legislation was passed in 1906, and in New York, where there was a high-profile debate during Hughes's unsuccessful attempts to have legislation enacted there appear to support McCormick's case. However, there are two problems in incorporating McCormick's account into a general explanation for the introduction of the direct primary. First, some states had enacted primary legislation without "muckraking moments," so such moments were not a necessary condition for its enactment.

Second, they were not a sufficient condition either. There appears to be no connection between the thirteen nonsouthern states McCormick specifically identifies as having "muckraking moments" (California, Indiana, Montana, Nebraska, New Hampshire, New Jersey, New York, North Dakota, Ohio, Pennsylvania, Rhode Island, South Dakota, and Vermont) and the introduction of the direct primary.[4] Of these states, only five (Nebraska, North Dakota, Ohio, Pennsylvania, and South Dakota) had passed wide-ranging direct primary laws by the end of 1908 – the final year of McCormick's study. Of the remainder, Rhode Island did not enact the direct primary during the Progressive era, while Indiana, Montana, and Vermont all did so quite late – as did New York, although the intense debate prompted there after 1905 really should count for the McCormick case rather than against it.

Clearly, in some states political scandal did help to push nomination reform further than it might otherwise have gone, but the impact of scandal on either elite or mass attitudes toward the direct primary does not appear to account for all such legislation. Yet, public opinion was an important constraint on political elites, and we return to that matter in Section 4. First, though, it is important to consider the role played by antiparty reformers in accelerating the use of the direct primary, especially in the East.

[3] McCormick, "The Discovery that Business Corrupts Politics," p. 263.
[4] McCormick, "The Discovery that Business Corrupts Politics," p. 262.

2. Reformers and the Invention of a "Solution"

In understanding the rise of the direct primary, the crucial period is the years between about 1897 and 1899, and not, as many would argue, between 1902 and 1908. Before 1897 nomination reform had centred mainly on efforts to provide for state laws that would enable the existing nominating system to work more effectively. In the two or three years after 1896, the direct primary came more into prominence as an alternative to the existing arrangements, even while many laws relating to the older system continued to be enacted. However, while ballot reform had produced acceptable results very rapidly, a similar outcome to nomination reform legislation was proving elusive. That was why there had been so much support among political elites for the idea of a National Conference in 1898. It is in these years between 1897 and 1899 that the direct primary started to be discussed more seriously as an alternative. But why?

We shall see shortly that the fact that the direct primary did come to be discussed in this way was of great significance for what was to happen in subsequent years. However, far more important than this aspect of agenda setting in explaining those eventual outcomes was the role of party elites in initiating laws reforming the caucus-convention system in the first place. It was these party-initiated reforms that had got political debate to the point at which direct nominations could be regarded as a serious alternative. Without the earlier discontent in the parties both about the ballot and the nominating system (in the decade before 1896), debate about direct primaries would still have been confined to a few "hobbyists" on the fringes of politics. It was because party elites had been so concerned with problems in the system of candidate selection that the direct primary could become a serious rival to the caucus-convention system. The direct primary emerged out of a process of party institutionalization that could not be concluded because wholly satisfactory systems of nominating candidates had not been put in place.

The argument developed in this book is that there were two main features of the attempt to regulate party nominations that contributed to the unlikely outcome of a reform – one that could be shown to be flawed – being adopted by party elites who might have been expected to protect their parties from such reforms. The first is that the problem of how to nominate candidates was highly complex and involved incompatible objectives; in public debate relatively little attention was paid to how, in practical legislative arrangements, these objectives might be reconciled, if at all. The second feature was that public debate about reform of the system was driven on by a belief among reformers, both inside and outside the parties, that successful reform was possible providing the correct "solution" was adopted; a sufficient number of them also believed they knew what that solution was. In part, their optimism was fanned by the very success of the official ballot legislation. However, the key to the eventual success of the direct primary was the absence of serious rivals to it. Consequently, amid the complexity of the issues surrounding nomination reform, attention came to be focused on the supposed "solution" rather than on anything else. Moreover, the main contribution of antiparty reformers to the outcome was to help keep public attention focused on the direct primary rather than on the complex nature of the nomination "problem." Despite the failure in Cleveland, the direct primary could be presented as a "quick fix" for at least some of the problems of party nominations, and its limitations were never really exposed to the scrutiny that they might have faced in other circumstances. In a sense, therefore, it was much more a matter of political elites "backing into" the direct primary than their being driven into it by their opponents.

This point can be illuminated by means of a light-hearted analogy. In the famous radio comedy, *The Hitch Hiker's Guide to the Galaxy*, a super-computer, Deep Thought, was asked to find the answer to the problem of life, the universe and everything. Millions of years later, Deep Thought announces the answer, which was forty-two. Confronted by anger and disbelief at that answer, Deep Thought noted, "I checked it very thoroughly . . . and that quite definitely is the answer. I think the problem, to be quite honest with you, is that you've never actually known what the question is."[5] Similarly, the "question" of nominating reform was plagued, from the early 1890s until after the widespread adoption of the direct primary, by confusion as to what precisely the "question" was. As noted in Chapter 2, some participants in the public debate were aware of this; in 1900, Amos Parker Wilder argued that nomination reform was different from ballot reform in this regard, but many of his fellow reformers ignored the point. Instead, complex issues tended to be reduced to oversimplified ones. The title of a 1909 article by Isaac M. Brickner, "Direct Primaries versus Boss Rule" – was typical of this, and the overall effects of such oversimplification were to obfuscate the issues, not least about the objectives of would-be reformers.[6] To see why there was a problem about the objectives of those engaged in the debate about nominations, it is necessary to refer again to the four variables that were discussed in Chapter 3 – participation, logistics, fraud, and control. Here, however, they will be considered in a different order, beginning with logistics.

(i) Logistics
The problem of "scale" was one that had been widely recognized and was one that tended not to divide party regulars from even reformers of the

---

[5] Douglas Adams, *The Hitch Hiker's Guide to the Galaxy*, London, Millenium, 1994, p. 147.
[6] Isaac M. Brickner, "Direct Primaries versus Boss Rule," *Arena*, August 1909, pp. 550–6.

most antiparty persuasion. Both increased population size and urbanization created problems of having people participate in electoral units that remained unchanged. Although some regular organizations might have found the chaos that could result from too many people trying to get to vote in a particular caucus advantageous, for the most part it hindered their activities as much as those of any independent-minded reformers. Consensus on this matter may be compared with one aspect of the earlier debate over the Australian Ballot; both party regulars and reformers wanted to prevent "knifing," in the form of party ballots that omitted the names of some official party candidates for lower offices. As was shown in Chapter 2, split-ticket voting of this kind created serious problems of party management for "regulars." Reformers also opposed the practice, but in their case because it made it more likely that some voters would have voted unwittingly for candidates whom they had not intended to support. However, simply because there was considerable agreement about the problems caused by changing "scale," they were not likely to feature much in political debate even though they were one of the main factors giving rise to discontent with older balloting and nominating practices. Similarly, after the mid-1890s, arguments about "scale" in relation to nominations were not prominent in public debate, even though alleviating those problems remained an important objective.

(ii) Fraud

Had the nominating problems of the late nineteenth century primarily been ones of fraud, it is doubtful that the path of regulation of party nominations would have led to the direct primary. The outright purchasing of votes, the stuffing of ballot boxes, or whatever was as easily controlled through regulating the conduct of caucuses as it was through a direct election. Furthermore, eliminating fraud *per se* was not likely to change political outcomes very much – cities and states would not have been governed by very different people even if had been eliminated completely; as was noted in Chapter 3, an important point made by Branson was that fraud was primarily a weapon used between rival professional politicians rather than as a means of keeping out of office middle-class political independents.[7] Nevertheless, fraud was an easy target to attack in public debate, and even professional politicians argued that it was in the "true interest of each party" to eliminate it.[8] Nor was this mere rhetoric. Fraud made for uncertainty in much the same way that "trading" and "knifing" at general elections did in the pre-Australian Ballot era. With some notable exceptions, therefore, many party elites were quite content to go along with the

[7] Walter J. Branson, "The Philadelphia Nominating System", *Annals of the American Academy of Political and Social Science*, 14(1899), p. 26.

[8] Edward Lauterbach, address to *National Conference on Practical Reform of Primary Elections*, New York, January 21, 1898, p. 114.

elimination of fraud in much the same way that they had supported the Australian Ballot.

As an objective, the elimination of fraud was not especially divisive, but, unlike "logistics," it continued to surface in political debates because self-confessed reformers found the language of fraud useful rhetoric against their opponents. It could be introduced seemingly to bolster the substantive point a reformer was making. A typical example of this is found in a discussion in a 1910 issue of the journal *Current Literature*. In this article, the author was seeking to counter the argument that one disadvantage of direct primaries was that candidates might be nominated with less than a majority of those voting, while in conventions those nominated did obtain majorities.[9] Although the author never mentioned or alluded to any practices that might actually be fraudulent, an "honest plurality" in a direct primary is contrasted with "a dishonest machine-made-majority" in a convention. In other words, the language of fraud was used to stigmatize party regulars, even though removing fraud was an objective that many regulars accepted; but, of course, regulars and reformers might well differ on the matter of how best to eliminate it.

(iii) Control

There were two important but separate objectives that fell under the heading of control. One related to the quality of elected public officials. Municipal reformers, especially, wanted to change the profile of such officials – they wanted "better" candidates running for public office and getting elected, and by "better" they meant ones who had particular sets of skills and attitudes that they believed were typically not found among most party candidates. In forums such as the annual meetings of the National Municipal League – which first met in 1894 – considerable attention was paid to ways of improving the quality of officeholders. Party regulars too were concerned with "quality" but, generally, they believed that the current nominating systems did provide what was required. In particular, parties would tend to filter out the completely incompetent – because they would prove to be an embarrassment in office – and they would provide for ethnic and territorial balance in the selection of a party slate, thereby satisfying the claims of different communities. Whatever the merits of these arguments, the important point is that while there was agreement between regulars and reformers, at the most general level, about the need for competent public officials, there was a sharp disagreement about the skills actually needed and the ability of parties to supply public offices with such people.

The spectrum of opinion on the second objective falling under the heading of "control" was even greater. This concerned the role of organization in politics. At one extreme were those reformers whose objective was to remove all organizational advantage from the nominating process, so

---

[9] For example, *Current Literature*, July 1910, p. 7.

that even the most unknown of outsiders could compete on equal terms with anyone else. At the other extreme were party regulars who wished to preserve advantages that parties currently enjoyed vis-à-vis political independents. In between were a whole variety of positions, including those of Boston Democrat Josiah Quincy, who was a strong partisan and a supporter of the role of party in organizing politics, but who was willing to make some concessions so that independents could play a role. Another intermediate position that could command some support was adopted by those municipal reformers who wished to limit the influence of party organization at the municipal level of politics but who supported its persistence in state and national politics. The crucial point is that there were sharply diverging positions on how "organized" politics should be, although the consensus of the mid-nineteenth century, that organized parties were central to democracy at the state and federal levels, was far from having been eroded even by 1910.

(iv) Participation

Reformers wanted to increase mass participation in the nominating process; democracy was to be restored by having more people involved in candidate selection. Given the ethos of participation that had dominated the history of American parties, this was not a matter on which most regulars could oppose them, even if they wished to. Indeed, many regulars were in favor of increased participation, providing that those attending caucuses were genuinely committed to the party rather than either disruptive infiltrators from the other party or those seeking to influence politics but lacking any commitment to the party. For example, having loyal supporters who would go out to vote in "his" wards was the basis of Jim Pendergast's power in Kansas City;[10] this was not unusual, for in the first decade of the twentieth century, there were few places where a "boss" was so secure that low participation rates worked to his advantage. Of course, other factors might incline regulars to reject the direct primary, but a desire to have lower participation rates was not usually one of them.

Broadly speaking, these were the main issues informing the positions taken by the principal types of participants in the nomination reform debate. As a crude summary, it can be said that "reform" was characterised by having too many objectives that its adherents wished to realize simultaneously; party "regulars" may have had fewer conflicting objectives, but they still had more than enough to make it difficult for them to decide where party interests might lie. As a result, the transformation of the nomination process in the eastern United States, at least, rarely developed into a series of battles between well-defined sides; the remainder of this section considers why this should have been the case.

[10] See Lyle W. Dorsett, *The Pendergast Machine*, New York, Oxford University Press, 1968, Chapters 1–4.

As has just been noted, the most extreme of the reformers wanted to elect better public officials, reduce much of the power of party organizations, and increase participation in the parties. Of course, there was no reason why these objectives should actually be compatible with each other, and the first two would seem as if they might involve social and political engineering on a massive scale. Most reformers did not draw this conclusion, though, because usually they connected the three objectives in the following way. The power of the organizations in the existing nominating systems tended to reduce participation because people could not be bothered to attend organization-dominated party caucuses; the organization used their ability to organize conventions to minimize the impact of those who opposed their preferred candidates; the candidates often chosen by these organizations were not of the calibre needed for public office. Now, of course, most reformers were not so naive as to believe that changing the nominating system was the only, or even the main, route to "better government," but reform of that system was seen as a way of helping to break organizations, getting better men into office, and increasing mass participation all at the same time. The reform agenda was not a simple one; or rather, it was not simple before the direct primary started to become identified as the "solution."

For many reformers, therefore, the point of eliminating party conventions was to stimulate mass participation in the selection of candidates, to reduce the power of party organizations to select their preferred candidates, and in doing so raise the quality of elected public officials. The belief that conventions more readily harbored fraud in the selection process also featured in the propaganda of at least some of those who were to advocate a more direct system of nomination. Thus, in the late 1890s, many of the more antipartisan opponents of the party convention came to propose a very simple remedy for a complicated set of problems, and F. M. Brooks's account of the nature of political power is typical of the simplistic accounts that were being propagated by then. In late 1897, he wrote:

It is the power to nominate which makes the "boss" and the "machine." Bosses cannot control the voters. They control and get their power from delegates, party workers, politicians, office-holders and office-seekers. Take away the power to nominate, and bosses and machines will cease to exist.[11]

Of course, not all those who believed that something "had to be done" about the process of selecting party candidates took this kind of view; the wide range of politicians who had endorsed the idea of a national conference on nominating reform in early 1898 included few who subscribed to Brooks's sort of idea. Yet, eventually, quite a number of such politicians would go along with the conclusion of the Brooks-type of

---

[11] F. M. Brooks, "The Nominating Ballot," *Outlook*, December 18, 1897, pp. 950–1.

argument, and support the direct primary as the "solution" to the nomination "problem."

There is an apparent paradox here, though – the very matter with which
this chapter has been attempting to get to grips. If the issues raised by
nominating reform were so complex, and also embraced people with widely
differing attitudes to party, why did they come to converge on a single
institutional reform, the direct primary? Movements with multiple objectives, and widely differing opinions among their adherents, would be
expected to find it difficult to shift the status quo firmly in one direction.
However, they did so in this case. There are two reasons for this unusual
occurrence – one relating to the "cause" and the other relating to its potential opponents.

First, there seemed to be an obvious "quick fix." Between about 1896
and the early 1900s attention in public debate started to shift sharply away
from the complex "questions" of nomination reform to a supposedly simple
"solution." The answer was not the incomprehensible "forty-two," of
The Hitch Hiker's Guide to the Galaxy, but the easy to comprehend state-
mandated direct primary election. The very complexity of the issues raised
about the then current nominating system had meant that usually they
were open to serious discussion only in a scholarly book like Frederick
Dallinger's; although such a level of debate was also possible at a forum
like the National Conference on Practical Reform of Primary Elections, this
could not be the stuff of practical politics. Indeed, had there not been an
obvious "quick fix" available, in the form of the direct primary, it may be
doubted whether mass-level agitation over nomination reform could have
continued for that long. The problems of the nominating system were not
ones that could easily capture popular imagination – unless they were highly
simplified.

Furthermore, the experience of the Australian Ballot had demonstrated
that institutional reform could work. With nomination reform there was,
additionally, a group of people, centred on those reformers whose commitment to parties was weak or even hostile, who believed that not only
was a "solution" possible, but that there was a uniquely optimal solution.
That solution was the direct primary, and, irrespective of what else it might
achieve, as an "answer to the problem" it did have one clear advantage over
the status quo – it would surely lead to quite large increases in participation
rates in candidate selections. As a consequence, issues such as how the
quality of elected public officials could be improved got pushed further back
on the political agenda. Some supporters of the direct primary took the view
that increased "quality" would follow directly from the people controlling
the nominations; those who were more sanguine about that could console
themselves with the belief that at least the direct primary would increase
voter participation in the parties, which was no bad thing, and the matter of
the quality of public officials could be dealt with subsequently.

That the direct primary had come to be seen rather widely by the early twentieth century, as "the solution," and not merely a possible policy to be tried out in limited experiments was the result of three factors. First, it was the only conceivable alternative that had been used already in a number of different localities. None of the other schemes used in various Pennsylvania counties, for example, had been used much outside that state. The direct primary had a track record, albeit a mixed one. Second, the fact that in many parts of the United States caucuses were no more than elections (for delegates) anyway meant that the direct primary did not have the appearance of an entirely alien reform; it had the supreme advantage of seeming to be a rather "unradical" radical reform. Third, from the mid-1890s onward, most antiparty reformers lined up in support of the direct primary, and that gave it a public prominence it would have lacked had there been a number of competing schemes that these reformers were advocating. This was the real contribution of those reformers to the eventual outcome. They lacked the clout to get the direct primary enacted, but they helped to shape public debate because they focused on a single supposed "solution."

However, if reformers focusing on a "solution" suggests a parallel with ballot reform, there are two important differences between the two cases. Unlike the earlier debate, where party elites found alternative reforms to the reform-sponsored POB, no such party-friendly schemes emerged, and the direct primary became the only option to some minor variation on the status quo. Yet, ballot reformers like Richard Dana actually had been far more radical than were their counterparts in respect of the direct primary. The Australian Ballot was a wholly new mechanism that party elites found could promote their own interests, even if it emanated from antiparty reformers. The direct primary was not an alien device; it was already in use in about one-third of all states by the mid-1890s, and its use was increasing. Those reformers promoting it did not have to "sell" a foreign device to potentially skeptical party elites. In short, with the Australian Ballot, the power of the reformers was to "sell a new idea" – to convince party elites to consider a device that might benefit them. With the direct primary, the power of the reformers was to help narrow the focus of political debate to the only widely used alternative to the caucus-convention system, and in doing so the reformers made it more likely that their preferred outcome would be realized.

However, acting alone, those reformers could never have succeeded. The role played by public opinion, discussed earlier in this chapter, in constraining elected politicians, was important but so, too, was the fact that, for a variety of reasons and in varying contexts, many party regulars were also willing to contemplate direct nominations. An interesting feature of nomination reform, therefore, was that a disparate set of political actors who were united mainly in their dissatisfaction with the status quo, could come together as a broad coalition supporting an apparent "solution" that could be shown to be seriously flawed. At the same time, it was much more difficult for the potential opponents of the direct primary to muster. It became a valence issue, akin to the politics of "Mom and Apple Pie"; in many circumstances most political actors had an incentive to show that they were in favor of it. After all, who could fight against a reform that would increase the number of people involved in candidate selection? Central to the tradition of American political parties since the 1830s had been their mass character, so to oppose a reform that would permit a restoration of the mass party base was to court unpopularity. For this reason, the potentially damaging evidence from Cleveland – that direct primaries did not place effective power in the hands of voters, that they lowered the standard of candidates running for office, and so on – did not have the devastating effect on the debate that might have been expected.

3. Consensus Over the Direct Primary: The Case of New Jersey

By the end of the nineteenth century, it was becoming difficult to mobilize against direct primary legislation – even in the case of urban counties. In previous chapters, it has been seen how, in many states, there was little opposition to the direct primary. This was true of Minnesota, first with its introduction in Minneapolis in 1899 and then two years later in the rest of the state. The level of opposition was also relatively low in other states; for example, in Massachusetts in 1903, when it was applied to some offices there, and also in Pennsylvania (in 1906) and Missouri (in 1907). By the beginning of the twentieth century, many elected politicians accepted the need for reform of the nominating system, and recognized that earlier legislation had not brought about the kind of change that had been evident with ballot reform. Hemmed in by long-standing attitudes to parties in America, on the one side, and by the growing debate about a supposed "solution" (the direct primary), on the other, state legislatures were increasingly turning to that "solution."

In addition to the cases discussed in detail in previous chapters, there is another state, not discussed so far, that is worth mentioning more briefly here – New Jersey. It illustrates how much historically based expectations of the role parties should play in American democracy shaped institutional change. Before 1902, New Jersey had not experienced any extensive or radical regulation of its nominating system, although there had been legislation on some aspects of party nominations in 1878, 1882, 1883, and 1898. Moreover, the extent of party control in the state cannot be doubted, since it continued to use the most party-friendly ballot, the "shoestring" ballot, until 1911. Yet, it was not a laggard on party nomination reform. The dynamic of party institutionalization was such that early aspects of institutionalization, especially the official ballot, prompted pressure for further reform. Not only did party elites know that there were serious problems for the parties with the existing nomination process, but also that such reforms would be popular electorally. Given the attention focused on it in public debate in the preceding few years, the direct primary was the obvious instrument to use in pushing institutionalization further. As Reynolds points out:

The origins of the direct primary can be traced to the efforts of party leaders around the state to bring further order and legitimacy to the candidate selection process. In their newly won status as "official" organizations, the Democratic and Republican leadership came under pressure to demonstrate that their nominees truly were the popular choice.[12]

Consequently, by 1902, the year before the passage of the statute introducing the direct primary on a statewide basis for some local offices, all of the urban counties in New Jersey had replaced caucuses with primaries, and in every county in the southern part of the state at least one of the two major parties was now using primaries.[13]

The legislation of 1903 mandated the use of the direct primary, at public expense, for ward and township officers. Of it, the *Jersey Journal* noted that the:

primary bill is drawing the fire of politicians of the heeler class of both political parties. The decent element in both parties, realizing that our present primary systems are a disgrace to the nineteenth century civilization, is heartily in favor of the reform.[14]

That the "decent element" was clearly in firm control of the parties was evident in the vote in the state legislature – the legislation passed with not a single dissenting vote in the assembly and only one in the senate. While it had the support of those with Progressive sympathies, it also had the far more significant support of both party organization leaders and legislative leaders. Of course, the offices brought under the direct primary after 1903 were not major ones, and it was not until further legislation in 1908 and 1911 that such offices were covered. However, the interesting points about the 1903 law are, first, that even minor offices should come under the law in a party-dominated state and that so little opposition was actually mobilized. The absence of opposition was made clear by Boots, writing fourteen years later, when he argued:

The principal objection of the political leaders to the bill were [sic] probably expressed by the Republican county committee of Essex: "It gave the municipal clerks too much power. They were likely to be partisan, find technical flaws in the petitions of independent men of an opposing faction or party and prevent intended

---

[12] John F. Reynolds, *Testing Democracy: Electoral Behaviour and Progressive Reform in New Jersey, 1880–1920*, Chapel Hill and London, University of North Carolina Press, 1988, p. 130.

[13] Reynolds, *Testing Democracy*, p. 131.

[14] *Jersey Journal*, February 9, 1903, cited in Ralph Simpson Boots, "The Direct Primary in New Jersey," Columbia University, Ph.D. dissertation, 1917, p. 21.

nominations. Independent voters might resent having primary ballots provided for them." . . . It will be conceded that these reasons for opposing the bill were not of great weight.[15]

That the introduction of direct primary legislation could be relatively consensual, as it was in this instance, is not surprising. In the absence of particular factors, consensus on the matter, as on any valence issue, was usual, and there were three additional factors that helped to bring about agreement in this case. First, as has been shown in previous chapters, doing something about the nomination process was an issue that most party elites had been addressing for more than a decade. It was not a matter that had been sprung on them by those opposed to party interests. Second, the range of alternative policies open to them for dealing with the problems of nominating now that there were many more voters, was limited by American public attitudes toward parties. Third, as the debate about the problems of the nomination process was transformed into one about a supposed "solution" – the direct primary – so what it was feasible for party elites to enact was further reduced.

The key argument being made here, therefore, is that the introduction of the direct primary was much more consensual than has usually been argued. Far from pushing party regulars into conflict with themselves, antiparty reformers played a rather different role. They helped to narrow the alternatives available to party elites by turning debate about nomination reform into an issue about the direct primary itself. That is, they helped to channel debate so that the direct primary was always likely to emerge as the subject of legislation. When it did so it would be a matter on which agreement could be reached between party elites. If that argument is correct, then it must be asked how we can account for the presence of conflict over primary legislation in some states. After all, we have seen in earlier chapters that the direct primary was not always a consensual matter. In fact, there were three main circumstances in which conflict could develop.

In those western states, where the direct primary became a device aimed at challenging the power of economic elites, the source of conflict is obvious. Party elites became divided between those who supported insurgency and those who sought to defend the economic interests, and the issue of the direct primary split these elites in predictable ways. (It must be remembered, though, that insurgency was not the cause of the direct primary in all western states – Minnesota being an obvious example.)

Another circumstance generating conflict over the direct primary was when it became clear how individual careers in a party would be affected directly by the introduction of the direct primary. This happened in Illinois, where it was known that it would benefit the incumbent governor, Charles Deneen. Deneen was able to prevail over his opponents on each occasion

[15] Boots, "The Direct Primary in New Jersey," p. 23.

a bill was introduced, although, in neighboring Wisconsin, Robert La Follette had failed initially (in 1901) in his attempt to do precisely the same thing. His opponents saw La Follette's own political ambitions as being dependent on its introduction, and this helped opposition to consolidate against the direct primary. Intraparty rivalries were often crucial, therefore, to the development of conflict on the issue. By contrast, because the direct primary did appear to be popular with mass electorates, competition *between* parties tended to help its introduction. Providing the majority party in the state was not split on the matter, the minority party would find opposition difficult. Once the majority party was divided, though, the broad coalition in its support might well not form. As was seen in Chapter 5, intraparty opposition in the majority party was important in wrecking direct primary legislation in New York, before its final enactment in 1913.

Finally, there is the unusual case of New York where the balance of power between the parties in the major cities and those elsewhere was tilted far more to the former. Because there were more politicians whose livelihoods depended on the kinds of practices that others were trying to restrict in the interests of party effectiveness, it became easier to mobilize opposition to the direct primary in New York. (The same effect had been evident over the Australian Ballot.) In turn, that could prompt the dispute developing into a partisan matter, and that would always complicate successful resolution of the issue.

Obviously, in any of these three circumstances public debate about the direct primary could be extensive, as politicians sought to line up winning coalitions to defeat or support the direct primary. In Illinois, New York, and Wisconsin, for example, it is easy to trace that debate through newspaper coverage at the time. When the matter was more consensual, it was something that was rarely discussed in the newspapers. The most extreme case was Pennsylvania, where the fact that it was a direct primary that was being introduced in the drive for nomination "uniformity" was hardly ever mentioned. However, in states like Missouri and New Jersey also, the legislation passed with little controversy, and it scarcely ranked as a matter of even secondary importance, let alone primary importance, for the newspapers. The same was broadly true of Massachusetts, although Governor Walker's late conversion to direct nominations gave slightly more prominence to the issue than in the other three states.

4. Could the Parties Have Done More to Protect Themselves?

One of the arguments that lies at the heart of this book is that the role of antiparty reformers in the introduction of the direct primary was much more restricted than has usually been believed. In this chapter, it has been argued that the real importance of such reformers was in helping to transform a debate about a highly complex issue – nomination reform – into one in which a "solution" (the direct primary) came to the forefront. Because of this change of focus, the direct primary was introduced more widely and more quickly than it would have been otherwise. While this was an important role, it is clearly a more restricted one than that usually claimed for these kinds of reformers. It might be argued that I have under-estimated that role by not considering whether these reformers succeeded in imposing on the parties a form of nomination that was more destructive of party interests than it need have been. Perhaps, it might be argued against me, the real significance of the reform is that it got the parties to accept a measure that was more extreme than others they could have adopted to meet the problems they faced? To see if this argument is plausible it is worth posing the question of whether party elites could have done more than they actually did to protect party interests when passing direct primary legislation. If they could have, then the claim that antiparty reformers did exert great power over the issue would have to be explored further. If, however, it can be concluded that party elites could have done little more than they did to protect party interests, then the argument for continuing to interpret the direct primary as the triumph of antipartism is much reduced.

Two aspects of the legislation, in particular, might be raised. First, whether more might have been done to restrict participation in party nom-inations to party adherents, thereby ensuring that nominations remained an essentially party activity. Second, whether ways might have been found of combining a direct primary with procedures providing for greater party organization influence over nominations, thereby reducing the likelihood that candidates would become the principal actors in the parties.

Who should participate in party primaries, and how participation could be regulated, was a matter that was the subject of intense debate through-out the period. It raised both theoretical and practical problems. The most antiparty viewpoint was that nominating a candidate was merely the first stage of a public election, and, therefore, all citizens had a right to attend a party caucus or vote in a primary. As John R. Commons put it in 1898: "Just as we do not leave the definition of citizenship and the machinery of naturalization to the private interests of any body of men, so we can not leave the definition of party membership to even the party organization."[16] The citizen himself had a right to vote in the primary of the party that he intended to vote for, and the test of whether he intended to vote for say, the Democrats, was whether he said he would vote for them. On this view, a party would be left at the mercy of all those who merely said they were Democrats, or Republicans, or whatever.

---

[16] John R. Commons, address to the *National Conference on Practical Reform of Primary Elections*, p. 22.

Horace Deming outlined a similar, although rather more ingenious, argument in an address to the National Municipal League in 1905. He rejected the idea that only "accredited members of any organization" had the right to participate in nominations. Instead, all those who shared the political principles a candidate was claiming to represent had a right to vote in that primary; their right stemmed from the fact that being a nominee for public office was "really to hold an elective public office – no less a public office because its term lasts only from the nominating to the general election."[17] Both Commons's and Deming's views meshed with the idea of what would shortly be called an "open primary" – that is, one that was not confined to those people who, in some sense, could display that they were party members and not merely that they wished to participate in party nominations.

However, not all reformers, even those well outside the parties, took the view of someone like Commons or Deming. In 1903 the reform journal *Outlook* noted, "A primary is not an election, and it is not unfair to ask the man who wishes to take part in a party nomination to accept, for the time being at least, party membership."[18] That same year, the academic, James Albert Woodburn, made a similar point:

No opponent of a party has a right to participate in its Primary. The law should protect a party from its enemies who may seek to disrupt or weaken it. The test of party membership, or party loyalty, is the most difficult matter in framing primary laws.[19]

Party elites, of course, generally concurred on both his points; they expected those who took part in party nominations to have a commitment of some kind to the party. However, the issue of what sort of commitment it was, and how that commitment could be revealed, let alone enforced, was proving difficult to resolve. To see why this was the case, it is useful to discuss how a European mass membership party typically deals with the matter.

There are two main devices mass membership parties employ to prevent their nominations coming under the influence of their opponents. First, only those who are party members are eligible to take part in candidate selection. A member is someone who formally joins the party, and who, in doing so, agrees to be bound by the rules of the party and who generally pays an annual fee. Members who break the rules – for example, by openly supporting another party or joining it – may be disciplined and ultimately

---

[17] Horace E. Deming, "Some Dangers of the Control by Permanent Political Organizations of the Methods of Nomination to Elective Municipal Office," *Proceedings of the New York Conference for Good Government and the 11th Annual Meeting of the National Municipal League*, Philadelphia, National Municipal League, 1905, pp. 361–2.

[18] *Outlook*, July 4, 1903, p. 537.

[19] James Albert Woodburn, *Political Parties and Party Problems in the United States*, New York and London, G. P. Putnam's Sons, 1903, p. 286.

expelled from it. Second, to make sure that new members are not "entry-ists" bent on undermining the party, rights of nominating candidates may be delayed until the member has been in the party for a certain length of time. Even long-serving members may have to endure this "qualifying" period should they move from one area to another; thus, the British Labour Party would not allow members who moved from one parliamentary constituency to another to take part in the nomination of Parliamentary or local government candidates until they had resided in that constituency for one year.

Now, although this is often not recognized by those who insist that American parties are radically different from their European counterparts, a number of key features of membership parties were, or could have been, mimicked by American party elites had they chosen to do so. Others could not, and identifying the ones that could not be copied is crucial to under-standing the dilemma facing American party elites at the beginning of the twentieth century.

Given their decentralized character, American parties could not have issued membership cards to party adherents on the European membership party model; at least they could not have done so efficiently, and the system would have been open to serious abuse in many urban areas. But they could have got the state to register party members for them, so that only party members could participate in the nomination process. Indeed, this is really what came to happen in "closed" primary states – the state was registering party members for the parties. So it was not that parties were moving toward becoming "public utilities" that accounts for their taking a differ-ent path from membership parties. Part of the reason for the failure of American parties to develop on at least "functionally equivalent" lines to membership parties lies in decentralization. In general, European member-ship parties neither retain members irrespective of their behavior nor expel them simply on whim – because either policy would tend to discredit the party as a whole, and not just in the locality in which that occurred. Party elites intervene when the interests of the wider party are threatened by local practices. Thus, the British Labour Party's problem with Militant Tendency in Liverpool in the 1980s threatened the credibility of the party nationally and not just on Merseyside; furthermore, the centralized nature of the party meant that it could act to remove members of Militant, even though the latter were in control of the party in the Liverpool area. In a more cen-tralized party, the party's "wider interests" are more easily protected from locally based factional interests. However, there would have been both less incentive for American state parties to act against such interests in one of their cities, and also fewer prospects of doing so successfully, given the high level of autonomy enjoyed by county parties.

The weaker "wider interest" of the party at the level of state politics meant that American parties themselves could never be trusted with polic-ing their own membership. The test of whether a member was really a "loyalist" or an "infiltrator" could not be left up to the parties, and certainly not the local parties, because decisions would likely rest in the hands of those who had a particular stake in including and excluding given individuals from "membership" in the party. Exclusion from a party, therefore, would have to be on grounds that could be handled under the embrace of state law; some of the flexibility that European parties would have in excluding unwanted members would thereby be absent in the United States.

Nevertheless, there were two other key differences between European membership parties and American parties. The first was that, for the European parties, nominating candidates and campaigning directly in elections were a relatively small part of the political activities of party members; elections were infrequent, so that candidates did not have to be nominated very often. American parties, though, were always having to fight elections; there were many levels of elected office, within each level there were many different kinds of public office that were elective, and terms of service were short. In brief, most American party "members" spent much of their time in activities directly related to candidate selection and election campaigns because that took up so much time each year for a party. If "members" were to be expected not to take part in nominations until they had served at least a year as a "member" then much of what they might be doing was not available to them. In terms of getting people to be involved in a party, being able to participate in nominations was that much more of an incentive than it was in Europe, where other kinds of political mobilization were a more important aspect of party work.

Moreover, one of the factors making it possible for European parties to "police" their memberships was that often they were not that large and, furthermore, most of their members did not move from one place to another.[20] This stability made it more possible to know who were "infiltrators" and who were possible troublemakers. But the United States had a tradition of large numbers of people being active in political parties – proportionately far more than would become members of European parties in the twentieth century – and the most populous parts of the country had high levels of residential mobility, much higher than in most of Europe. This meant that it could be far more difficult in America to know whether someone was a party loyalist or not. More important, however, unless a person could be involved in party activity immediately they might not be

---

[20] As Scarrow points out, one of the reasons that confusion arises in the English-speaking world about membership parties is that Duverger's highly influential analysis (of the early 1950s) introduced the term "mass party": "To the ears of English speakers . . . a "mass" party sounds confusingly like a party which has a 'massive' membership – something that a *parti de masses* may or may not possess. The same confusion arises when the term "mass-membership party" is used as a substitute for Duverger's 'mass party' label." Susan Scarrow, *Parties and their Members: Organizing for Victory in Britain and Germany*, Oxford, Oxford University Press, 1996, p. 19.

available at all because they would have moved somewhere else. Consequently, there was a strong argument for having American party "members" become involved in all aspects of party life as soon as possible; supplementing this was the point that, in not purging the party "rolls" regularly, a party might become victim to fraud – through the impersonation of those who had moved away, and so on.

These factors reinforced party decentralization in shaping the form that tests of party loyalty might take. Generally, it was not acceptable to restrict nominating rights to party members who had been registered for, say, at least a year – partly because this would make fraud more likely and partly because it went against an ethos of participation in all aspects of party life.[21] Consequently, few party elites argued against the idea of new members having nominating rights nor did they argue against annual updating of "membership" registration. Given this, it became difficult to see how acceptable tests of "loyalty" could be devised that would confine "membership" to those who were actually committed to the party. One form of test was to get the would-be member to state (or possibly swear) that he had supported the party at the previous election. Yet, under the Australian Ballot, there was no possibility of proving that the person had done so. Alternatively, or additionally, the person could be asked to state that they intended to support that party at the general election – but this, too, was unenforceable. Assuming that parties were not accorded the right simply to reject those who would register as "members" of their party – and that would have been subject to the objections mentioned above – there was no means of guaranteeing that parties did not have on their lists, as registered party voters, people who were at best indifferent to the party and, at worst, trying to create trouble.

The result was that there was no means of making even a "closed primary" especially "closed." The best that could be done was to have registration as early as possible in a year, compatible with there not being too many "ineligibles." This would mean that a voter was forced to choose party registration before it became evident which candidates might run, and which party, therefore, might be strategically the better choice with which to register. This still gave parties more protection from infiltrators than did "open primaries" but the level of protection was not that high. Thus, party decentralization, the importance of nominating as an activity of party work, an ethos of mass participation in the party, and a mobile electorate all combined to make it impossible to solve the problem of party loyalty satisfactorily. This meant that, as America moved from being a highly partisan

---

[21] Greater restrictions could be considered for the potentially more disruptive category of party switchers, who might be acting strategically. The Massachusetts law of 1903 did not allow those switching party affiliation to vote in their new party's primary until twelve months had elapsed – except in the case of municipal elections.

society in the mid-nineteenth century to a much less partisan society by the mid-twentieth century, the parties' "membership," too, became one less based on partisanship. There was little that the party elites could have done to prevent it. They were constrained by the factors just mentioned. Even if they had required state officials to collect a fee for them – that is, party membership dues – from those registering as party "members," they could not have created a form of organization comparable to that of the European membership parties. Instead, they were left with "closed primaries," and that was about the best that they could do to protect themselves.

Thus, it was not incompetence or a lack of imagination about what might happen to the parties eventually, or even their being outwitted by antipartisan reformers, that led to nominating powers being distributed so widely. There was no better way of protecting the parties from "nonmembers," assuming that reform could not run counter to the widely held view that parties should be arenas of mass participation. The older, informal, methods of regulating participation in the party had relied on the knowledge available in face-to-face societies that a particular person was or was not a supporter of the party; a nonsecret ballot, together with evidence of other aspects of their political behavior, made it possible to conclude whether they were or were not loyal to the party. Increased scale necessitated a move away from informal procedures, but in the particular circumstances of American politics it was not possible to produce similarly effective ways of excluding nonloyalists.

As it was, the cause of party "closedness" was given a boost by the "Doc" Ames fiasco in Minnesota in 1901–2 (see Chapter 4, Section 6). The Ames experience appeared to expose the dangers of an open primary – any would-be candidate could get those loyal to him personally to enroll in a party, thereby eliminating party as a significant intermediary in the nomination process. The lesson was not lost on politicians. Some states, such as Massachusetts, that had been planning to adopt an open primary switched to a closed one, as did Minnesota itself. While some of the states that adopted various forms of direct primary between 1903 and 1910, including Wisconsin, used an "open primary" (despite the Ames experience), most did not. In 1908, only four states had open primaries, and that number did not increase over the next twenty years.[22] As with the Australian Ballot, antipartisan attitudes did not dominate in decisions about the type of primary to be used, and, in general, party elites ended up with arrangements that they preferred. In the circumstances, it is far from clear that anything else could have been done to protect the influence of party in this regard. Indeed, the prevalence of the closed primary in the first decade of

---

[22] Miller McClintock, "Party Affiliation Tests in Primary Election Laws," *American Political Science Review*, 16(1922), p. 467, and Merriam and Overacker, *Primary Elections*, p. 69.

the twentieth century suggests that the power of antiparty reformers in controlling nomination reform did not extend beyond the power to promote it as a "solution."

The other respect in which it might be claimed that party elites could have done more to protect party influence over nominations was in formalizing a role for parties at the pre-primary stage. The basis for this argument is that such proposals did emerge subsequently. As noted in Chapter 5 (Section 5), by 1909 Governor Hughes of New York was proposing the use of preprimary conventions that would endorse candidates. This legislation failed, but subsequently a few states – notably Colorado (from 1910) and South Dakota (in 1916–17) – adopted versions of the basic scheme.[23] Between then and the mid-1960s, a total of nine states were to legislate for this kind of endorsing convention at one time or another.[24] Under the Colorado version candidates who could obtain a certain percentage of the delegates' votes at the convention (at first 10 percent, and later 20 percent) would have their names entered on the primary ballot. The candidate with the largest share of the convention vote would have his or her name placed first on the ballot; this gave him or her an advantage among informed voters who would know that this was the party's "designated" candidate and an advantage also among the uniformed, who disproportionately tend to vote for the first named candidate. Thus, it provided a double benefit for the most popular candidate at the convention, who in many cases would be the one who had been most effective in mobilizing party regulars.[25]

Certainly, preprimary conventions of this kind did help to preserve the nominating influence of party organizations in the states in which they were used. For example, states with endorsing conventions have had lower proportions of contested primaries.[26] Had these conventions been adopted more widely party control over nominations may have been greater – at least in the period from 1900 through the early 1960s. However, two arguments can be made against the claim that preprimary conventions were a missed opportunity by party elites to preserve party power. The first is that by themselves, and in the longer term, they may well have been unable to

---

[23] Merriam and Overacker, *Primary Elections*, p. 76.

[24] R. John Eyre and Curtis Martin, *The Colorado Preprimary System*, Boulder, Col., Bureau of Governmental Research and Service, University of Colorado, 1967, p. 6.

[25] The Colorado law was not a "pure" version of the preprimary endorsing convention because state law did provide for candidates who failed to get the required proportion of the vote at the convention to gain access to the primary election by collecting a large number of signatures from eligible party voters. The Hughes version was not a "pure" version either, however. Hughes left the designation of candidates to party committees, which were more restricted in membership than caucuses would be, and so his plan, too, allowed candidates to gain access to the ballot providing they acquired a certain number of signatures in support of their candidacy.

[26] Malcolm E. Jewell and David M. Olson, *American State Parties and Elections*, Homewood, Ill., Dorsey Press, 1978, p. 137.

prevent the demise of party influence in the nominating process; they did not in Colorado, where party control weakened dramatically in the second half of the 1960s.[27]

The second point is that the Hughes Plan was not produced until most states had already enacted primary laws. It was devised by a reformer to deal with the particularly entrenched political parties in New York, and was initially, therefore, a solution tailored to a particular problem. The reason that it did not figure in earlier debates about direct primaries is that it would have been regarded as a cumbersome solution. Instead of simplifying the nomination process, it added an extra stage. First delegates would attend party caucuses (as previously), then there would be the party convention (again, as before) and finally there would be a primary election open to all registered party voters. (In Hughes's version, the first stage was designation by party committees, but these were committees that would have to be set up under law, and could not consist of just those committees that a party happened to have.) With the benefit of hindsight the preprimary convention system can be seen as a way of tying candidates to parties, but the problem most party elites and most antiparty reformers were focusing on earlier was that of caucuses, and the links between them and conventions; that was what the legislation had been directed toward in the 1890s, and it was to that issue that the idea of direct elections was conjoined. Even if a prominent politician had engaged in a leap of imagination and seen the advantages of preprimary conventions it may be doubted whether this would have had much impact on political debate. It was a relatively complex solution, and the attraction of the direct primary in the form that it had been used hitherto was that it was a simple device that was already being used in a number of places. Unlike the Indiana type of ballot reform, which was able to provide a viable alternative to the POB model, the preprimary convention could probably not have offered a serious challenge to the ordinary form of the direct primary.

The significance of the preceding discussion is this. Once the caucus-convention system was found wanting, and alternatives to it were being considered, it was unlikely that party interests could have been better protected than they actually were. In retrospect, it is clear that the preservation of party power depended on that earlier nominating system not being abolished. Yet, the failure of legislation in the 1890s to deal with its obvious limitations increased the possibility that other "solutions" to the problems it posed would become attractive. As the one "solution" that had been used quite widely already, the direct primary was probably the only practical alternative to a caucus-convention system for which support had declined to the point at which it was difficult to defend effectively. What party elites

[27] See Alan Ware, *The Breakdown of Democratic Party Organization*, Oxford, Clarendon Press, 1985.

appear to have done was as much as they could to protect the power of party in the nomination process. They were not outwitted by antipartisans committed to destroying party power. When it was clear where party interests lay, they tended to defend them effectively, and in opting for the closed primaries they demonstrated that they could do so.

5. Concluding Remarks

The main thrust of the argument presented here has been that, between the mid-1890s and the early twentieth century, both the nature of American public attitudes toward parties and antiparty reformers helped to ensure that the only well-known alternative to the caucus-convention system became the one reform on which attention would be centred. While this role was not insignificant, it is important to place it in context and not to overstate it. Nomination reform was being undertaken already in most states, and had been further encouraged by the apparent success of ballot reform; of the alternatives to conventions, only the direct primary had been used in a number of states and it had been growing in use. That the antiparty reformers (and others) came to focus exclusively on the direct primary did not change the direction that reform was taking; rather, it helped to speed up acceptance of the direct primary among party elites.

In this context, it is worth recalling Schattschneider's famous remark that "the definition of the alternatives is the supreme instrument of power. . . . He who determines what politics is about runs the country."[28] From one perspective, it appears that antiparty reformers could be seen as powerful because of the part they played in helping to set the agenda for nomination reform in the decade or so after the mid-1890s. However, what happened in this case was very different from the examples of agenda setting that Schattschneider had in mind. As his discussion of the "system of 1896" illustrates, Schattschneider was concerned with circumstances in which political conflict was transformed; his argument was that conservatives were able to transform a radical agrarian protest into sectional politics. In his view, what politics was about was different after 1896 because of the actions of certain political elites. The change in the debate about nomination reform was not transformative in quite this way, nor, indeed, in the way that the debate about the party ballot in the 1880s was. By focusing on the direct primary, antiparty reformers ensured that the complexities of the issues relating to nomination reform tended not to come to the fore in public debate, and instead it was the supposed "solution" to which attention was drawn consistently. However, this "solution" was not a new way of understanding the matter – its possible relevance to the problem of

[28] E. E. Schattschneider, *The Semisovereign People*, Hinsdale, Ill., Dryden Press, 1975, p. 66.

nominations was known already. Again, it is far from clear that this focus on the direct primary led to other possible reforms not being evaluated, because, arguably, there were no such alternatives. In the end, the contribution of the reformers was really to speed up the experimental use of the direct primary in particular states, and to facilitate its use over a wider range of offices than would have happened otherwise.

Constrained as they were by public attitudes to parties, and engaging in a public debate that increasingly was about direct nominations, elected politicians, therefore, came increasingly to disregard the fact that the impact of such nominations on party interests was largely unknown and that they could have adverse consequences for the nomination process. Caution was abandoned in favor of a "quick fix." The result was the enactment of a reform that, in the long term was to contribute to the transformation of America's parties in ways that those who passed such legislation could not have foreseen, and would not have endorsed.

C

WHAT HAPPENED NEXT?

8

Reaction and Aftermath

By the end of 1915, the direct primary had become the most widely employed nominating system in the United States. All but three states (Connecticut, New Mexico, and Rhode Island) used it for selecting candidates to at least some elective offices. Most of these forty-five states nominated virtually all offices in this way – 78 percent of states in the east and 95 percent of western states did so. In an obvious sense, candidate selection had been transformed. But how much had actually changed, and how much of the change that there had been could be attributed to the impact of direct nominations? These are questions that are addressed in the middle of this chapter. Following that, we consider the adoption of the presidential primary, and its relation to the direct primary. First, however, attention will be paid to a matter that was largely forgotten toward the end of the twentieth century, but which is important in understanding the rise of the direct primary: namely, that in the decade and a half after 1915, attempts were made in many states to abandon direct nominations.

1. Reaction Against the Direct Primary

Between 1919 and 1926, more than 70 percent of the nonsouthern states that had enacted direct primary legislation (twenty-six of thirty-four states) experienced attempts by legislators either to repeal or reduce in scope direct nomination provisions. In the 1925 legislative session alone, such efforts were made in nineteen states.[1] The revolt against the direct primary was evident throughout the country. Omitting Utah, in which most offices were still not directly nominated anyway, there were only seven states in which little effort was made to revert to the caucus-convention system. Although only two were in the east (Delaware and Pennsylvania), while five were in the west (Arizona, California, Nevada, North Dakota, and Oklahoma), the

---

[1] *Congressional Digest* 5, No. 10 (October 1926), p. 260.

vast majority of western states were still subjected to similar pressures to those in the east.

At first, the opponents of direct nominations enjoyed some success. In 1919 Idaho restricted their use to county offices. In 1920 Kentucky made the direct primary optional, instead of mandatory, for statewide offices, and in 1921 New York abandoned the use of direct nominations for statewide offices.[2] Thereafter, the closest repeal efforts came to enactment were in Colorado (1925), where the state governor vetoed a bill; in Vermont (also 1925), where the lieutenant governor cast the decisive vote against it in the state senate; and in New Jersey (1926), where a bill to repeal the direct primary was lost in the legislature by only one vote.[3] For all the agitation, outright repeal of earlier legislation was always unlikely, and even restrictions on its use were difficult to build into popular causes.

Publicity for the repeal campaign was provided, in part, by well-known politicians, of whom Coolidge's vice president, Charles Dawes, was the most prominent. Not surprisingly, though, the main opposition to direct primaries was centered in the party organizations themselves. This was revealed in a minisurvey of state governors and state party chairmen published in 1923.[4] Of nine nonsouthern governors, five declared themselves in favor of the direct primary, four were opposed to it, and one was neutral; two of its opponents were from states that either did not use the direct primary (Connecticut) or made only limited use of it (Utah).[5] Among nine state party chairmen, opposition was much more pronounced with seven chairmen coming out against direct nominations, while only two supported them.[6] Individual political careers could be made or broken, depending on the nominating system deployed; thus, among the more visible public office holders, there were many by the 1920s who could see how their own careers had benefitted from the reformed nominating system. The attitude of state governors was especially important. Given that usually they possessed the power of vetoing legislation, opposition at that level could be crucial to the success of repeal efforts.

---

[2] Nevada had been the first state to repeal direct nominations (1915), but it was restored in 1917.

[3] Helen M. Rocca, *Nominating Methods*, Washington, D.C., National League of Women Voters, 1927, p. 37.

[4] William E. Hannan, "Opinions of Public Men on the Value of the Direct Primary," *Annals of the American Academy of Political and Social Science*, 106(1923), pp. 55–62.

[5] The governors in favor of the direct primary were those of Kansas, Illinois, Nevada, Wyoming, and Wisconsin. The states whose governors opposed it were Colorado, Connecticut, Nebraska, and Utah. The governor of New Hampshire was neutral.

[6] The party chairmen opposed to direct nominations were from Arizona (Democrat), Massachusetts (Democrat), New Jersey (Republican), Oklahoma (Republican), Vermont (Democrat), West Virginia (Democrat), and Wyoming (Republican). The supporters were two Republicans from Michigan and Wisconsin.

However, it would be a mistake to see the failure of those efforts as hinging solely on the political ambitions of individual politicians. There were other substantial obstacles in their paths. First, there was the basic problem in the decentralized American political system that the status quo was easier to defend usually than to attack. *Centeris paribus*, it should have been easier to preserve the caucus-convention system at the earlier period than to bring about its reintroduction.

Second, what fragmentary evidence there is in relation to public opinion suggests that dissatisfaction with the direct primary was much less prevalent among mass publics than it was among those active in party politics. (The main evidence derives from referendums, where all repeal efforts failed.) This would not be surprising; it was the latter who would more likely be aware of the difficulties that direct nominations could pose. For most citizens, the direct primary still appeared to be a superficially fair system of selecting candidates. Public opposition to repeal would not have been a decisive factor, though, had there been an overwhelming majority of elected politicians in its favor, but there was no such clear majority among them.

Third, by the early 1920s an important and large group had been added to the national electorate – women. Although in the 1920s women's electoral participation was lower than men's, and although the impact of women's organizations on that vote was small, those organizations were opposed to repeal. They saw such a move as reinforcing a political style of male-dominated, "smoke filled," rooms, and thereby as opposed to the interests of women. As Freeman had argued in her study of the entry of women into American party politics: "Although the strength and organization of the major political parties varied from state to state, party leadership everywhere had the same attitude: They wanted women as voters and workers but not as leaders or decision makers."[7] To return to the caucus would remove what power women had as primary voters. This was a point made at the time by Charles Merriam; he observed that women formed only about 5 or 10 percent of delegates to conventions but constituted 40 percent of primary voters.[8] Consequently, those state legislators who worried about the public reaction to their stance on repeal now had to consider the impact that women might have on their electoral prospects, and this, too, contributed to an unwillingness to go along with it.

But what had led to the widespread reaction against direct nominations only a decade or so after their introduction? As always, with any proposed

[7] Jo Freeman, *A Room at a Time: How Women Entered Party Politics*, Lanham, Md., Rowman and Littlefield, 2000, p. 150.
[8] Charles E. Merriam, "Nominating Systems," *Annals of the Academy of Political and Social Science*, 106(1923), p. 4.

institutional change, there were some instances of an impetus emanating from a belief that political enemies would fare much worse under a different set of rules. A good example of this was Nebraska, where in 1918 the renomination, and subsequent reelection of incumbent US Senator, George Norris, provided the spur for changing the nominating rules again.[9] Norris had become unpopular with many of his Republican supporters because of his unenthusiastic support for America's involvement in World War I. However, in a state with an open primary, and faced with four opponents, he won renomination in 1918, but with only 36 percent of the vote. Not surprisingly, both in the primary and in the general election, he enjoyed significantly increased support from those of German origin. Following the 1918 election, the new Republican governor, a fierce opponent of Norris, led the effort to repeal Nebraska's direct primary legislation, and in both 1919 and 1921 he succeeded in getting the legislature to pass bills restoring the convention system of nomination – by wide margins. (In 1919 the bill applied to all statewide offices, except that of governor, while the 1921 legislation applied only to national committeemen.) On both occasions the law was reversed by initiative referenda placed on the ballot by German Americans, with the active support, of course, of George Norris.

Nevertheless, personal animus was not the main factor in providing for reaction against the direct primary, even though there were instances in which it was important. More fundamental was that a decade or so of experience with direct nominations had made evident to politicians in all states the sorts of problems that had been exposed in Cleveland in the 1890s. In exchange for getting rid of the difficulties associated with caucuses and conventions, politicians had introduced a nominating system that could not provide for balanced tickets (and, thereby, the demands for representation by particular localities and ethnic groups), could greatly increase the cost of nomination for some offices, and could lead to the selection of unqualified, unsuitable, or unelectable candidates. Interestingly, though, in the 1920s one of the main objections often made in public to direct nominations was one that could have been quite easily corrected – that a candidate could be nominated, as was George Norris, with less than 50 percent of the vote.

The significance of the objection is that it enabled opponents of the direct primary to cast doubt on the democratic credentials of the mechanism. Since part of the problem in selling their case was that the direct primary appeared to mass publics as superficially the more democratic device, it was a useful tactic. But it was no more than a tactic; several states had already adopted the obvious solutions to the problem, and there would have been few barriers to its introduction were the antimajoritarian features of some primary

---

[9] See Burton W. Folsom, "Tinkerers, Tipplers and Traitors: Ethnicity and Democratic Reform in Nebraska during the Progressive Era," *Pacific Historical Review*, 50(1981), pp. 52–75.

laws to have been seen as their main liability. Maryland and Minnesota (both in 1912) had started to use the Alternative Vote electoral system for their primaries. The other possible solution for ensuring majority nominations – the run-off election – was deployed in six southern states, five of which had adopted it before 1917. Indeed, at various times other states had also used forms of so-called preferential voting to ensure that nominees were not the choice of merely a small minority.[10] The solutions to the problem of vote fragmentation were well known. The far more intractable problems posed by direct primaries for the parties were, first, interest aggregation, because nomination decisions were now individualized, rather than being considered as part of a "package." This increased the likelihood of intraparty tensions, and also the risk that unelectable tickets might result. The second problem was that the direct primary both reduced the ability of the party to control the "quality" of candidates selected, and in some cases made it more possible that wealthy individuals might triumph over poorer rivals having broader support among party activists.

As Helen M. Rocca noted at the time, the renewal of the debate from 1919 onward about the direct primary was centred by would-be repealers on the claim that direct nominations "weakened or destroyed party responsibility."[11] Under the heading of declining party responsibility, it was possible to include many of the difficulties the parties were facing under direct nominations – including those of interest aggregation and weak or unsuitable candidates. "Party responsibility" was a good rallying cry because most voters might be presumed to prefer "responsible parties" to "irresponsible parties." Both sides on the repeal issue had a stake in emphasizing that the direct primary had made a difference – but had it? Had the role of party in the American states changed during the previous decades, and to what extent were any such changes the result of the transformation in nominating systems? It is to these issues that we now turn.

2. The State of the Parties in 1930

When examining the state of the parties in about 1930, it is useful to divide America into three separate regions – the eleven states of the old Confederacy, the twenty western states, and the seventeen states in the east. Within each region there were important differences in the role played by party, so that, for example, California was no more typical of the West than was New York typical of the East. In fact, these two states, often cited as exemplifying politics in their own region, were highly unusual in a number of important respects. Consequently, all generalizations about each of the

[10] Charles E. Merriam and Louise Overacker, *Primary Elections*, Chicago, University of Chicago, 1928, pp. 82–5.
[11] Rocca, *Nominating Methods*, p. 39.

regions must be treated carefully. Nevertheless, there were important regional differences, and by 1930 there was much greater heterogeneity in American party politics than there had been forty years earlier.

In the South, party, as such, had collapsed in most places, and it is in this region that there was the most sustained early development of candidate-centered politics. The individual politician became important in the South because party competition had dissolved completely during the 1890s. The South was without parties or their functional equivalents. As Key was to observe in 1949:

> The South, unlike most of the rest of the democratic world, really has no political parties. . . . The one-party system is purely an arrangement for national affairs. The legend prevails that within the Democratic party in the southern states factional groups are the equivalent of political parties elsewhere. In fact, the Democratic party in most states of the South is merely a holding company for a congeries of transient squabbling factions, most of which fail by far to meet the standards of permanence, cohesiveness, and responsibility that characterise the political party.[12]

In some states, such as Florida, individualism was so rampant in the electoral arena, that there was nothing apart from the individual candidate. In others, such as Virginia, factions centered on particular politicians affected the electoral environment in which individuals operated. However, as the quotation from Key indicates, virtually the entire South was devoid of permanent partylike structures.

In a sense, the South's party structures had started to diverge from those in the rest of the country once the Whig party collapsed in the 1850s. Republican party organizations never penetrated southern society in the way that the Whigs had or that the Democrats continued to after the Civil War. The Republicans' constituency was mainly whites in mountain areas who had supported the Union in the War and the newly enfranchised African Americans of the Black Belt. Local Republican party organizations developed in these areas after the war, and persisted even while the GOP became uncompetitive at the state level from the 1870s onward. By 1890 such organizations were still in existence, but in the next two decades the systematic restructuring of politics to exclude black Americans from voting destroyed both the Republican party and also the Democratic party. Faced with no opposition, and more important, no possibility of opposition from any electoral organizations, the Democratic parties in the South disappeared. It became a region of partyless politics and individual politicians. The direct primary played no direct role in bringing this about. Rather, in part, it was introduced to bring order and legitimacy to a system in which parties were ceasing to function.

To some extent – though only to some extent – a transition to a candidate-centered style of politics was evident in the West as well. It was

---

[12] V. O. Key, Jr., *Southern Politics*, New York, Alfred A. Knopf, 1949, p. 16.

most highly developed in California, but political observers saw other parts of the West also as being centred more on individual politicians than on parties. For example, in 1940 the political scientist Thomas C. Donnelly said of the eight Rocky Mountain states: "The attachment to personalities is much stronger than the attachment to parties." However, he went on to add:

Once a leader merits the voluntary support of a body of followers, they seem to remain unusually devoted to him regardless of his record on party issues. The character of the man rather than his party allegiance is the thing that registers with the westerner.[13]

The point about meriting voluntary support is important. In these states politics was still not dominated, as it was in California, by "self starters" who from the beginning of their careers had to organize their own nomination and election. In most of the western states, party still mattered in getting started in a political career; it was only when that career was established that the politician would acquire his own "body of followers" with whom he could assert his independence from his party.

In the 1930s, party was more important in most western states than in California, because many of the structures and practices of nineteenth-century politics were still in place in those states. For example, when in power, the main source of income for the Democratic party in Utah was the "tax" of between 1 and 5 percent on the salaries of state employees; the "tax" was collected by a party agent.[14] Similarly, when in power in New Mexico, the Democratic party there levied "a regular monthly assessment of 2 percent on the salaries of all political employees of the state to finance its activities, and special assessments in campaign years" were sometimes also levied.[15] In Colorado, the modified version of the Hughes Plan for selecting candidates, together in Denver with the use of a large multimember district for state legislature seats, ensured a key role for parties as an intermediary between individual politicians and mass electorates.[16] These are but three examples of how, in the West, older practices and party-oriented institutions prevented a collapse into an entirely candidate-dominated system within a state.

Nevertheless, if party was still an important electoral intermediary in the West, Donnelly was correct in seeing personality as providing a counter-vailing source of political power. This was most apparent with those most

---

[13] Thomas C. Donnelly (ed.), *Rocky Mountain Politics*, Albuquerque, University of New Mexico Press, 1940, p. 8.

[14] Frank Herman Jonas, "Utah: Sagebrush Democracy," in Donnelly, *Rocky Mountain Politics*, p. 31.

[15] Thomas C. Donnelly, "New Mexico: An Area of Conflicting Cultures," in Donnelly, *Rocky Mountain Politics*, p. 240.

[16] Alan Ware, *The Breakdown of Democratic Party Organization, 1940–1980*, Oxford, Clarendon Press, 1985, pp. 59–67 and 119–31.

high profile of officeholders, U.S. Senators, and some of them, such as
Idaho's William Borah, could and did act independently of their party
organizations. But independence from party was possible with some other
major offices as well. Perhaps the most interesting cases were those where
independent sources of power were then channelled through the party, for
mutual benefit. One example was the Denver mayor for much of the 1920s
and 1930s, Ben Stapleton, whose organization was very much a personal
one, focusing on city, not state, politics; however, he attached this organization to the Democratic party.[17] Such cases expose the fact that the relationship between the individual politician and the party need not be one of
tension as one of mutual reinforcement. Stapleton stabilized his power base
through his role in the Democratic party, while the party benefitted because
it was more sure of the availability of his resources in election campaigns.
Necessarily such cases complicate any overall assessments that can be made
of the role of party in the western states.

But, if the individual politician was more important vis-à-vis party in the
west than in the east, did this represent a change since the 1890s? And what
role, if any, did nomination reform play in bringing it about? With the
exception of California, most western states were unlike those in the South,
in that the role of party did not appear to have changed dramatically since
the 1890s. For example, neither Donnelly nor his fellow contributors
saw the Progressive era as a watershed in the role of party in the Rocky
Mountain states. To the contrary, Donnelly believed that it was the relatively small populations of states in the region that had led to the personal
links between voters and politicians.[18] To this might be added the further
argument that the relatively recent settlement of the western states meant
that parties there had never developed the close links to voters that their
counterparts in the east had. Reinforcing the point is one made by Shefter,
and noted in Chapter 4, that the western parties did not build highly structured and broadly based organizations in the nineteenth century because
they had other means of acquiring political resources.[19] So, if these arguments are accepted, should it be concluded that the role of party had not
really changed much in the West – that the politics of personality evident
by the 1930s had always been an element modifying the role of party?

There are reasons for believing that parties had lost power relative to
candidates, and the unusual and extreme case of California can illuminate
some of the pressures that were evident elsewhere. Institutional reforms
eroded the power of party at the local level. In particular, several changes
in the rules of the game tended to wither what vitality local parties had

---

[17] See Ware, *Breakdown of Democratic Party Organization*, pp. 63–5.
[18] Donnelly, *Rocky Mountain Politics*, p. 8.
[19] Martin Shefter, *Political Parties and the State*, Princeton, N.J., Princeton University Press,
1994, p. 177.

enjoyed – the city-manager system of local government, the creation of separately elected boards for particular public functions, nonpartisan elections for local government, and California's unique cross-filing primary all did so. Attempting to take party politics out of city government had only limited success in large urban areas (such as San Francisco) where there was already intense party competition. There parties could adjust to the new rules. Where devices such as nonpartisan elections did constrain parties was in those cities in which the Republican party had been dominant. The incentive for covert partisan activity by Democrats in such conditions was limited, and on the Republican side it became clear that the interests of local businesses could be protected through informal linkage between Republican-inclined, but overtly nonpartisan, incumbents and challengers.

Many of the localities in which this style of politics came to be practiced were small, but a city as large as Oakland could still see party removed from the arena of local government. In effect, incumbents in Oakland would coopt a successor when a council seat became vacant, and the new incumbent would then use the advantages of office to consolidate their position at the subsequent election.[20] Even when demographic changes might otherwise have made Democratic party revival possible, the advantages accruing to incumbency provided little incentive for the party to support challengers. Consequently, control by business-dominated elites, broadly Republican in their sympathies, persisted for decades. Oakland is perhaps the most extraordinary example, because there even the influx of large numbers of African Americans into the "lowlands" during World War II could not facilitate a sustained Democratic revival at the local level.[21] The tendency for nonpartisan elections to restrict the potential for covert partisan competition in cities originally dominated by the Republican party was reinforced by the cross-filing primaries in California's partisan elections. It weakened party competition by allowing candidates to compete in the other party's primary election; the beneficiaries were incumbents who would use their name recognition to overcome opposition to them, even in the other party. For example, in 90 percent of state senate districts in 1944 one candidate won the nomination of both parties.[22]

Over time, the impact of this in California was to limit the activities of local parties, and in doing so it produced a much more individualistic style of electoral competition – one in which it was a candidate who went in

[20] Jeffrey L. Pressman, "Preconditions of Mayoral Leadership," *American Political Science Review*, 66(1972), pp. 511–24.

[21] Democrat-backed candidates succeeded in winning some seats on the Oakland city council in 1947, but that group lost power in 1947 and it was nearly three decades before the Democrats again had any influence in city government. See Ware, *Breakdown of Democratic Party Organization*, pp. 52–3.

[22] V. O. Key, Jr., *Politics, Parties and Pressure Groups*, Fourth Edition, New York, Thomas Y. Crowell, 1958, p. 429.

search of party support rather than parties grooming candidates for public office. Consequently, by 1930, party as such had a much less direct impact on the recruitment of candidates to public office in California than it had enjoyed thirty years earlier. What someone had done for the party in the past was now far less significant in securing nominations than how he or she might help in the future the interlinked groups of politicians who called themselves either Democrats or Republicans. The contrast can be drawn by considering William Randolph Hearst's father who secured his nomination to the U.S. Senate seat in 1886. The Senate was known as the Millionaire's Club in the nineteenth century, because money mattered so much in securing the support of state legislators who controlled the nominations to it. However, legislators tended to reward individuals who had a track record within their own party. George Hearst was no exception. He was estimated to have spent half a million dollars to secure the seat, but he was not a parvenu in Democratic party circles. For example, he had used his own money six years earlier to bail out a party newspaper in San Francisco, and had subsequently obtained the party's support in that city to further his political ambitions.[23] By 1930, such tests of past loyalty to the party cause were less necessary for political advancement.

Since the beginning of the century, California had become much more candidate-centered than most other states in the West. However, many of these other states also now required that local elections be legally nonpartisan, so that the question remains of why party tended to retain more of a role there than in California. Certainly, the cross-filing primary strengthened individualism among politicians in the Golden State, by making it easier for incumbents to control their own political careers. That cannot account for all of the difference, though. Two related factors made California atypical. First, it was easily the largest, and the most industrialized, of the western states during the Progressive era. The breadth of the socioeconomic divisions within the state tended to deepen the fervor of the assault on the parties – parties that had been the vehicles of the dominant economic interests in the state. Thus, not only did California go further than other western states subsequently in dismantling party structures – through such devices as cross-filing – but there persisted an antagonism to party that was generally weaker elsewhere. Second, as the historian George Mowry once remarked, the progressive politicians in California were characterized by "an extreme individualism."[24] Their inability to work together contributed to the collapse of Progressivism in the state, but, more

---

[23] *New York Times*, January 19, 1887; W. A. Swanberg, *Citizen Hearst*, New York, Bantam Books, 1971, pp. 26–7.

[24] George E. Mowry, *The California Progressives*, Berkeley, University of California Press, 1951, p. 288.

important for the argument being developed here, it meant that there would be no legacy of political cooperation for the 1920s. A politics of individualism suited conservatives who could protect business interests through nonparty channels, while on the nonconservative side the previous twenty years had seen individual political ambition triumph over cooperation, once the structures that held the old-style politics together had been removed.

As in California, elsewhere in the West local bases for parties were undermined by the introduction of city-manager systems of government and nonpartisan elections. The potential for the politics of personality – for candidate-centered, rather than party-centered politics – was, thereby, much greater in 1930 than forty years earlier. But that potential was not fully realized, in that there were still institutions and devices at the state level – such as the "taxing" of state employees – that enabled parties to retain resources and prevent the extreme form of individualism, of the California variety, replacing party politics. Moreover, in none of the western states, including California, could the introduction of direct primary elections *per se* be said to account for any reduction in the role of party. While direct nominations certainly had not helped parties to sustain their role neither, in general, do they appear to have weakened them that much. This point becomes even more evident when we turn to consider the eastern states.

In the east, party organizations adjusted to the introduction of the direct primary, and they continued to play their traditional intermediary role between candidates and mass electorates. McCaffery's conclusion about the effect on the Republicans in Philadelphia, which was noted in Chapter 5, was true also of parties in most cities and in most states: In theory, the direct primary made selection of party candidates for public office fairer and more competitive, but, in practice, it did not affect the ability of party organizations to control nominations.[25] Indeed, paradoxically, the passage of direct primary legislation coincided with the first half of what might be regarded as the "golden age" of American urban party machines. Until the end of the nineteenth century, the so-called machines of major urban areas were highly unstable in that citywide control was usually difficult to sustain. Most bosses drew their strength from particular localities, and it was through a series of alliances that power over an entire city was possible. Intraparty rivalries and competition left those who were dominant in a city at any given time open to threat from their rivals, who might well be their temporary allies. With the notable exception of William Tweed, there are few city bosses before the last decade of the nineteenth century whose names became that well known. By contrast, in the period from 1890 to

---

[25] Peter McCaffery, *When Bosses Ruled Philadelphia: The Emergence of the Republican Machine, 1867–1933*, University Park, Pennsylvania State University Press, 1993, p. 182.

1930, a number of such politicians became famous – the Pendergasts (of Kansas City), Big Bill Thompson (of Chicago), George Cox (of Cincinnati), and so on.

In that forty-year period, it became more possible than it had been earlier for a politician to control his city's party and to do so over an extended period. The constant civil wars within the nineteenth-century parties had been replaced by more stable intraparty relationships. This stability meant that even reforms such as the city-manager system might have little effect in changing the role of party. Thus, Mayhew noted of Pendergast's machine: "It operated with no trace of difficulty in a model nonpartisan council-manager system introduced in 1925, and reached out like Jersey City's Hague machine to take over the state government during the New Deal."[26] Clearly, the ability to centralize patronage within the party was a key element in facilitating stability, as McCaffery has shown in the case of Philadelphia.[27] In turn, the incentive to centralize depended on how local government was organized. Finegold argues that the structure of local government would be reflected in the structure of local party organizations, so that governmental consolidation, of the kind seen in New York in 1898, tended to lead to the centralization of power in a party.[28] Because of that centralization in urban parties, and even more than in other party organizations, their overall operations were largely unaffected by the revolution in the procedures for candidate selection.

Nevertheless, there would appear to be a paradox here. If party control over nominations was not threatened, why were party organizations throughout the country in the 1920s agitating for repeal of direct primary laws? There are three considerations that are relevant in resolving this.

The first is that, although many party organizations still had a great deal of influence over most offices they would deem important to their interests, they had lost some control. Popular incumbents, such as Nebraska's George Norris, were now more able to thwart the wishes of a majority of their party's leaders and activists than had their predecessors in the 19th century. Thus, while it is true that "party organizations, party machines, and politicians had to manage the primary as they had always taken care of party affairs," they could not always do so effectively.[29] Especially when there were divisions within a party organization, little control might be exercisable. Consequently, at a more local level it was possible in some districts for an unsuitable candidate, backed by friends and relatives, to secure the

---

[26] David R. Mayhew, *Placing Parties in American Politics*, Princeton, N.J., Princeton University Press, 1986, p. 100.

[27] McCaffery, *When Bosses Ruled Philadelphia*, Chapter 4.

[28] Kenneth Finegold, *Experts and Politicians: Reform Challenges to Machine Politics in New York, Cleveland and Chicago*, Princeton, N.J., Princeton University Press, 1995.

[29] V. O. Key, Jr., *Politics, Parties and Pressure Groups*, p. 412.

party's nomination. Despite the charges of corruption usually levied against nineteenth-century parties, it was usually not in their interest to nominate the incompetent and those whose venality was unrestrained. Such candidates were more likely to succeed under the direct primary, because the parties were less able to "filter them out," yet the party concerned might be blamed for any scandals that emerged subsequently. The full consequences of both this, and the impact of the primary on intraparty relations, became apparent to party organization leaders only when the direct primary had been operating for a few years; once it did, they then pursued its repeal.

A second factor was that, despite machine centralization, even in the eastern machines there was evidence that the politics of personality was becoming more significant. The parties' ability to determine who would be their candidates was being undermined by the ability of candidates to separate themselves from their parties. Most obviously, the direct election of U.S. Senators from 1914 onward reduced the intermediate role that parties played in determining which of the would-be aspirants (usually among the wealthy) would actually secure a Senate seat. As in the nineteenth century, not all Senators were millionaires, but far from ending the link between wealth and the Senate, First Amendment rights merely changed the optimal strategy for those seeking a seat. Particularly, in relation to incumbents, party became rather more peripheral than it had been, simply because the wealthy could now use their money to buy publicity for themselves among voters.

Perhaps the more important change, though, was in relation to the mayors of major cities. Someone like Chicago's Big Bill Thompson, mayor from 1915–23 and 1927–31, represents an intermediate figure between the party-dominated mayors of the nineteenth century and the largely self-selected mayoral candidates of the last thirty years of the twentieth century. Thompson had been a party stalwart in the city's Republican party. Without such a background, he could not have become mayor.[30] However, once in office he differed from his nineteenth-century predecessors in having far more freedom to build (and to change) his own electoral coalitions. In 1915, Thompson had presented himself as broadly supportive of the kind of reforms, including Prohibition, that might appeal to native-born Protestants. They were abandoned when Thompson noticed that the balance of voting power was shifting to various ethnic groups in the city. As an individual, he was able to change his electoral coalitions far more swiftly than would his party, were such a decision being taken collectively among its leaders. Thompson's ability to make these kinds of switches depended, in part, on the expanded role of government in the changed

---

[30] On Thompson, see *Big Bill Thompson, Chicago and the Politics of Image*, Urbana and Chicago, University of Illinois Press, 1998.

circumstances of the early twentieth century. Thompson was a booster of city redevelopment, an issue that enabled him to appeal to a broad range of voters, even while he was alienating major bodies of public opinion through, for example, his opposition to American involvement in World War I. Issues such as urban redevelopment facilitated individual political entrepreneurship among American political executives, because it enabled them to identify themselves, rather than their party, with it. To bolster his individual appeal, Thompson adopted the style of the showman – again a marked change in style from nineteenth-century politicians. His forte was the big parade, usually with himself riding a horse and wearing a cowboy hat – drawing attention to, and greatly exaggerating his exploits in the west as a young man. (In this regard he was merely copying the lead of his fellow Republican, Teddy Roosevelt.)

Thompson, like a number of politicians in that era, had become semi-detached from his party. He was not completely detached in the way that politicians would be after the 1960s, but his relations with party organizations were different than they had been for elected politicians three decades earlier. It is against this sort of background that the opposition of party organization elites in the 1920s to the direct primary must be understood. In the East, as well as in the West, personality was important now in politics. It mattered not just in presidential elections but could matter in state and city elections – at least so far as the head of the ticket was concerned – and it mattered in U.S. Senate elections. Personality had been of less consequence in the nineteenth century, and the main effect of this change was to reduce the power of party organizations. Clawing back a little of that power through repealing direct nomination legislation represented an obvious strategy for them.

Party organizations were threatened in another way, though, and this brings us to the third factor prompting their concern with the politics of party nominations. The traditional base of Jacksonian politics was being rapidly eroded, despite the apparent health of many urban machines in the 1920s. In Yearley's words, during the mid-nineteenth-century:

... in the Northern states, government and party could not realistically be divorced from one another ... parties counted on financing themselves by tapping public power and the fiscal resources of government.[31]

During the last two decades of the nineteenth century, and in the first twenty years of the twentieth century, that base was removed by reforms in the recruitment of local government personnel, and in the administration, budgeting and financing of those governments. The result was not an end to

---

[31] C. K. Yearley, *The Money Machines: The Breakdown and Reform of Governmental and Party Finance in the North, 1860–1920*, Albany, State University of New York Press, 1970, p. xiii.

politics at the local level, but a reconfiguring of municipal politics away from the parties. In concluding his study of these reforms for the period 1880–1920, Schiesl argued:

... "politics" had not been exorcised from city management. Indeed, four decades of structural reform had intensified rather than depressed partisanship among administrative officials. They emerged as a new political force and derived most of their authority from such metropolitan constituencies as business interests, civic organizations, and research bureaus. In consequence, the machine bureaucracy, popularly based, was being replaced by career agencies, professionally organized. These reformed bureaucracies, while relatively free of corruption and malfeasance, constituted the new power centres in urban affairs and were more entrenched than the bases of the political machine.[32]

In the municipalities, the main foundations of patronage politics had been removed by the 1920s, even while its best-known practitioners appeared to be thriving. In 1932, it was estimated that 60 percent of municipal employees were appointed under civil service rules.[33] The long-term prospects for party machines were poor, and their short-term prosperity depended on, first, the much greater organization of, and resources available to, criminal activity during Prohibition, a development that provided alternative sources of finance to some parties. Second, the New Deal helped subsequently to inject cash into organizations that could neither control local business in the way that they had, nor could provide the kinds of jobs that were attractive to employees. Between the late 1930s and late 1940s, most of the erstwhile machines collapsed. This was in the future, though. In the 1920s, what was clear was that, as the old base of the parties had eroded, so formal control over some functions, such as candidate selection, was crucial for the vitality of party organizations. In their narrow, more electorally oriented, role parties in the cities needed control over candidates, if they were to be significant as electoral intermediaries.

Reform outside the municipalities was much slower; in 1932 it was estimated that only 14 percent of employees were covered by civil service rules, and this provided the basis for the continuation of traditional styles of organization.[34] Nevertheless, ever since the passage of the Pendleton Act in 1883, the trend had been toward the restriction of party involvement in public employment. Although it took decades for this Act to have much affect, the general trend at the federal level, as well as at other levels of politics, had been toward transforming the relationship between government and party; by the 1920s there was no mistaking the direction of that change.

---

[32] Martin J. Schiesl, *The Politics of Efficiency: Municipal Administration and Reform in America, 1880–1920*, Berkeley, University of California Press, 1977, p. 191.

[33] Charles Edward Merriam and Charles Foote Gosnell, *The American Party System*, Third Edition, New York, Macmillan, 1940, p. 196.

[34] Merriam and Gosnell, *The American Party System*, p. 196.

Deprived of some of the resources that had helped sustain party power, party organizations had to become much more concerned with preserving the ultimate source of their control over their candidates – control of the nominating function; in part, it was for that reason that there was so much more at stake in the battle over direct nominations in the 1920s than had appeared to be the case a decade or two earlier.

3. The Delayed Impact of the Direct Primary

The transformation of the major American parties, from being "married" to government, to a relationship with government that involved much less interdependence, was slow. Although the spread of the civil system at federal, state, and local levels was well advanced by 1930, it would be several decades before the process was complete. Nevertheless, many urban political machines had collapsed by the end of the 1940s; even the partial rejuvenation provided by the New Deal was no more than temporary. In a number of places the return of young ex-servicemen to their home cities after the war provided a catalyst for electoral challenges to the remaining old style organizations. However, while, as a general conclusion, this summary statement is correct there are two important qualifications to it.

First, in some counties traditional forms of party organization survived at the city level, and even thrived after 1945. The Democratic organization in Chicago revived under Richard Daley; and the Republican party in sub-urban Nassau County, New York persisted in the old practice of "taxing" county employees a portion of their salaries, which was then paid into party coffers, and in doing so, they retained tight party control.[35] These kinds of centralized operations were unusual by the 1970s, but those that there were showed few signs of becoming moribund. Second, pockets of patronage sur-vived, even in areas where most offices were covered by civil service rules. The fragmentation of American local government facilitated this persis-tence, so that, for example, the Brooklyn Democratic party was still a center of old-style patronage in the 1970s, even though much local government in New York City was no longer so overtly venal.

Nevertheless, apart from the isolated cases, like Chicago, in which a high degree of integration between party and government survived, by the early 1950s most American parties had become, in one important respect at least, more like parties in many other democracies. They were sufficiently sepa-rate from government that the working of the institution depended on other suppliers of resources. Money was provided by individuals, businesses, and, often, candidates, while party activists provided their labor during election campaigns. While a relatively smaller proportion of Americans were now

---

[35] Mayhew, *Placing Parties in American Politics*, pp. 38–9.

involved actively in the organization of electoral politics than in the nineteenth century, the parties were more than capable of providing essential electoral services for their candidates. The type of activist started to change as so-called amateur activists, attracted more by public policy issues than anything else, began participating in the Democratic party in the early 1950s and later that decade in the Republican party. Yet, these activists were still operating within the confines of party organizations, so that they were no more a challenge to the viability of those organizations than were their predecessors.[36]

With the exception of both the southern states and the exceptional northern state, party remained a significant intermediary organization in most states until the 1960s. In general, politics could not become fully candidate-centered because candidates needed the parties to get themselves nominated and elected. Even incumbent Senators usually found that party was a useful asset, although their elections were the most candidate-centered ones in the decades from the 1920s to the 1950s. Of course, there were significant variations in the degree to which candidates operated independently of their parties – variations that were both regional and between levels of office. A state legislature candidate in New York had much less scope for electoral-related activity outside the party than a congressional candidate in Oregon. Yet, for both of them, the incentives for largely independent political action were limited. County and state party leaders still had access to activists who might help to deny renomination to an uncooperative maverick. Parties alone had the resources for fighting general election campaigns, which would otherwise be costly for the individual candidate. These ties between party and candidate were not usually strong enough to have facilitated the kind of party discipline found in parliamentary democracies, but they were more than adequate for keeping politics essentially party-centered until the 1960s.

Nevertheless, the introduction of the direct primary had made one important difference to candidate-party relations. When there were splits within a party organization, the relative power of the candidate would increase. Moreover, as Key argued in 1958, the direct primary actually tended to facilitate intraparty divisions:

The direct primary procedure seems in general to make more difficult the domination of the nominating process by the party organization and the interests affiliated with it. That result comes about in part because the primary encourages cleavages among the political professionals and careerists by permitting them to carry their differences to the primary voters for settlement. The selection of candidates may even become the fortuitous result of the interaction among many centers of influence.[37]

---

[36] See Ware, *Breakdown of Democratic Party Organization*, Chapter 4.
[37] Key, *Politics, Parties and Pressure Groups*, p. 422.

Thus, between the 1910s and the 1950s party control over nominations, and influence over their candidates once selected, was less complete than it had been in the preceding decades, though in many cases party was still the most significant factor affecting the selection of candidates. Had there been no change after the 1950s the importance of the direct primary might still have been that it "created new conditions of work for party leaders, conditions that affected their manner of operation and influenced the nature of party itself."[38]

The main impact of the direct primary was not experienced until the 1960s – more than fifty years after it was adopted by most states. By that time all states had started to use it – Rhode Island (1947) and Connecticut (1955) being the last to succumb.[39] Changes in campaign technology fundamentally shifted the balance between candidates and parties. Moreover, without the widespread use of the direct primary, the technological advances – television, computer-analyzed opinion polls, and so on – would not have had the effect that they did, because candidates would have had to work through party leaders to build support for their nomination at a convention. The interaction between the new technologies and direct nominations worked in two ways to restrict the role of party. First, these technologies made it much easier for the candidate to appeal directly to primary voters, bypassing, if necessary, party leaders and the activists whom the latter could mobilize. Second, by increasing the relative importance of money over campaign labor as an electoral resource, the new technologies devalued the one asset with which most individual candidates could not hope to rival the parties. Moreover, once candidates started to build up their own campaign organizations, to exploit the new technologies, so the appeal to party activists of working in party campaigns diminished, and the individual candidates were then able to start recruiting their own campaign workers on a scale that had not been possible hitherto.

In other words, the substitution of new campaign resources for older ones also facilitated the taking over by candidates of the older resources from the parties. Nor was this the only respect in which party could be said to have imploded. There were many lower levels of office for which individualistic campaigning made less sense because the expense of many of the new technologies would not justify their use in contests for such offices. However, as local parties themselves found it relatively less easy to raise money to finance their activities, and had fewer activists whom they could deploy on party-organized campaigns, so candidates at these levels also had to turn to more individualistic electoral campaigning. The parties were now incapable of performing a role that no other institution could perform adequately.

---

[38] Key, *Politics, Parties and Pressure Groups*, pp. 412–3.
[39] Mayhew, *Placing Parties in American Politics*, pp. 24 and 27.

The transformation in the relationship between party and candidate was rapid. At the beginning of the 1960s television was used primarily in presidential rather than subnational election contests. By the end of the decade, the more individualistic style of campaigning was to be found in most congressional elections and in some contests below that level. Symbolically the turning point is often seen as Milton Shapp's successful bid for the Democratic gubernatorial nomination in Pennsylvania in 1966.[40] Shapp was a wealthy "outsider" who used his money to finance an appeal directly to the primary electorate against the candidate endorsed by the party organization. From then on, it became clear that the optimal strategies for building a political career had changed.

There are many ways of illustrating this change. For example, consider the effect of party endorsement in a primary on the success rate of endorsees. Some states require by law that one candidate is formally endorsed before a primary, while in others party rules permit them to do so. How often do party-endorsed candidates win primaries compared with those who are not endorsed? Even in a candidate-centered era, it would be expected that a high proportion of endorsees would win. Many would be so clearly superior to their opponents that they would be the obvious endorsee for party activists. Others might be endorsed just because they were expected to win, and those attending endorsing conventions might be swayed by the need not to make powerful enemies unnecessarily. Consequently, while the absolute rate of success of endorsees is not likely to be revealing, any change in their success rate would be. Data compiled by Jewell and Morehouse covers two periods: 1960–80, which includes years before candidate supremacy; and 1982–98, which postdates the period of transition. Whereas 91 percent of endorsees won their primary election in the earlier period, only 74 percent did so in the later one.[41] The declining influence of party on candidate selection is evident here.

However, parties as political intermediaries have not been completely eliminated. To the contrary, there is considerable evidence that in some ways they have revived in the last twenty years. At all levels, party organizations became more professional. Nationally, they are less heterogeneous than they were, as both electoral realignment in the South and the erosion of the liberal, northeastern wing of the Republican party since the 1970s have removed the main minority wings from the two parties. Since the early 1980s greater party cohesion in Congress has been apparent. Again, since the 1980s, major public officeholders and the congressional parties have become much more active in raising funds that they can use for seed money

[40] Robert Agranoff, *The New Style in Election Campaigns*, Boston, Holbrook Press, 1972, p. 7.

[41] Malcolm E. Jewell and Sarah M. Morehouse, *Political Parties and Elections in American States*, Fourth Edition, Washington, D.C., CQ Press, 2001, p. 109.

for likely candidates in their party. Finally, Supreme Court decisions in the 1990s increased the incentive for the parties to raise soft money that could be used in support of candidates. In all these ways, party matters more than it did in the American polity. Nevertheless, with respect to the relation between candidates and their parties, these changes cannot counterbalance the shift in that relationship that was prompted by the interaction between technological change and the direct primary in the 1960s.

What happened at that time provides confirmation of Ranney's verdict, cited in Chapter 1, that "[T]he general adoption of the direct primary by the states from the early 1900s onward is, in my opinion, the most radical of all the party reforms adopted in the whole course of American history."[42] That it took more than fifty years to convert a previously party-centered polity into a candidate-centered one should not detract from Ranney's conclusion. Of course, it would not have had the effect that it did had it not been for other features of the polity in which it occurred – for example, long-standing judicial interpretations of the First Amendment, which have constrained any attempts to restrict who or what can spend money during election campaigns. Direct primaries would have had a wholly different impact on parties if they had been introduced in a different institutional context. But, given that context, the way that they interacted with the new campaign technologies of the 1960s to change the incentive structure facing individual candidates has been all too apparent. To a large extent, therefore, it is the direct primary that accounts for the divergence of America's parties from those in other democracies during the twentieth century, and for the transformation of a polity that had been so party-centered for much of that democracy's history.

4. Changes in the Direct Primary Since the 1920s

When the direct primary was first introduced, political parties kept firm control over it in the sense that the form the primary took tended to protect party interests. Thus, for example, in 1928 Merriam and Overacker reported that only four states used either an "open" primary or something rather close to that.[43] The remaining forty-four states had some form of "closed" primary.

Moreover, only in California was the "cross-filing" primary introduced, although earlier many states, especially in the West, had banned party labels from local government ballots and prohibited parties from formally endors-

---

[42] Austin Ranney, *Curing the Mischiefs of Faction: Party Reform in America*, Berkeley, University of California Press, 1975, p. 121.

[43] Merriam and Overacker, *Primary Elections*, p. 69. The four states were Montana and Wisconsin, which had fully "open" primaries, and Michigan and Vermont, where the voter could change his or her party affiliation on the day of the election.

ing candidates in such elections. Nevertheless, during the remainder of the century, the parties' ability to control the primary was much reduced. By 2000, only just over half the fifty states (twenty-six) employed some version of the "closed" primary.[44] Again, during the early decades of the twentieth century, most states had used a form of ballot that encouraged straight-ticket voting. More than 60 percent of states had provisions for "straight-ticket levers," or their equivalent, on the ballot, but seventy years later only 40 percent of them had this facility.[45]

During the course of the twentieth century, the role of party in the nom-ination of candidates was diluted. Not only did "open" primaries become more numerous, but new forms of primary, even less conducive to party control, were introduced. Alaska and Washington pioneered the "blanket" primary, in which voters may not merely decide in which party's primary they will vote when they are about to do so, but they also may decide to vote in the primary of one party for one public office and in the other party's primary for other offices. In the 1970s, Louisiana further reduced the role of party in its primaries. There is but a single "primary" in Louisiana in which all candidates (Democrat and Republican) must run. If a candidate secures 50 percent of the total vote he or she is then held to have won the general election. If no candidate secures this total there is a run-off election between the two leading candidates, who, in some circumstances, might be candidates of the same party. Unlike the blanket primary, this arrange-ment does not generate an incentive for a Democrat, say, to vote for a Republican – unless there is no Democratic candidate whatsoever in the contest. However, it disadvantages party interests in a different way. A party that has multiple candidacies for a particular office, and in which the party's vote is fragmented between the different candidates, could find that none of its candidates reach the run-off stage. Indeed, that party's candidates may have polled more votes in total than the candidates of the other party, but it is the latter whose representatives reach the run-off election.

So far neither the "blanket" primary nor the Louisiana "nonpartisan" primary have been adopted in many states – although the latter has been used in "special" elections in Texas. Nevertheless, in an electoral world that is dominated by candidates, rather than parties, it is increasingly likely that some politicians may see it as in their interest to introduce legislation requir-ing the use of one of these forms of primary, or some variant on them; when their own interests conflict with those of a majority of party activists, they may be tempted to further weaken the role of party. This was the key factor in explaining how Proposition 198 came to be passed by voters in California in 1996. Moderate Republicans, who had seen an electable U.S. Senate candidate go down to defeat at the hands of conservatives in 1992,

[44] Jewell and Morehouse, *Political Parties and Elections in American States*, p. 103.
[45] Larry J. Sabato, *The Party's Just Begun*, Glenview, Ill., Scott Foresman, 1988, p. 224.

decided to change the rules of the game to give their kind of activists more chance of nominating a candidate.[46] While the U.S. Supreme Court struck down that legislation, there is a possibility that its original supporters may seek to overcome that failure by sponsoring an initiative referendum on the Louisiana style of primary.

This "fraying at the edges of party control" is happening slowly. Not all politicians will benefit from more "candidate-centered" primary systems, and the bias in favor of the legislative status quo in America means that widespread change is unlikely in the near future. There is not a perceived crisis to drive such reform as there was one hundred years ago when the direct primary started to replace the caucus-convention system in most states. Nevertheless, over time the number of states deploying primaries that reduce the intermediary role played by party in the electoral process may well increase.

5. The Direct Primary and the Presidential Primary

The passage of direct primary legislation in the first decade of the twentieth century had an effect on presidential selection as well. It spurred the passage of laws providing for presidential primaries, a proposed reform that is more recent in origin than the direct primary itself. There was little discussion of it in the nineteenth century. Florida took the lead, passing legislation in 1901 allowing parties to elect delegates to their national conventions through primaries. In 1905, Wisconsin mandated the use of primaries in selecting delegates, but there was no provision for a delegate to indicate which candidate he would support. Pennsylvania also passed legislation early, in 1906, but the parties did not make use of it in the 1908 selection process. In 1910, Oregon became the first state to establish a presidential preference primary in which the delegates to the National Convention were required to support the winner of the primary at the convention. Other states followed that lead, and in 1912, twelve states either selected delegates in primaries, used a preferential primary, or both. The number of states deploying presidential primaries increased at the next two elections, reaching its maximum of twenty in 1920, and thereafter there was a slow decline. From 1936 onward, only about thirteen or fourteen states used them, and this number remained relatively stable until the post-1968 reforms.

Despite the fact that Wisconsin and Oregon were in the vanguard in mandating the use of presidential primaries, their pattern of growth was different from that of the direct primary. With the latter, the western states

---

[46] Bruce E. Cain, "Party Rights and Public Wrongs," *Public Affairs Report*, 41, no. 4 (September 2000), p. 5.

TABLE 8.1. *Use of Presidential Primary in 1920 by Size of State*

	Five or Fewer Congressional Districts	Six to Eleven Congressional Districts	Twelve or More Congressional Districts
Provision for Presidential Primary in 1920	Montana New Hampshire North Dakota Oregon South Dakota Vermont	California Maryland Nebraska West Virginia Wisconsin	Illinois Indiana Massachusetts Michigan New Jersey New York Ohio Pennsylvania
No Provision for Presidential Primary in 1920	Arizona Colorado Connecticut Delaware Idaho Maine Nevada New Mexico Rhode Island Utah Washington Wyoming	Iowa Kansas Kentucky Minnesota Oklahoma	Missouri

had been quicker to enact legislation after 1906, although most eastern states were using direct primaries extensively after 1915. The presidential primary was used far more in the east than in the West, and, despite Florida's early legislation, it was little used in the South. In 1920, for example, more than two-thirds of eastern states (twelve out of seventeen) had provision for a presidential primary compared with just over one-third of western states (seven of out of twenty). The typical state not employing the presidential primary was a small or medium size state in the West. Nevertheless, it was size of population rather than region that was the crucial variable; there was a preponderance of western states not using it simply because so many of them were small. For these purposes three categories of nonsouthern states may be considered: small states (those having five or fewer congressional districts in 1920), medium size states (those with between six and eleven districts), and large states (those with twelve or more districts) (see Table 8.1). Of the nine large states, only Missouri did not use a presidential primary in some form in 1920. However, while nearly 90 percent of these states had primaries, only 50 percent of medium-sized states had them (five out of ten). Usage was lower still among small states, with only one-third of the eighteen states using it in 1920. The proportion of small eastern states not using it is exactly the same as that of small western states, indicating that region was not the important variable.

Why was region not important in the way that it had been for the direct primary? The crucial point is that for state politicians, whether "regular" or "reformist" in their orientation, far less was at stake in presidential selection. National affairs impinged on the states only in so far as congressional delegations protected state interests in their chamber; the actions of a president had little effect on the conduct of public life within a state. Furthermore, presidential selection involved a series of complex negotiations between a variety of political elites at (and before) the National Convention, so that the possible input from any one state was necessarily limited. By contrast, other public offices seemed to have more impact on people's lives. Thus, as was seen in Chapter 4, the campaign for the direct primary in the West became part of an assault on the structures of power dominated by economic interests. That was why generally, after 1906, it was introduced more quickly there than in the east. However, such considerations could play no such role in the case of the presidency because of the nature of the office and the means by which nominees were chosen. No one state could change that process; all it could do was change its own procedure in relation to the selection of delegates and in mandating their voting behavior at National Conventions.

This explains why there was no "western bias" in the introduction of the presidential primary, so there remains the issue of why its introduction seems to be related to population size. This returns us to the point, made in Chapter 3, that the underlying nomination problem in the late nineteenth century related to scale. Informal procedures of the kind that had been introduced in the 1830s were inadequate in a political universe containing far more people. Formal rules were required because the informal constraints that worked in a face-to-face society could not work in a much larger one. It was for that reason that the larger states had been at the forefront of nomination reform between the mid-1880s and 1900. Delegate selection for National Conventions, and the behavior of delegates at these Conventions, posed similar, although much less pressing, problems. In general, it was the smaller states that were less affected by problems of scale, because in those states the older informal mechanisms of social regulation could still be effective.

Nevertheless, a presidential primary imposed costs on state political leaders, in terms of loss of influence over the bargaining process at the National Convention, especially when delegates were mandated to vote for the winner of the state's primary. This was to be relevant in the subsequent development of presidential primaries. To explain the point, it is useful to begin with an argument made by James Ceaser:

In order for the new system [of presidential nomination] to produce the kind of candidacy sought by many of the Progressive theorists, namely an outside campaign in which the candidates would take their case directly to the people, a large percentage of delegates, probably well over the number needed for the nomination, would have to be chosen in the primaries. Unless this number was obtained, the party organizations would continue to maintain control and candidates would have to tailor their outside strategies to fit the requirements of their inside strategies.[47]

If an insufficient number of states moved to selecting mandated delegates in primaries, the candidates would move back toward strategies of bargaining with state political leaders. This is what happened. Even in 1920, the high tide in the use of presidential primaries before the 1970s, primaries were largely incidental to the final outcomes. Among Republicans, Hiram Johnson obtained more primary votes than anyone else – nearly one-third of the total – but the nomination went to Warren Harding, who won less than 5 percent. For the Democrats, by far the largest number of votes went to unpledged delegates, and the nomination went to James Cox who had obtained a mere 15 percent of the total primary vote.

Given this record, it was impossible for its supporters to put forward the kind of defense that could be made of the direct primary – namely, that it appeared to be a more democratic device than caucus-convention systems. However, in one sense, the presidential primary was not doomed by this outcome. Although there was now little incentive for party leaders to have state voters commit delegations to "outside" candidates who might have little hope of ultimate success, this did not mean that outright repeal of the presidential primary was necessary. By a variety of devices – running as favorite sons themselves, warning off potential "outside" candidates with threats to oppose them if they entered a primary, and so on – state governors could often keep control of their National Convention delegations in much the same way that they could with the older mechanism. This explains why there were still so many presidential primaries in the decades between the 1930s and the 1960s: It was not necessary to abolish them formally in order to prevent the fragmentation of power.

This period is usually called that of the "mixed nominating system," one in which presidential primaries existed alongside delegate selection through the caucus-convention system. Most states employed the latter, and most delegates were chosen through them. Primaries were used by "outside" candidates as a way of trying to foist themselves on their party – always unsuccessfully, no matter how well they did in the primaries. Primaries were also

[47] James W. Ceaser, *Presidential Selection: Theory and Development*, Princeton, N.J., Princeton University Press, 1979, p. 221.

used at times by those pursuing an "inside" strategy, as a way of demonstrating to party leaders that they did have electoral popularity. However, such candidates were always selective in which primaries they chose to enter, or to contest seriously, and that meant that in any given election year there were relatively few primaries that were contested fiercely. As with the West Virginia primary of 1960, a victory in such a primary could greatly assist an inside strategy, but, in general, the role of primaries was limited in the "mixed system."

The "mixed system" worked reasonably well until 1968. The disastrous Democratic Convention of that year then set in train a series of events that led, eventually, to a report that recommended reform of rules governing the selection of delegates. This point is important because, unlike the circumstances leading up to the adoption of the direct primary, the reforms that led to the dominance of the presidential primary in the 1970s were the result of a series of events and decisions in a very brief period. The "mixed nominating system" was highly stable; there were not serious problems inherent to it that might have led to political elites reevaluating that process. Indeed, given the decentralized nature of national parties, it is hard to see how such reevaluation might have been effective. It took a highly divisive convention to trigger change; as a sop to the dissidents, proposals to establish a commission of enquiry into delegate selection were presented, and, on a close vote, they were adopted. While there is disagreement as to whether the majority on the McGovern-Fraser Commission intended that the presidential primary would increase in importance, or even whether they merely foresaw that eventuality, the impact of their report was to do just that. The complexity of the new rules meant that state parties now had an incentive to abandon the use of state caucuses and adopt primaries. Between 1972 and 1976 their use doubled, and more important, most delegates were now selected through primaries. The primary had become the dominant mechanism in presidential selection.

However, this raises the same question that was asked in relation to the direct primary: Why did party elites go along with reforms that, with hindsight, seemed to be so much against party interests? At the conclusion of his massive study of the reform process within the Democratic party, Byron Shafer put the matter this way:

How could . . . politics result in the constriction of the regular party, especially when most – almost all – of the key decisions in reform politics had to be taken by regular-party officials, inside the party itself? . . . the answer is deceptively simple. For it lies in a continuing pattern of decision-making within the regular party, a pattern which stretches back perhaps a hundred years and which was applied – and wrongly applied – to the particular incidents in reform politics between 1968 and 1972. . . . [It] has to do with a set of associated, continuing traditions in American party politics. These include a coalitional approach to party affairs and a brokerage approach to party leadership. They imply accommodation – "cutting the deal" –

whenever possible. Calculation by participants in the politics of party reform which accord with this general pattern – recall again that the key negotiations during this period were conducted almost entirely within the regular party – were everywhere."[48]

Shafer's explanation is broadly compatible with the account of the rise of the direct primary presented in this book. That, too, was the result largely of decisions taken by party elites in support of their own, or what they perceived to be their party's, interests. It was the result of "deal cutting." In the case of the direct primary, though, there was often a conflict between the interests of an individual politician and the long-term interests of his party, and, in any case, it was often difficult to determine where party interests really lay.

Although the crisis that produced the reformed presidential selection rules after 1968 was solely in the Democratic party, the Republicans were drawn into reforming their own party. As Democratic state legislators moved toward supporting a presidential primary, as the way of most easily conforming with new party rules, their Republican counterparts were faced with an unfortunate choice. Their nominating system appeared to work well, but if they did not follow the Democrats in using a primary their opponents would benefit from the greater publicity that such events attracted. This leads to an important point; primaries – whether direct or presidential – were well suited to the demands of campaigning in the television age. It was easy for television to make a "drama" or a "horse race" out of a primary election; it was much less easy for them to turn party caucuses or conventions into such spectacles. Thus, in return for losing control over the presidential nominating process, state party leaders found that they had produced a system that created greater public awareness of their party's nomination activities in an election year.

At the time, many experts failed to predict one of the main consequences of the new primary-dominated presidential nominating system. It was expected that the rules for the proportional allocation of delegates to candidates, depending broadly on their share of the vote, would produce many brokered National Conventions. In fact, the dynamics of the new nominating system are such that the very opposite has happened. A frontrunner emerges after the early primaries and all rivals then fall by the wayside; since 1972, there has always been one candidate in each party who has a clear majority of delegates committed to him by the start of the National Convention. This means that in its operation the modern presidential nominating system resembles a kind of multistage direct primary: the convention plays no role, other than a formal one, in nominating a candidate. Unlike a direct primary, though, the elections are not all held on the same day. The logical conclusion might be to turn this "quasi-direct primary"

[48] Byron E. Shafer, *Quiet Revolution: the Struggle for the Democratic Party and the Shaping of Post-Reform Politics*, New York, Russell Sage Foundation, 1983, pp. 527–8.

into the real thing – by requiring every state to hold a primary and to hold it on the same day. Among other results, it would have the advantage of reducing the formal campaign period, thereby making the process less gruelling for candidates. But logic provides no reason for making a change. Obtaining agreement from all the states to bring a national primary about would be extremely difficult; smaller states, notably New Hampshire, would lose the publicity they generate once every four years. Consequently, unless there is a major scandal or crisis that prompts such a change, it is unlikely that the direct primary principle will be extended formally to presidential nominations in the near future.

6. Concluding Remarks

By the 1930s, the wave of opposition to the direct primary within party organizations had largely died out. By the end of the previous decade, it had been clear that repeal (or even major revision) of primary legislation was difficult to achieve. Moreover, the onset of the Great Depression and the New Deal changed the focus of attention of party politicians in a number of ways. The direct primary could be accepted by politicians as just part of the context in which American parties had to operate; the parties adapted to it. It was not until a few decades later, when campaign technology and strategy was changing, that it became so apparent that the very foundations of party power had been removed by reforms of about sixty years earlier. Even in its most "party-friendly" form – for example, a completely closed primary – it was a mechanism that facilitated the dominance of candidates in the electoral process. However, during the course of the twentieth century, the ability of state parties to protect party interests was reduced, the "open" primary became far more common, and new versions of the primary, that eroded party power even more, started to appear.

In an obvious respect, change within American parties has been slow. By comparison with, say, the rise and decline of mass membership as an organizing principle in many European parties during the twentieth century, the transformation in candidate selection in America since the introduction of the direct primary may appear to be less radical. But in many respects, these changes in America's parties have been just as dramatic when viewed in a broader context. The direct primary was much longer in its gestation than is usually acknowledged, and it took decades for its full effects to be evident, but the long-term change to a candidate-centered polity has been just as significant as the superficially more apparent transformations in the European parties.

9

Conclusions

In answering the question – Why was the direct primary introduced by so many states between 1899 and 1915? – it is important to distinguish between several different aspects of the answer.

The first has to do with long-term pressure from within the parties for reform of the caucus-convention system in selecting candidates. The informal practices of that system, which had worked reasonably well at the height of the Jacksonian democracy, were performing much less well with population expansion and urbanization. With the decreased effectiveness of older methods of control, parties found themselves now using nomination practices that brought them into disrepute and which made it more diffi-cult to coordinate intraparty activities. However, any proposed reform of the system would be constrained in two ways. On the one hand, the decen-tralization of the parties meant that reforming them by creating party rules would never be sufficient, because parties at the state level (and below) would be unable to provide enforcement. That is why it became necessary to use state law to effect reform; the many statutes that were enacted in the 1890s are not evidence of the parties being "punished" by antiparty reformers, but, rather, that institutionalization was possible only through mechanisms external to the parties. On the other hand, any reform had to be compatible with the Jacksonian ethos that parties were *the* means of effecting democracy, and any redesign of them had to be directed toward maximizing participation within them. Arguably, one of the reasons that in the twentieth century American parties ended up by being much weaker than their European counterparts was that so much had been expected of them during the nineteenth century. The persistence of a belief that parties should be vehicles for mass participation precluded any reforms that might have reduced participation in the nominating process, and correspondingly advantaged any schemes that were likely to increase it.

The second aspect concerns change in the 1890s. There were two devel-opments in that decade that were to further limit the direction that reform of candidate selection took. The evidence of the Australian Ballot reform helped to foster a belief among party elites that successful institutional reform of parties was achievable. With the official ballot, it had been possible to eliminate practices at the polling booth that both generated adverse publicity for the major parties and also made it difficult for them to prevent electoral "treachery" in their own ranks. The decline of split-ticket voting in the 1890s demonstrated that party control over mass electorates could be retained, even with institutional reforms that appeared to limit a party's scope of action. This encouraged a belief in there also being solutions to the problems posed by the caucus-convention nominating system, which similarly would be compatible with party interests. However, at the same time, it was becoming clear that, although the various legislative reforms of the 1890s were improving the nominating system in some respects during that decade, fundamental problems of ensuring that opinions expressed at early stages of the nominating process were somehow reflected in decisions at the final stages remained. Even when procedures were regulated by law, there were still too many opportunities at various stages of the process for major strands of opinion to be shut out of the nominating system.

The third aspect relates to why it was the direct primary, and not some other possible reform, that had emerged by the end of the 1890s as the only alternative to some version of the status quo. The direct primary had many advantages over potential rivals. It had been used in rural counties in some northern states, and its use was increasing. Since many caucuses, especially outside New England, had never been anything more than elections, the direct primary did not have the appearance of a wholly alien system; it was not an institution of foreign origin that could be criticized as being incompatible with American political values. It also could be expected to meet the demand that popular participation in parties should increase. Consequently, those who were most committed to reform, and this included those individuals who were most opposed to parties, came rapidly to alight on the direct primary as the one mechanism that was worth promoting in public debate. By the second half of the 1890s, the direct primary was the "only game in town." Thus, unlike contemporary debates in Britain about its electoral system, in which reformers are not agreed on a single proposal, here was a reform debate in which the alternatives were being narrowed down quickly early on. Finally, the growing use of the direct primary in the South, for entirely different reasons than would apply in the north, provided a model for northern politicians, even though many of them were all too aware of the differences in the dynamics of southern party politics.

This leads us to the fourth aspect. What drove politicians to move beyond merely experimenting with direct nominations in some counties and to provide for their more wide ranging use? One possible answer that this study has refuted is that the reform was simply imposed on politicians by reformers intent on weakening the parties. Most certainly, the popular characterization of the process as a conflict over control of the cities, pitching urban party machines against their local opponents, cannot be sustained. In most states, neither of these protagonists had sufficient seats in the state legislatures for this to be a dominant feature. In most states, it was rural legislators and those from small cities who held the balance of power – and by some margin. In fact, the introduction of the direct primary was very much "politics as usual." Nomination reform was the kind of issue that would be popular with an electorate that had been socialized into a political system that had valued mass participation in politics via the parties. Consequently, party competition in some states, and the fear of it developing in others, led party leaders to embrace the direct primary. In yet other states, it was intraparty rivalries that led otherwise "regular" politicians to champion it. Moreover, there were significant regional differences. The faster enactment of direct nominations in the western states after 1906 was precipitated by a desire among reformers to remove the power base of economic elites within the parties. Such full-scale assaults on the parties were largely absent in the east.

Party politicians were not the "victims" of antiparty reformers who somehow imposed a debilitating reform on them. Certainly, this was not the terms in which those politicians who were in a position to promote reform understood what was happening. Some of them, like Robert Luce, favored direct primaries out of a belief that it would make parties more effective. Others, like Charles Deneen, saw it as a means of bolstering their own political careers. Yet others, like Samuel Pennypacker, came to see it as part of a strategy for stymieing a Democratic party revival. Among those who opposed it, there were those, as in New York, for whom intraparty rivalries formed the basis of their stance. Moreover, the direct primary was rarely an issue that was thought to pose a threat to the very existence of the parties. To the contrary, the stronger the party organization, the more able it would be to adapt its operations to ensure continuity of control over the nomination process.

Long after the legislation of the early twentieth century, the relatively low level of conflict generated by the direct primary in many states appears curious. This is not because we might have expected politicians then to understand that other bases of party power were already being undermined, and that this would make control over nominations so much more crucial in future decades. We cannot have such expectations of politicians in the situation they were facing. And, usually, they did do what they could to protect party interests – for example, in most states they required the use of both non-POB ballots and closed primaries. Rather, their behavior may appear curious because, by the early 1900s, there was already considerable evidence that the direct primary was a flawed reform. Both the experience of Cleveland in the 1890s and the "Doc" Ames scandal in Minnesota (1902), shortly after its introduction there, were precisely the kinds of setbacks that might have allowed the direct primary's opponents to mobilize against it effectively. The difficulty of utilizing adverse publicity against direct nominations, even when supported by such evidence, illustrates how much the pressure to do something about the "nomination problem" was a concern for many politicians.

This "pressure" was not external; it was not a response to demands from those they would rather not heed. It was the pressure that came largely from more than a decade of trying to legislate improved procedures for selecting candidates, when none of the improvements seemed to be producing the kinds of positive results that had been evident earlier with ballot reform. It was party politicians who had started off the process of party institutionalization, and for whom there would be important benefits should suitable arrangements be devised.

However, in "doing something," American politicians were constrained in ways that European politicians would not have been. The Jacksonian ethos of participation-through-parties precluded reforms that might have removed some of their problems without weakening the base of party power. The parties could not require would-be members to serve a long apprenticeship before they acquired rights to participate in the nomination process. Because there were so many elective offices in the United States, nominating candidates and running election campaigns were far more central to the work of a party than they were elsewhere. To have required a long apprenticeship – say, by demanding that a person be registered for at least two years – would have run counter to an important political value. Replacing older, informal, methods of denying nomination rights to those who had been "treacherous" meant opting for a system of state regulation of membership in which parties could now do little to control their own members. Given annual voter registration, the most that could be expected was an apprenticeship of a few months, and, even under a closed primary, there were no means of proving that a member had been or would be disloyal. Under the older system, there were informal methods of excluding such people, under a state-regulated system there were no effective methods. By contrast with the more centralized European parties, the newly institutionalized American parties had subjected themselves to rigid regulation under the law. The laws may not have appeared rigid when introduced, but the more formal restrictions inherent in legal regulation were to deny American parties what their European counterparts had – flexibility in the application of procedures to particular cases.

Yet, this leads us to the key issue of counterfactuals. Under what conditions could the outcome have been very different, and if it had been different, would the long-term relationship between parties and candidates have been more like that in Europe? A central argument here has been that the fragmentation of power in American parties meant that effective institutionalization was possible only if the law was used to regulate parties.

But the rigid nature of legal regulation as a tool meant that it could not possibly create the kind of reform that a more centralized party could enact internally. Legislation would either provide too few constraints on the discretion of party leaders or far too many. Thus, a law might just involve regulating how delegates to conventions were to be selected, but, by itself, that could not ensure that such delegates would either not be offered inducements to vote a particular way at a convention, or that "honest" delegates would not be outmaneuvered procedurally at it. In other words, there were limits as to how much relatively narrow procedural reform could ensure "fair" outcomes at conventions. Or, rather, the law could do so but only by restricting the flexibility of a party meeting in a convention. For example, legislation could require that delegates vote only for candidates for whom they had been authorized by those who selected them. This is not only a possible solution, but, for example, it is now required in many states in relation to presidential selection. However, such legislation necessarily prevents the emergence of compromise candidates, the dropping of some candidates in favor of others to balance the ticket, and so on. In other words, it destroys the flexibility of party-controlled nominations in precisely the way that direct primaries did. It was not so much the direct primary, *per se*, that reduced party autonomy in America, but the fact that the only way of controlling party behavior was by legal devices.

Herein lies one of the unique problems that faced American parties. Institutionalization by law would either fall short of remedying all the problems the parties faced, or it would do so by making party merely a vehicle for transmitting automatically the preferences of the lowest level party supporters into nomination outcomes. By contrast, a more centralized party would not face such stark choices. Party rules could be "bent," suspended in particular circumstances, or whatever, as the way of reaching necessary accommodations in order to present potential party voters with an optimal set of candidates. With centralization, particular instances of the nonapplication of rules do not necessarily lead to their being disregarded more generally in the party. That is the advantage centralized parties have – they can more easily control their political environment, through not being bound by absolutely rigid regulations. Because law was the only medium for party institutionalization in America, there was no possibility of establishing a nomination framework that would both generally safeguard the interests of supporters and also provide party leaders with flexibility in choice of candidates. The granting of discretion (in law) for party leaders to disregard a popular choice for nomination – because, for example, he or she is known by them to "have skeletons in the closet" – is incompatible with a law granting sovereignty to party supporters in the choice of candidates.

Consequently, the only alternative to direct primary laws was legislation that would also have been candidate-centered, in that it could have granted party supporters sovereignty only by mandating delegates to vote for particular candidates, and for no one else. The American parties were thus torn between Scylla and Charybdis. On the one side, the pressures to do something to prevent abuse of party power were strong. On the other side, the only solutions that would work were ones that might weaken the ability of parties to act as effective intermediaries in candidate selection. But what of a possible compromise solution on the lines of the Hughes Plan? Suppose it had emerged earlier, could the party elites have evaded the stark choice they faced? There is no doubt that such a scheme would have helped to preserve some party power, but there is no reason for believing that it would have been especially attractive to these elites. It added yet another stage to a process that was already complex. It was not a relatively simple reform, in the way that the official ballot had been. Because of this its popular appeal would not have been great. It would also have been difficult to "sell" to reformers, and that, too, would have made it more difficult to "sell" to mass publics.

Now let us consider a slightly different counterfactual. Suppose that the insurgency movement in the West had been held at bay; let us imagine that party regulars displayed more subtlety in dealing with their "young Turks," so that La Follette failed to win the governorship of Wisconsin, for example. Under those circumstances what would have happened to the direct primary? After all, this was a mechanism that had become increasingly the subject of experimentation in the states, with the eastern states in the vanguard. One plausible line of argument is that the experimentation period would have been extended, but as the disadvantages of the direct primary became evident, so the "experiments" would be curtailed. In place, by 1920 or so, we might imagine a "mixed" nominating system, with a number of states using direct nominations for selecting some kinds of candidates and the caucus-convention system for others. The kind of balance evident later in presidential selection might have been evident here, too.

However, even if this scenario is thought initially to be convincing, on reflection it is far from clear that the "solution" would have proved stable in the long term. The advent of the new campaign technologies from the 1960s onward would have provided an incentive for some individual office-holders in major offices to push for the introduction of direct nominations for the offices they held already or for those to which they aspired. These technologies provided an opportunity for such officeholders to free themselves from the electoral fortunes of their parties, and political ambition would have provided them with an incentive to do so. From time to time, even before the 1960s, state governors might well have pushed for the extension of the direct primary, citing the usual arguments about the expansion of mass participation and so forth. It is worth remembering that the three states that had not adopted the direct primary by 1915 did all do so later; interestingly, in each case it was introduced before the age of television campaigning in state or local elections. In other words, the kinds of political actors who might most expect to benefit from an extension of the system of direct nominations were often well placed to initiate a campaign for it within their own state. (By contrast, no one in a position to do so had much incentive to extend the presidential primary system until after 1968. Few politicians within a state were likely to benefit from a move that would advantage mainly politicians from outside it who were seeking the presidential nomination. It took a radical, and unpredicted, change in the rules of the presidential nominating game to change the incentives facing politicians in the states.)

The stability of the "mixed" nominating system for the presidency does not provide a model, therefore, on which a hypothetical future for American parties can be constructed *sans* political insurgency. It is at least arguable that, in the case of the direct primary, the equivalent of Pandora's Box had already been opened by about 1906 – even if La Follette had failed in Wisconsin, and Oregon had collapsed into the Pacific Ocean. As an alternative to existing methods for selecting candidates, the direct primary would always prove attractive to those politicians who could see how their own political futures might be promoted by distancing themselves from their party. That is why someone like Charles Deneen is so much better a role model for understanding how the direct primary fitted into American political and governmental structures than Robert La Follette ever was. With Deneen the personal ambition was concealed much less well by a political rhetoric emphasizing the triumph of democracy through nomination reform; La Follette was just as ambitious, but he succeeded in persuading far more people, then and subsequently, that he was not reforming, in part, for his own advancement: Deneen's humbug was easier to detect.

There have been Deneen-like figures around in the United States since the end of the nineteenth century – politicians who saw how the link between their political ambitions and their actual (or potential) electoral coalitions would depend on removing caucuses and conventions from the nomination process. Certainly, by the 1960s, there would have been a great many more of them than there had been earlier, probably, but even in the first half of the twentieth century there was always the possibility that, in particular states, further extensions of the direct nomination principle would have occurred. Moreover, the experience of the South, with the rise of the individual politician there, may have provided models for Deneen-like politicians in the north during the decades after 1910.

The fragmentation of governmental power in the United States, and the consequent decentralization of its parties, had two effects on the rise of the direct primary. First, it limited the kind of party institutionalization that could develop, thereby making direct nominations the only plausible alternative to the status quo. Second, it provided a political context in which individual candidates could more easily escape from the constraints of party than would have been possible in more centralized parties. This would have continued to provide a source of pressure for direct nominations even in the absence of the "big push" in the West provided by insurgency.

The combination of party decentralization and an ethos that valued mass participation through the parties meant that party institutionalization in America was always likely to go down a path that would increase the power of candidates. The demand for widespread participation through parties could be reconciled with the requirements of institutionalization only by formally linking the outcome of candidate selection procedures to supporters' preferences between candidates. The direct primary did that, had done it already in a number of counties, and was relatively easy to understand. This provided it with a considerable advantage in becoming the chosen mechanism. There is, therefore, a sense in which the direct primary did not actually change the nature of American parties; that change might have been predicted given the fragmentation of America's political institutions, and hence its parties.

There is an obvious parallel between the argument outlined here and one developed by Leon Epstein, with the crucial difference that Epstein sees a political culture of antipartism, and not institutional fragmentation, as the primary cause. He argues:

I regard the twentieth-century regulatory treatment of American parties, distinctive though it is on the democratic universe, as a response to durable historical circumstances. In this light, the direct primary itself is not so much a cause of candidate-centered politics, as it is an institutionalized means for pursuing such politics in a civic culture that is broadly hostile to party organizational control. The means to be sure, are consequential. Without the direct primary and the related presidential preference primary, candidate-centered campaigns might not have flourished so handsomely in the United States although they would probably have existed in greater degree than elsewhere.[1]

Like Epstein, I regard the direct primary "as a response to durable historical circumstances." Like him, I believe that a changed balance in favor of the candidate would have developed in the twentieth century, even if the parties' legislators had not enacted the direct primary, seemingly against the interests of the parties themselves. However, unlike Epstein, I can find no evidence to support the view that it was a distinctive political culture that explains the rise of candidates over parties. Rather, American parties could respond to the changed circumstances that were prompting party institutionalization only by means that would eventually weaken the power the parties had enjoyed in the nineteenth century.

Stanley Hoffmann once observed that the American political tradition is alleged to be like the French, in that they share "a belief in each country's

---

[1] Leon Epstein, *Political Parties in the American Mold*, Madison, University of Wisconsin Press, 1986, pp. 155–6.

being an exception."[2] (By comparison, it might be added, the British simply regard their political tradition as normal, while that of other nations is in varying degrees not quite so normal as theirs.) Ever since the Frenchman de Tocqueville noted the "exceptional" political development evident in the United States, American analysts have invoked cultural differences as the mainspring of America's distinctive politics. There are two points to make clear about this in concluding this study.

First, it may well be the case that some American values are important explanatory variables in relation to its political development. All that has been argued here is that there is no evidence that antipartism was responsible for the direct primary, and that there is evidence supporting an alternative hypothesis. Second, it is at least arguable that, by the late twentieth century, antipartism had become more prevalent in the United States than in other democracies. Indeed, it might well be expected that the reduced power of parties to control political outcomes would have helped to fuel doubts among mass electorates about their relevance to those outcomes. If Americans are now more "disappointed" in their parties than citizens elsewhere, it may well reflect what was done to the autonomy of the parties in the twentieth century. However, not only is this not the argument usually produced in support of political culture explanations, but the argument cannot apply to the early twentieth century. Attachments to parties remained strong then, and there is no evidence that genuinely antiparty sentiments ever percolated beyond a rather small minority of so-called good government types. The politicians who enacted the direct primary had nearly all made their careers in political parties, and most would continue such careers. Politicians as diverse as Robert Luce, Samuel Pennypacker, and Charles Deneen were party politicians; they differed from their opponents who rejected the direct primary either because they took different views from them on the effect of primary legislation on parties, or they saw their own careers as benefitting from changing the rules of the nominating game.

What undermined America's parties one hundred years ago was not so much that too many people were hostile to them but that, arguably, too much had been expected of them. Nothing illustrates this better than the name by which the first mass-based party was often known by its supporters in the nineteenth century – The Democracy. Parties had been not just an instrument for defending particular interests, or promoting particular principles; they had been the means by which the people were to be involved in their government. By the end of the nineteenth century, however, much more complex relations within American society and a more diverse economy meant that the parties could not now fulfill the enormous

---

[2] Stanley Hoffmann, "France Self-Destructs," *New York Review of Books*, May 28, 1992, p. 25.

expectations that many Americans had had of them. The problem was that these expectations had not really changed; parties were supposed to be forums for high levels of mass participation. Ironically, in trying to make sure that they lived up to the ideal, America's politicians helped to propel them down a path in which they became arguably less important political intermediaries than parties in other democracies.

Index

Abrams, Richard M., 18, 132
Alternative Vote system: to eliminate nonmajority candidates, 231
Altschuler, Glenn C., 10
antipartism and antiparty reformers, 6–12, 14, 111, 160; and ballot reform, 23, 24, 27, 40, 43–5, 55; as shaping debate on direct primary, 199, 209–10, 213, 215, 223, 256. *See also* Progressive reformers
Argersinger, Peter H., 48
Arkansas: and early use of direct elections, 99
Australian Ballot. *See* ballot

Baldwin, Simeon, 187, 192–3
ballot and ballot reform: Australian, 22, 25, 256; variations of Australian, 41–3; shoestring, 43, 44, 211; pure office block, 41, 43, 45, 48–51, 52, 53; blanket, 46; pure party column, 52, 54; compared to nomination reform, 55–6
Barry, Brian, 144
Bartels, Larry M., 169–70
Bass, Herbert J., 37
Berry, William H., 140
Binney, Charles C., 79
Black, Frank: as example of partisan support for reform, 38
Blaine, James G., 177, 186
Borah, William: as example of candidate-centered politics, 234
Branson, Walter J., 73, 104, 205

Britain: and patterns of party strength, 166. *See also* parties: American compared with European
Brock, William R., 88, 89
Brooks, F. M., 67, 107, 112, 208
Bryan, William Jennings: impact on Democratic party, 176, 177
Buenker, John D., 68
Burnham, Walter Dean, 163, 168
business and monopolies: political power of, 200, 201, 213
Butler, Edward, 146

California, 231, 235–7
Cameron, Simon, 173
candidate-centered politics, 8, 262; in South, 232; in West, 232–5; in California, 235–7; in East, 237–8, 239; limits on, 242–3; in 1960s, 244–6
candidates: quality of under direct primary, 106, 109, 116, 206, 209, 220, 238; nonmajority under direct primary, 230–1
caucus and convention system, 153, 183, 255; defined, 57–9; discussion versus election at, 60; variations on, 60–3; as synonymous with elections, 101, 102, 197
Ceaser, James, 251
city-manager system, 235, 237
civil service reform, 24, 72–3; and decline in party power, 241–2. *See also* corruption, fraud, and scandal
Cleveland, Grover, 38